CAPITAL AND THE DISTRIBUTION
OF LABOR EARNINGS

CONTRIBUTIONS
TO
ECONOMIC ANALYSIS

126

Honorary Editor
J. TINBERGEN

Editors
D. W. JORGENSON
J. WAELBROECK

NORTH-HOLLAND PUBLISHING COMPANY
AMSTERDAM · NEW YORK · OXFORD

CAPITAL
AND THE DISTRIBUTION
OF LABOR EARNINGS

MICHAEL SATTINGER

Miami University of Ohio

1980

NORTH-HOLLAND PUBLISHING COMPANY
AMSTERDAM · NEW YORK · OXFORD

ISBN: 0 444 85397 9

Publishers:

NORTH-HOLLAND PUBLISHING COMPANY
AMSTERDAM · NEW YORK · OXFORD

Sole distributors for the U.S.A. and Canada:

ELSEVIER NORTH-HOLLAND INC.

52 VANDERBILT AVENUE

NEW YORK, N.Y. 10017

Library of Congress Cataloging in Publication Data

```
Sattinger, Michael.
   Capital and distribution of labor earnings.

   (Contributions to economic analysis ; 126)
   Bibliography:  p.
   1.  Wages.  2.  Employment (Economic theory)
3.  Labor economics.  I.  Title.  II.  Series.
HD4909.S27           331.2'1        79-22687
ISBN 0-444-85397-9
```

Printed in the Netherlands

INTRODUCTION TO THE SERIES

This series consists of a number of hitherto unpublished studies, which are introduced by the editors in the belief that they represent fresh contributions to economic science.

The term 'economic analysis' as used in the title of the series has been adopted because it covers both the activities of the theoretical economist and the research worker.

Although the analytical methods used by the various contributors are not the same, they are nevertheless conditioned by the common origin of their studies, namely theoretical problems encountered in practical research. Since for this reason, business cycle research and national accounting, research work on behalf of economic policy, and problems of planning are the main sources of the subjects dealt with, they necessarily determine the manner of approach adopted by the authors. Their methods tend to be 'practical' in the sense of not being too far remote from application to actual economic conditions. In addition they are quantitative rather than qualitative.

It is the hope of the editors that the publication of these studies will help to stimulate the exchange of scientific information and to reinforce international cooperation in the field of economics.

The Editors

To my parents,
BARBARA and IRVIN

PREFACE

My interest in the size distribution of earnings began over ten years ago when, as a graduate student at Carnegie-Mellon University, I read D.G. Champernowne's 1953 stochastic process paper at the suggestion of Partha Dasgupta. Some time later, Michael J. Farrell suggested that I read A.D. Roy's little-known 1951 paper relating the concept of comparative advantage to the distribution of earnings via self-selection. Without a doubt, Farrell's suggestion is responsible for putting me on the track which eventually led to this book. The existence of comparative advantage is fundamentally inconsistent with the point of view taken in most analyses of the distribution of earnings and leads inevitably to the consideration of the general problem of the allocation of workers to jobs.

Although the basic ideas of the 1975 *Econometrica* paper on comparative advantage were completed when I was a graduate student, I chose another topic as a doctoral thesis because I could not demonstrate the empirical relevance of the concepts. I returned to the subject matter in a 1971 Stony Brook working paper. Hendrik Houthakker kindly read the paper and wrote me concerning earlier work by Jan Tinbergen, which I had not known about. It seems that I had rediscovered a methodology first used by Tinbergen in a 1947 paper on the distribution of labor incomes (published in English in 1951). Because his paper did not employ the concept of comparative advantage, however, I did not originally regard it as an important predecessor. Only after I had read the paper five or six times (a profitable number for a Tinbergen paper) did I realize its conceptual contributions and its importance. After publication of my 1975 comparative advantage paper, Tinbergen corresponded with me often and provided valuable and insightful comments on my work, for which I am extremely grateful.

During the 1974–1975 academic year, I was fortunate to spend a year as a visiting assistant professor (adjunktvikar) at the Institute of Economics, University of Aarhus, Denmark. My colleagues there, among them Niels Bolwig, Jørgen Gelting, Svend Hylleberg, Niels Westergaard-Nielsen and Ebbe Yndgaard, encouraged my interest in the distribution of earnings and provided me with valuable comments and discussion.

Back at Stony Brook, Edward Ames gave me mature and competent advice on the development of my ideas. Others at Stony Brook who assisted me are William S. Dawes, Javier Ruiz-Castillo, David Swinton, John Wile and John Winn.

This book was written at Miami University in Ohio. I am greatly indebted to my colleagues here for their advice and support. In particular, Donald Cymrot, T. Windsor Fields, Gerald Flueckiger, Daniel Seiver and Dennis Sullivan read through parts of the manuscript and offered criticisms and suggestions. I am also indebted to my chairman, William McKinstry, and the academic community here for the sane and orderly working environment which I found so conducive to work. At all times I have received complete cooperation and assistance from the administration, library and computer staff. I particularly want to thank Albert Kaled and Christine Noble of the Academic Computer Service for their assistance. I further wish to acknowledge the support and encouragement given to me by the North-Holland Publishing Company.

Over the years I have received research assistance from a number of students. These include Bruce Fein, Mindy Cagen, Carol Jachman, Jean LaRosa, Cheryl Savage and Shou-Heng Liu. For typing, I am indebted to Jeanette Corlett, Mimi Farr and Kathy Porter Fox.

Of course, none of the above are in any way responsible for remaining errors in the manuscript or for any views that I have expressed.

It is at this point in a preface that an author usually acknowledges the' bounteous support of his or her trusting and expectant government. Unfortunately, federal support was not forthcoming. In a very real sense, then, this project was paid for (through my forgone activities) by myself, my wife, my children, my colleagues, my students and my university. My wife, Ulla, and my children, Graham, Andrew and Nicholas, bore the greatest burden. To all I am grateful for their tolerance and patience.

Like a child, a manuscript has a life of its own. It gets out of hand sometimes, does not cooperate, refuses to conform to the outline neatly laid out for it, and produces unexpected surprises. While the manuscript did not develop exactly as I had planned, I have prepared it as well as possible with the abilities and resources at my disposal. After leaving my hands, the manuscript and the ideas it contains will be judged on their own merit; my person and my reputation will no longer be relevant. But as the author, I am not indifferent to its success: my hope is that the book will be received seriously and read with care.

Oxford, Ohio   *M.S.*
April 1979

CONTENTS

Introduction to the series   v
Preface   vii
List of tables   xiii
List of figures   xvi

Chapter 1.   Introduction   1

Chapter 2.   A Critique of the human capital approaches   13
    1.   Introduction   13
    2.   The Mincer model   14
    3.   The Becker-Chiswick model   15
    4.   Marshall's objections   20

Chapter 3.   Some of the literature   23
    1.   Introduction   23
    2.   Tinbergen's theory of the distribution of earnings   24
    3.   Comparative advantage   29
    4.   The scale of resources effect   32
    5.   Capital models   35
    6.   Conclusions   37

Chapter 4.   The inequality multiplier: An aggregate analysis   39
    1.   Introduction   39
    2.   Assumptions of the model   40
    3.   The inequality multiplier   42
    4.   Effects of capital intensity on earnings inequality   45
    5.   Wage differentials   48
    6.   Relation to partial elasticities of complementarity   51
    7.   Technological progress   55
    8.   Graphical analysis   57
    9.   A theory of poverty   60
    10. Unobserved sources of variation in earnings   64

11. Implications for growth accounting   66
12. Summary and limitations of the analysis   68

Chapter 5. The assignment of workers to jobs   69
1. Introduction   69
2. Preferences   72
3. Comparative advantage   77
4. Scale-of-resources effect   79
5. Scale-of-resources effect with comparative advantage
present   85
6. Scale-of-resources effect with Cobb-Douglas production
function   88
7. Relation to capital-skill complementarity   90
8. Some observations on the assignment problem   91

Chapter 6. Differential rents   95
1. Introduction   95
2. Assumptions   97
3. Wage and rent functions   98
4. Reserve prices and the unemployment of labor and
machines   101
5. Examples   104
6. Perfectly elastic supply of capital   113
7. Nature of the model   116

Chapter 7. The empirical application of the theory   119
1. Introduction   119
2. Transition to an empirical model   119
3. Industry capital to labor ratios   122
4. Capital concentration over time   124
5. The relation between capital intensity and labor quality 126
6. The measurement of inequality   132
7. Implications of the data for earnings inequality   134
Appendix: Data sources   136

Chapter 8. Earnings inequality over time   139
1. Introduction   139
2. Male income inequality, 1949–1969   140
3. Upper income shares   147
4. Conclusions   152
Appendix: Data sources   153

Chapter 9.   Cross-section studies 155
    1.   Introduction 155
    2.   Data 156
    3.   Results 168
    4.   Alternative schooling variables 177
    5.   Further effects of schooling 181
    6.   The effect of the average level of education on inequality 183
    7.   Poverty 186
    8.   Conclusions 189
    Appendix: Data sources 190

Chapter 10.   Wage differentials 193
    Appendix: Data sources 200

Chapter 11.   Disaggregated analysis 203
    1.   Introduction 203
    2.   Data 204
    3.   Results 205
    4.   Upper and lower tails 206
    5.   Productivity, growth and other variables 210
    6.   Effects of sectoral shifts 215
    7.   Conclusions 222
    Appendix: Data sources 223

Chapter 12.   The distribution of earnings by industry 225
    1.   Introduction 225
    2.   A neoclassical theory of the demand for a distribution of workers 226
    3.   Demands for workers by schooling levels 229
    4.   The demands for workers by earnings levels 237
    5.   Unionization and concentration 242
    6.   Conclusions 244
    Appendix: Data sources 245

Chapter 13.   Hierarchies 247
    1.   Introduction 247
    2.   Pareto coefficient 248
    3.   Nonproduction workers 251
    4.   Conclusions 258
    Appendix: Data sources 258

Contents

Chapter 14. To be continued   259
            1. Introduction   259
            2. The effects of capital variables   260
            3. The effects of schooling variables   261
            4. Revisions in human capital theory   262
            5. Work to be done   264
            6. Concluding remarks   267

References   269

Author index   277
Subject index   279

LIST OF TABLES

7.1   Manufacturing industry data, 1959
7.2   Nonmanufacturing industry data, 1959
7.3   Manufacturing industry data, 1969
7.4   Nonmanufacturing industry data, 1969
7.5   US capital concentration, 1948–1972
7.6   Education versus capital intensity, 1969, thirty industries
7.7   Earnings versus capital intensity, 1949
7.8   Earnings versus capital intensity, 1969
7.9   Elasticities of inequality measures with respect to change in bracket population
7.10   Time series of capital and education variables
8.1   Income inequality, males 25 and over, 1949–1969
8.2   Income inequality, males 25–64, 1949–1969
8.3   Income inequality, males 25–34, 1949–1969
8.4   Income inequality, 1949–1969, linear relation
8.5   Correlation coefficients for variables in table 8.2
8.6   Top 1 percent, 1917–1948
8.7   Top 5 percent, 1917–1948
8.8   Correlation coefficients for variables in tables 8.6 and 8.7
9.1   Selected data for 1959 cross-section estimations
9.2   Selected data for 1969 cross-section estimations
9.3   Male earnings and income inequality, 1959
9.4   Earnings and income inequality, males and females combined, 1959
9.5   Correlation coefficients for tables 9.3 and 9.4
9.6   Male earnings and income inequality, 1969
9.7   Male earnings and income Gini coefficients, 1969
9.8   Earnings and income inequality, males and females combined, 1969
9.9   Male earnings and income inequality, linear form
9.10   Correlation coefficients for tables 9.6 and 9.7
9.11   Male earnings and income inequality, alternative capital variables
9.12   Male earnings and income inequality, alternative schooling variables, 1959

9.13   Male earnings and income inequality, alternative schooling variables, 1969
9.14   Educational differentials
9.15   Male income inequality by schooling level
9.16   Poverty rates, 1969
9.17   Poverty rates, alternative schooling measures, 1969
10.1   Correlation coefficients for variables in tables 10.2–10.5, 1920–1970
10.2   Building trades, 1925–1970
10.3   Drivers and helpers, 1937–1970
10.4   Manufacturing skilled and semiskilled versus unskilled, 1925–1948
10.5   Occupational wage differentials, 1947–1968
11.1   Changes in mean earnings by industry, 1949–1969
11.2   Distribution of earnings by industry, 1949
11.3   Distribution of earnings by industry, 1969
11.4   Changes in distribution of earnings by industry, 1949–1969, thirty industries
11.5   Changes in distribution of earnings by industry, 1949–1969, twenty manufacturing industries
11.6   Changes in distribution of earnings by industry, 1949–1969, thirty industries
11.7   Changes in distribution of earnings by industry, 1949–1969, twenty-five industries
11.8   Changes in distribution of earnings by industry, 1949–1969, twenty manufacturing industries
11.9   Correlation coefficients for thirty industries
11.10   Correlation coefficients for twenty manufacturing industries
12.1   Schooling levels by industry, 1969
12.2   Schooling levels, sixty-five manufacturing industries, 1969
12.3   Expected schooling levels, sixty-five manufacturing industries
12.4   Deviations of actual from expected schooling levels, sixty-five manufacturing industries, 1969
12.5   Correlation coefficients for variables in tables 12.2–12.4
12.6   Mean earnings by industry, 1949 and 1969
12.7   Proportions of workers in upper and lower tails, twenty-five industries, 1949
12.8   Proportions of workers in upper and lower tails, twenty-five industries, 1969
12.9   Proportions of workers in upper and lower tails, twenty manufacturing industries, 1949
12.10   Proportions of workers in upper and lower tails, twenty manufacturing industries, 1969

12.11   Proportions of workers in upper and lower tails, sixty-five manufacturing industries, 1969

12.12   Effects of concentration and unionization, twenty manufacturing industries

12.13   Effects of unionization, thirty industries

13.1   Pareto coefficients, 1969

13.2   Ratio of production or nonsupervisory workers to total employees

13.3   Ratio of nonproduction to production workers, 1948–1970

13.4   Ratio of nonproduction to production workers, Cochrane-Orcutt regressions

LIST OF FIGURES

2.1   Mincer model
2.2   Becker–Chiswick model
3.1   Job choice in Tinbergen's model
4.1   Inequality multiplier greater than one
4.2   Inequality multiplier less than one
4.3   Rotation, inequality multiplier greater than one
4.4   Rotarion, inequality multiplier less then one
5.1   Equilibrium wage function, $\sigma < 1, \rho < 0$
5.2   Equilibrium wage function, $\sigma > 1, \rho > 0$
5.3   Equilibrium wage function, $\sigma = 1, \rho = 0$

Chapter 1

INTRODUCTION

The size distribution of labor earnings[1] may be interpreted in two very different ways. The traditional view is that earnings are factor *rewards* for the provision of different factor services. The major research questions then concern the magnitude of the rewards for different factor services and the distribution of those factor services among the labor force. For example, current research is directed towards identifying the magnitude of the factor rewards for schooling, job experience, innate ability and social background and towards explaining the distributions of these characteristics of individual workers. This approach may be called the individual characteristics approach, since it relates the distribution of earnings to the distribution of individual characteristics.

In contrast, the analysis undertaken in this book treats earnings as factor *prices*. As with all prices, earnings play an allocative role in the economy. They determine the assignment of workers to jobs. The distribution of earnings therefore arises as the outcome of a particular equilibrium of the economy. The major research questions concern the complete description of the supplies and demands for workers and the relation between the equilibrium earnings distribution and these supplies and demands.

This book, in following the second interpretation, investigates the relation between the distribution of capital among jobs and the distribution of labor earnings. Although some work has already been done, most economists are not aware of the formal relation between capital and the distribution of earnings. Capital is clearly relevant to the functional distribution of income (that is, the

---

[1] The size distribution of labor earnings is the description of the relation between each level of earnings (within a specified time period) and the number of workers with labor earnings equal to that level. A typical means of describing this relation is to use a population density function. Let x be the level of earnings and let $f(x)$ be the number of workers with earnings equal to x. Then $\int_{x_1}^{x_2} f(x) \, dx$ is the number of workers with earnings between x_1 and x_2. The size distribution of labor earnings is then described by the function $f(x)$.

division of national income among payments to capital, labor, land and other factors), but the relevance of capital to the division of labor payments among individual workers is not apparent. The major goal of this book is to explain why capital is central to questions concerning the size distribution of earnings among individuals and to demonstrate empirically that the predicted relationships are robust.

How can capital affect the distribution of earnings? Consider a simple economy in which all workers earn their income by renting identical machines and producing identical goods in a single-good economy. Suppose, furthermore, that only one individual can work with a machine. One way of describing the abilities of workers is by reference to the amounts of output they produce. A worker's output can be taken as a measure of his or her productive ability, a postulated single-dimensional variable describing differences among workers. However, the distribution of outputs (which we now take as the distribution of productive abilities) is not the same as the distribution of income. From each worker's output must be substracted the rent for the machine. This rent is the same for all workers, regardless of their output. Therefore, the distribution of labor income will be of the same shape as the distribution of productive abilities, but it will be shifted to the left by the amount of the machine rent. Labor incomes or earnings would then be more unequally distributed than productive abilities.

Now consider what happens when the economy switches to a larger machine (representing more capital). The outputs of individual workers would go up (although perhaps not in the same proportion), but the rental cost of the machines would also go up. The outcome for earnings inequality depends on the increase in outputs relative to the increase in machine rental costs. Earnings inequality could go down or up, depending upon how the new levels of output are related to the old outputs and to the change in machine rents. In this way changes in the amount of capital per worker can affect the inequality of labor earnings.

Let us now examine the nature of a theory of the distribution of earnings based on the individual characteristics approach (which treats earnings as factor rewards). The first step in this analysis is to postulate the existence of a function relating the earnings of an individual to the individual's earnings-relevant characteristics. This relation may be called the earnings function. The second step takes the factor rewards discovered in the first step as given and relates the distribution of earnings to the distribution of individual characteristics.

Suppose a social scientist, in implementing the first step, collects a large data base consisting of detailed information about individuals, including their earnings in a given period. The information may consist of the amount of formal schooling each individual has received, the quality of the schooling, the individual's age or work experience, his or her socio-economic background, childhood intelligence quotient, or cognitive or noncognitive skills. Using this data base, the social scientist observes a statistical relation between the characteristics of the individuals and their earnings, called the earnings function. What is the nature of this observed relation? What does it describe? What is the extent of its validity? From the observed relation between individuals' characteristics and their earnings, what can be inferred about the relation between the distribution of earnings and the distribution of individual characteristics?

The earnings function estimated by the social scientist is valid in the following sense. It identifies the sources of differences in earnings among individuals: that is, it identifies the earnings-relevant characteristics of individuals. Furthermore, the earnings function estimates the valuations placed on those differences by the society from which the data are taken. In other words, the earnings function estimates the magnitudes of different factor rewards. The estimated earnings function therefore validly predicts the source of the difference in earnings between two individuals with different characteristics.

Suppose now that the society or economy changes. One source of change may be in the distribution of individual characteristics. Can the earnings function be used to predict the resulting change in the distribution of earnings? That is to say, can we assume that the earnings function will remain unchanged as the distribution of individual characteristics changes? In general, the answer is no (the special conditions that must hold are discussed in Chapters 2 and 4). The earnings function explains why an individual's earnings are what they are in a given state of the economy. But what is exogenous to the determination of a given individual's earnings is endogenous to the determination of the entire distribution of earnings. As the distribution of individual characteristics changes, the valuations placed by the economy on the individual characteristics change. As a result, the earnings function shifts. The earnings function cannot therefore be used to predict changes in the distribution of earnings resulting from changes in the distribution of individual characteristics.

A second source of change in an economy is in conditions unrelated to particular individuals. There can be technological change or capital accumulation, for example. As Tinbergen has observed (1975a, p. 54; 1975b, p. 39), these variables are the same for all observations used to estimate the earnings function. Therefore their effect on the distribution of earnings cannot be observed. When these variables change, the earnings function changes and the distribution of earnings changes. The earnings function does not even suggest the influence of variables unrelated to particular individuals. Its use as a methodological device has caused economists to ignore major determinants of changes in the distribution of earnings.

Let us now examine three areas where our understanding of economic problems may be revised by interpreting earnings as factor prices. Nowhere has the individual characteristics approach had such a diversionary effect on the economic literature as in the subject of poverty. In the thirteen years or so since the war on poverty began in the United States, the reductions in poverty rates have been achieved by increasing the transfers to the poor. The amount of pretransfer poverty remains virtually unchanged (Plotnick and Skidmore, 1975, p. 137). The US economy is generating as much poverty now as it did when the war on poverty began. But, except among radical economists, the research agenda has not concerned the question of why there is a specific amount of poverty in the US economy. Instead, most research has been directed towards identifying who is poor and towards the specification of characteristics associated with poverty. The implicit assumption is that the rate of poverty would be generally the same if the US population were placed in a different economy. Such research is useful for the design of assistance programs. But listing who is poor and what their characteristics are does not constitute a theory of poverty, any more than a set of New York telephone books constitutes a theory of urban population. The study of poverty should include not only an examination of the characteristics of individuals that result in their inadequate earnings but also the reasons why the economy places such a low valuation on their labor services.

A second area where our ideas may be revised is in studying the interaction between education and ability in the determination of an individual's earnings. In particular, some economists have attempted to establish the extent of complementarity between education and ability. The problem with these attempts is that the nature of the relations being estimated have not been adequately identified. Does the estimated relation describe individuals, for example the way in which ability affects the amount the individual learns or benefits from the education process? Or does the estimated relation describe the society in which the individuals are placed, and the valuations the society puts on different combinations of the attributes education and ability? The relation between an individual's earnings and his or her education and ability is a composite of two relations. The first is the relation between an individual's education and abilities and his or her employment-relevant characteristics. The second is the relation between these employment-relevant characteristics and the earnings that an individual with this set of characteristics receives in the existing state of society. It is necessary to study both of these relations separately in order to produce interpretable results.

The treatment of earnings as factor prices is also relevant to the attempt to divide the source of earnings inequality up among categories of heredity, environment and covariance between the two. Although there has been some recognition that this division can vary from economy to economy, the proportions of variance attributable to each source are treated as natural constants and are not themselves explained. In their estimation, they are not treated as being endogeneously determined. In contrast, if earnings are regarded as factor prices, the important research questions concern the determinations of the market valuations placed on inherited characteristics versus environmental characteristics, rather than simply their estimation. For example, Chapter 4 presents a model in which the inequality in the productive abilities of workers is not necessarily equal to the inequality in their earnings; the two are related by a parameter called the inequality multiplier. That is, the (one-dimensional) differences among workers are exaggerated or moderated by the circumstances of the economy in which they are placed. What is needed in the literature is a theory that explains the proportions of earnings inequality attributable to hereditary versus environmental sources in terms of the characteristics of the state of the economy.

Remarkably, the general approach taken in this book is not new. Mincer's seminal paper presenting the human capital approach appeared in 1958. Champernowne's seminal paper on the stochastic chance model of income distribution appeared in 1953. But even earlier, in a paper first published in Dutch (a perfectly acceptable language) in 1947 and later translated into English in 1951, Tinbergen presented a model in which the distribution of earnings is derived as a solution to the problem of allocating heterogeneous labor to heterogeneous jobs. As with all prices, earnings therefore play an allocative role, and the distribution of earnings and the valuations placed on individual characteristics depend on the particular equilibrium of the economy. In an independent contribution, Roy (1951) developed the implications of comparative advantage for the assignment of workers to jobs and developed some of the consequences for the distribution of earnings. Tinbergen's and Roy's contributions will be discussed in Chapter 3.

One reason that the ideas of Roy and Tinbergen have not received greater attention is that their points of view are so obvious. Most economists would take it for granted that the distribution of earnings depends both on supply and on demand variables. Most economists would take it for granted that there exists comparative advantage in the performance of jobs by workers. Perhaps because these starting points are so obvious, many economists studying the distribution of earnings have not bothered to consider the full implications for the distribution of earnings. Yet these implications are so extensive that they may substantially revise our understanding of the nature of the distribution of earnings. In a similar manner, the introduction of the obvious principle of rational expectations into the study of dynamic cobweb models of markets has eventually, after a long period of gestation, led to a complete revision of our understanding of macroeconomics and monetary phenomena.

Ironically, in discussions of the literature, the contributions of Tinbergen and Roy have often been placed in the category of ability theories, as if they implied that the distribution of earnings could be explained by reference to appropriately defined innate abilities. The irony of this classification is that the theories imply just the opposite: that the distribution of earnings cannot be explained solely by reference to any set of worker characteristics, including ability. For example, following Roy's analysis, suppose there exists comparative advantage in the performance of jobs by workers. It follows that workers differ in their relative performances at those jobs. By the same token, the jobs also differ in the relative earnings that workers would receive. The ratio of two workers' earnings may be two to three at one job and three to four in the other. Therefore, the distribution of jobs in the economy will affect the distribution of earnings. The theory of comparative advantage in individuals is not just a theory of abilities, a theory of the initial difference among workers; it is also a theory of jobs and the differences in earnings among a given group of workers generated by those jobs.

The treatment of earnings as factor prices leads to a substantially different ideology than the individual characteristics approach. By far the most ideological fervor in income distribution has been concentrated on the functional distribution, the division of national income among the categories of labor, capital, land and other factors. This fervor arises from the question of whether income from certain sources is legitimate or justified, not whether the resulting distribution is equal or unequal. If income from the ownership of capital is illegitimate or unjustified, then it is illegitimate or unjustified no matter who receives it, even if the recipients are widows or orphans. This is certainly a defensible position. Fortunately, it is not my own, and I do not have to defend it. The position rests on the argument that whether or not an income is justified depends on the individual's contribution to production. The major ideological point of this book is that an individual's contribution to production cannot be related or attributed solely to his individual characteristics; his absolute and relative contribution to production depend upon the economy in which he is placed. If in the existing state of an economy an individual is in poverty, earning 30 percent of the average income, and if in an alternative state of the economy the individual would earn 60 percent of the average income and be out of poverty, to what extent can we attribute the individual's poverty to his own characteristics? If one worker's marginal product is four times that of another worker's when there is £20,000 capital per worker, and his marginal product would only be twice the other worker's if there were £10,000 capital per worker, does it make sense to explain that his earnings are four times as high as the second worker's because his marginal product is four times as high? The answer is no. The marginal product of a worker's labor is not a characteristic or property of the worker.

Of course it is already known that in a simple sense an individual's earnings do not depend only on his individual characteristics. Treating labor as an aggregate, the marginal product of labor depends on the quantities of the cooperating factors, capital and land. In particular, whether a person's earnings are high or low depends on how much capital has been accumulated in the economy. The point of the previous discussion is that not only do the absolute levels of workers' marginal products depend on the capital intensity of the economy, but the relative marginal products of workers (one worker's marginal product divided by another worker's marginal product) also depend on the capital intensity of the economy.

The ideological importance of the results of this monograph is that they establish a close connection between earnings inequality and capital accumulation and technological change in a market economy. In the absence of countervailing influences, market economies may tend towards more earnings inequality. But earnings inequality in any case is not an inevitable, incurable consequence of a market economy. The evolution of a market economy can be accompanied by policies to ameliorate any ill effects. The net conclusion of this book is therefore positive.

Once the individual characteristics approach and its implicit assumptions are shed, a wide range of possible influences on the distribution of earnings becomes apparent. Corresponding to these possible influences is a wide range of potential policies to affect the distribution of earnings. Unlike most policies to affect the pretransfer distribution of earnings, these policies would not require the manipulation of individual characteristics or, for that matter, the manipulation of individuals.

However, this monograph is directed towards the positive problem of describing the generation of the distribution of earnings. The normative conclusions and policy prescriptions deserve cautious and leisurely consideration and are therefore left to future work.[2]

The next chapter presents a critical analysis of the attempt to use human capital theory to explain the distribution of earnings. The human capital approaches are of particular interest because they clearly try to use a theory of individual behavior to draw inferences about aggregate phenomena and therefore fall under the heading of the individual characteristics approach discussed previously.

Chapter 3 presents a discussion of some (but not all) of the literature. This literature has generally been neglected, excluded or misinterpreted in previous "surveys", and therefore is discussed extensively here.

---

[2] The normative aspects of the pretransfer distribution of earnings have been studied by Tinbergen (1970) and Ritzen (1977), among others.

Chapters 4, 5 and 6 contain the major theoretical content of the book. Chapter 4 presents a straightforward aggregate model of earnings inequality. Instead of relating the characteristics of workers directly to their earnings, the model relates the characteristics of workers to the level of production. Workers are assumed to differ according to a single parameter, which can be interpreted as measuring a worker's skill, or alternatively his human capital or productive ability. Output per worker is then assumed to depend on the amount of capital per worker and on the average skill per worker. Using this production function it is possible to derive the linear relation between the marginal product of a worker's labor and his skill. It is then possible to relate the distribution of marginal products, and therefore the distribution of earnings, to the distribution of skill. The two distributions are not in general the same. The amount of earnings inequality, as measured by the standard deviation divided by the mean, equals the inequality in the distribution of skill times a coefficient called the inequality multiplier. This inequality multiplier is given by the elasticity of output with respect to the average skill per worker divided by one minus the elasticity of output with respect to the capital to labor ratio. The inequality multiplier therefore depends on the production function, and it is possible to apply to earnings inequality some of the sophisticated analysis that has already been applied to the functional distribution of income. In particular, it is possible to analyze the conditions under which the inequality multiplier is identically one and the conditions under which capital intensity and average skill affect it. The major hypothesis studied in the analysis is that earnings inequality increases as capital intensity increases and decreases as the average skill per worker increases, everything else the same. This relatively simple model brings out the reason why the distribution of earnings depends both on the distribution of workers' characteristics and on the economy in which they are placed. Furthermore, it identifies the restricted conditions under which the previous analysis of the distribution of earnings is valid.

Chapter 5 develops the assignment problem. Given heterogeneous jobs and heterogeneous workers, which worker will be at which job in equilibrium? In the simple case, workers can be characterized by a single parameter and similarly jobs can be characterized by a single parameter. These parameters are then related, via what is called an assignment principle, to the economic outcome (typically production) of a given worker in combination with a given job. One of these assignment principles, based on preferences, is discussed in the context of Tinbergen's paper in Chapter 3. A second principle, comparative advantage, is also discussed in Chapter 3, but is presented in more detail in Chapter 5. The most important assignment principle is the scale of resources effect. Instead of describing the distribution of jobs explicitly in terms of some abstract parameter (such as an ordinal measure of difficulty in the case of comparative advantage), it is possible to specify the distribution of jobs implicitly in terms of the distribution of cooperating factors, in this case units of capital or "machines" as they are called in the text. That is, the existence of a machine creates an implicit demand for labor and an implicit offer curve for labor of differing productive abilities. The intuitive reasoning behind the scale of resources effect can be presented very simply in terms of a matrix of outputs obtained from two individuals at two machines:

Matrix of outputs

	Machine 1	Machine 2
Worker 1	5	10
Worker 2	10	20

In the above matrix, five units of output are obtained if worker 1 uses machine 1 in a given period of time, ten units are produced by worker 1 using machine 2, and so on. The ratio of outputs for the two workers is the same at both machines, so that in a simple sense there is no comparative advantage. However, if worker 1 is assigned to machine 1 and worker 2 is assigned to machine 2, the total output will be 25 units. This is greater than the 20 units obtained if worker 1 is assigned to machine 2 and worker 2 is assigned to machine 1. In this simple case the more productive worker is assigned to the more productive (and presumably larger) machine in equilibrium. Chapter 5 analyzes the conditions under which in a market economy more productive workers will be assigned to larger machines, representing more capital. Also, it is possible to infer from the matrix of outputs the range in which the difference in machine rents must fall and the range in which the difference in worker earnings must fall in equilibrium.

Chapter 6 develops the differential rents theory of the distribution of earnings. Of course, David Ricardo is responsible for the first differential rents theory. In his model of the determination of land rents land is heteregoneous, differing by fertility, and labor is homogeneous. There is therefore no assignment problem. Chapter 6 in a sense generalizes Ricardo's differential rents model to two heterogeneous factors of production. In the model developed in that chapter, machines that differ in size represent one factor of production. Labor, differing in an innate characteristic – productive ability – is the other factor. Only one unit of labor can work with one machine. In equilibrium, a rent function relating the rent for a machine to the machine size and a wage function relating the wage rate to a worker's productive ability are determined by the partial differentials of the production function with respect to machine size and productive ability. The important conclusion from this model is that the distribution of capital among jobs affects in a predictable way the distribution of earnings among workers. In particular, the more unequal the distribution of capital among jobs, the more unequal will be the distribution of earnings.

The model combines elements of both classical and neoclassical economics. As in neoclassical economics, relative wages and relative machine rental costs are determined by the marginal contributions to production of a larger machine size or greater productive ability on the part of the worker. But the absolute levels of wages or machine rents are arbitrary. They depend on the reserve prices of labor and capital, which also affect the unemployment of labor or capital units.

Chapters 7–10 provide the major empirical work investigating the validity of the theories in Chapters 4, 5 and 6. Chapter 7 provides a transition between the theoretical work and the empirical work. It discusses the measurement of variables, tests the underlying assumption that more productive workers will be assigned to more capital intensive jobs in equilibrium, and discusses implications of the data for changes in earnings inequality over time. Chapter 8 contains the time-series tests of the theories. Two data sets are used. The first is for income inequality for 1949–1969. The data are taken from a time-series study by Chiswick and Mincer (1972). The second set uses data on upper income shares collected by Kuznets (1953) covering the period 1917–1948.

Chapter 9 uses cross-section data by state from the 1960 and 1970 US Censuses of Population. The capital to labor ratio and concentration of capital among jobs are not measured directly but are inferred from the industrial composition of employment. The chapter further investigates the determinants of educational differentials, income inequality within schooling levels and poverty rates. The results of Chapters 8 and 9 strongly support the differential rents theory of Chapter 6 and also give strong support to the argument of Chapter 4 that increases in productive ability (as measured by increases in the mean level of schooling) reduce earnings inequality rather than raise it, as predicted by the human capital approach.

Chapter 10 examines whether the results that have been obtained for earnings and income inequality are consistent with changes in wage differentials over time. Because the measure of the concentration of capital among jobs is not available for all time periods under consideration, the demand variables used are the capital to labor ratios for manufacturing and for nonfarm nonmanufacturing and the ratio of manufacturing employment to total nonfarm employment. The results are consistent among wage differentials and between wage differentials and earnings inequality. Both depend negatively on the manufacturing capital to labor ratio and the ratio of manufacturing employment to total nonfarm employment and positively on the nonfarm nonmanufacturing capital to labor ratio.

Chapters 11, 12 and 13 extend the analysis to include other demand variables. Chapter 11 considers the extent of temporal continuity in the distribution of earnings by industry. Using thirty manufacturing and nonmanufacturing industries, the analysis demonstrates that the best predictors of the proportions of workers in the upper and lower tails of the 1969 industry distributions of earnings are the corresponding proportions in the 1949 industry distributions of earnings. Changes in the capital to labor ratio, in the ratio of production workers to total employment, in productivity and in output occasionally have significant effects on the proportions, but these effects are small compared to the differences among industries. The inference drawn from this analysis is that shifts in production and employment among industries will have much stronger effects on aggregate earnings inequality than changes in the distribution of earnings within industries, for example arising from capital-skill complementarity. However, there are ambiguities in trying to draw conclusions about the aggregate distribution of earnings from shifts in production and employment. These ambiguities arise from alternative interpretations of the distribution of earnings within an industry, and are discussed at length in Chapter 11.

Chapter 12 examines the determinants of the distribution of earnings within industries. Essentially, reduced form demand functions are estimated in which the distribution of schooling and the distribution of earnings for workers within an industry are related to various characteristics of the industry, such as the capital to labor ratio, the ratio of production workers to total employment, and the ratio of research and development to value added. These results suggest that other characteristics of an industry besides the capital to labor ratio strongly affect the types of labor hired in the industry. At the aggregate level the distribution of jobs according to these demand characteristics will then affect the aggregate distribution of earnings.

Chapter 13 presents a preliminary study of two aspects of the upper tail of the distribution of earnings within an industry. The theory of organizational hierarchies provides a link between the shape of a hierarchy and earnings inequality in the upper tail, as measured by a parameter of the Pareto distribution. Section 2 of Chapter 13 relates the shape of hierarchies within industries, as estimated from the upper tail of the distribution of earnings within the industry, to various features of the industry. Section 3 examines the size of hierarchies within industries, as measured by the number of nonproduction workers. The empirical work demonstrates that within an industry the ratio of nonproduction workers to production workers increases as the ratio of capital to production workers goes up. However, the coefficients of this relation vary substantially from industry to industry. It follows that the number of nonproduction workers in the economy depends not only on the capital to labor ratio for the economy but on the industrial composition of employment.

Chapter 14 summarizes the conclusions of this work as well as the limitations and omissions. There remains a substantial amount of work to be done. Many of the implications of the general approach taken in this monograph are left to future work.

Chapter 2

A CRITIQUE OF THE HUMAN CAPITAL APPROACHES

1. Introduction

Although there are many other ways of looking at the personal distribution of earnings, by far the dominant approach has been the human capital school of thought. The reasons are obvious from the literature. The human capital methodology makes apparent a large number of research questions and empirical relations to be investigated and suggests many economically meaningful statistics that can be calculated. This chapter does not question the basic assumption behind the human capital approach, the argument that people take future benefits and costs into account in making current decisions, and that education and training can be regarded from the individual point of view as investments. But this assumption has been combined with less tenable assumptions in the human capital treatment of the distribution of income.

Certainly, there have been many critical discussions of the human capital approach to the distribution of earnings (the most notable being Blaug, 1976; Lucas, 1977; Rosen, 1977b; and Tinbergen, 1975b). But the human capital literature has not been revised to account for these criticisms.

In one of the de Vries lectures, Tinbergen (1975b, p. 37—55) discusses a number of criteria for evaluating the nature and validity of estimated relations. One of the points is that in an estimated relation in which a price appears, such as the earnings function, one must clearly specify whether the estimated relation is a supply, demand or reduced form equation in order to interpret it. But the interpretation of the earnings function in the human capital literature is ambiguous. There is a good reason for this ambiguity. There are in fact two distinct inconsistent human capital models of the distribution of earnings.

Mincer's model (1958, 1974) is the one most economists associate with the human capital school of thought. It is based on the assumption that individuals select among alternative schooling levels so that all differences in the present values of lifetime earnings are eliminated. As will be shown in section 2, this assumption simplifies the supply side of the market for individuals at a given schooling level. In contrast, the model developed by Becker and Chiswick (1966) simplifies the demand side of the market for individuals at any given level of education. Section 3 demonstrates that the Becker-Chiswick model requires the efficiency units assumption.

2. The Mincer model

The basic assumption underlying Mincer's schooling model is that individuals will choose among alternative levels of schooling on the basis of the present value of lifetime earnings. If one level of schooling offers a higher than average present value of lifetime earnings, individuals would acquire that level of schooling until the wage rate for that schooling level were reduced and its present value of lifetime earnings were brought into line with the present value for other levels of schooling. As a result, in equilibrium, the present value of lifetime earnings will be the same for all levels of schooling. If one also assumes that the length of the working life is the same for all levels of schooling, then the assumption imposes a simple form on the earnings function, the relation between an individual's earnings and his years of schooling. This earnings function takes the form $\ln E_s = \ln E_0 + rs$, where s is the number of years of schooling beyond the minimum, $\ln E_s$ is the logarithm of earnings of an individual with s years of schooling, $\ln E_0$ is the logarithm of earnings of an individual with the minimum years of schooling, and r is the discount rate used by individuals to calculate the present value of lifetime earnings. Mincer's schooling model therefore explains completely the earnings function.

But the earnings function does not by itself constitute a theory of the distribution of earnings. Even if schooling levels entirely determined the earnings of individuals, one would still need to know the number of individuals at each schooling level.

Consider the supply of individuals at a particular schooling level, holding the earnings for other schooling levels and the discount rate fixed. By the assumption that present values of lifetime earnings are equalized in equilibrium, this supply curve is perfectly elastic, i.e. it is horizontal, as shown in fig.2.1. (Taubman, 1978, similarly draws a horizontal supply curve in presenting his discussion of the human capital model in a textbook on income distribution.) The number of individuals with a particular level of schooling is therefore completely determined by the location of the demand curve. By explaining completely the relative earnings of individuals with different levels of schooling, Mincer's schooling

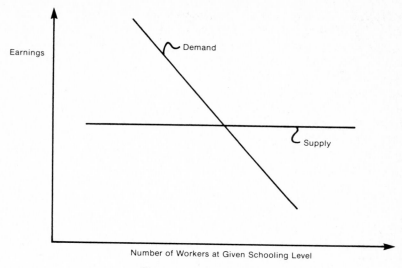

Figure 2.1. Mincer model.

model can give no explanation of the numbers of individuals at each level of schooling. Given the assumption that the present values of lifetime earnings are equalized, the distribution of earnings is then determined entirely by the demands for individuals with different schooling levels.

Suppose we are interested in the course of earnings inequality over time. This clearly depends on changes in the distribution of schooling over time. But what is the source of changes in the distribution of schooling? With no change in the discount rate, in the wage for the minimum years of schooling or in the underlying assumption that the present values of lifetime earnings are equalized, there is no change in the supply curves of individuals for each level of schooling. Instead, all changes in the distribution of schooling arise from changes in the demands for individuals at different schooling levels. Because these demands are nowhere brought into Mincer's analysis of the distribution of earnings, only a mechanical explanation of earnings inequality has been produced.

3. The Becker-Chiswick model

The previous section indicates that by making simplifying assumptions about the supplies of individuals to different schooling levels, the determination of earnings inequality is given by the demand side. It seems reasonable to ask whether there is also a simplifying assumption about the demand side which would allow one to explain the distribution of earnings in terms of models of the supply behavior or human capital investment behavior of individuals. The answer is yes. The efficiency units assumption provides the necessary simplification.

The efficiency units assumption has a long and little noted history. It is the silent partner of the labor theory of value. To express the value of goods in terms of an invariant unit of measurement (labor), it is first necessary to express the different qualities of labor in terms of different quantities of a single unit of measure. In developing the labor theory of value, Ricardo assumes, without very much evidence of doubt, that heterogeneous labor can be expressed in terms of efficiency units (1953, pp. 20–21):

> In speaking, however, of labour, as being the foundation of all value, and the relative quantity of labour as almost exclusively determining the relative value of commodities, I must not be supposed to be inattentive to the different qualities of labour, and the difficulty of comparing an hour's or a day's labour, in one employment, with the same duration of labour in another. The estimation in which different qualities of labour are held, comes soon to be adjusted in the market with sufficient precision for all practical purposes, and depends much on the comparative skill of the labourer, and intensity of the labour performed. The scale, when once formed, is liable to little variation. If a day's labour of a working jeweller be more valuable than a day's labour of a common labourer, it has long ago been adjusted, and placed in its proper position in the scale of value.

In other words, the relative amount of labor represented by two types of labor is unaltered by changes in the economy, and the relative quantities of labor can be measured by the relative wage rates. Early in his discussion, Marx similarly adopts the efficiency units assumption, with remarkably little discussion (1967, p. 44):

> Skilled labour counts only as simple labour intensified, or rather, as multiplied simple labour, a given quantity of skilled being considered equal to a greater quantity of simple labour. Experience shows that this reduction is constantly being made. A commodity may be the product of the most skilled labour, but its value, by equating it to the product of simple unskilled labour, represents a definite quantity of the latter labour alone. The different proportions in which different sorts of labour are reduced to unskilled labour as their standard, are established by a social process that goes on behind the backs of the producers, and, consequently, appear to be fixed by custom. For simplicity's sake we shall henceforth account every kind of labour to be

unskilled, simple labour; by this we do no more than save ourselves the trouble of making the reduction.

Again, it is being assumed that there is a fixed, invariant relation between any two types of labor, so that one type of labor can be expressed as a fixed quantity of the other type. A somewhat later classical economist, Sraffa (1960, p. 11), similarly relies on the efficiency units assumption:

> We suppose labour to be uniform in quality or, what amounts to the same thing, we assume any differences in quality to have been previously reduced to equivalent differences in quantity so that each unit of labour receives the same wage.

Samuelson (1971, pp. 404—405) has discussed the importance of the efficiency units assumption for the labor theory of value. In particular, the presence of comparative advantage (another classical concept) in the performance of jobs is inconsistent with the efficiency units assumption and is therefore inconsistent with the labor theory of value. A change in demand would then cause a change in the trade-offs between two types of labor. Other consequences of the efficiency units assumption for Marx's economics have been discussed by Morishima (1973, pp. 180—181) and by Bowles and Gintis (1977). However, the concern here is with the efficiency units assumption itself, and not with the labor theory of value or exploitation.

Under the efficiency units assumption, a worker's labor can be expressed as a fixed multiple or proportion of an arbitrary standard worker's labor. Suppose an individual with s years of schooling provides labor equal to b_s times the labor of an individual with the minimum years of schooling. The demand for workers with s years of schooling will then be perfectly elastic at a wage rate equal to b_s times the wage rate for workers with the minimum years of schooling. The demand curves will therefore be horizontal, as shown in fig. 2.2, and the number of individuals at each schooling level will be determined by the locations of the upward-sloping supply curves. Under the efficiency units assumption, therefore, the distribution of earnings and changes in it are determined by the supplies of individuals at each level of education.

By a subtle reinterpretation of its terms, the expression for the earnings function can be made to incorporate the efficiency units assumption. Suppose now that r is the rate of return to schooling, which can vary from individual to individual, instead of the discount rate. (The point that r is interpreted differently in different human capital models has been made previously by Lucas, 1977). Then $\ln E_{si} = \ln E_0 + r_i s_i$, where s_i is the number of years of schooling beyond the minimum, r_i is the rate of return for individual i (assumed here to be the

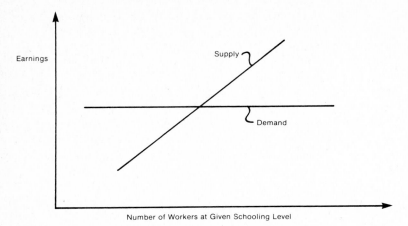

Figure 2.2. Becker-Chiswick model.

same for all years of schooling), $\ln E_0$ is the logarithm of earnings for an individual with the minimum years of schooling, and $\ln E_{si}$ is the logarithm of earnings for individual i with s years of schooling. Because this relation uses rates of return and not the discount rate, the relation holds for all distributions of schooling, not just in equilibrium when the present values of lifetime earnings are equalized, as in Mincer's model. Individual i's labor is then equivalent to and a perfect substitute for E_{si}/E_0 units of the labor of an individual with the minimum years of schooling; this ratio is unaffected by the distribution of schooling among individuals or by any other characteristics of the economy. Taking variances on both sides of the expression yields a legitimate theory of earnings inequality, with the variance of schooling explained exogenously on the basis of supply considerations.

For a complete development of the model, however, one must also provide a separate theory of the supply behavior of individuals; this is no longer provided by the hypothesis of equalized present values of lifetime earnings. Furthermore, the rate of return to an individual's schooling is determined by the effect of schooling on an individual's productivity, i.e. it is determined by the production function. If the rate of return is not explained in the model, the explanation for the earnings function and for the distribution of earnings is incomplete.

The Becker and Chiswick development of the human capital model is somewhat more complicated than the above expository model, and correspondingly harder to pin down. The starting point for the analysis (as presented by Chiswick, 1974, p. 37) is the relation $\ln E_{N,i} = \ln E_0 + \Sigma_{j=1}^{N} r_{ij}^* + U_i$, where N is the number of years of human capital investments, $\ln E_0$ is the logarithm of earnings if no human capital investments are made, U_i is a residual term, r_{ij}^* is the rate of return for individual i for the jth year of training adjusted for the proportion of income invested in each year, and $\ln E_{N,i}$ is the logarithm of earnings if individual i undertakes human capital investments for N years.

The possibility that the rate of return varies for different stages of human capital investment (and presumably decline with continued investments) means that a potential theory of the investment behavior of individuals can be developed by assuming that individuals invest in themselves up to the point where the marginal cost of borrowing equals the marginal rate of return on human capital investments. This theory of the supply side (referred to somewhat misleadingly as a supply and demand model) has been developed by Becker (1967 or 1975, pp. 94–144).

Nevertheless, because the Becker–Chiswick analysis uses rates of return instead of discount rates, the relation $\ln E_{N,i} = \ln E_0 + \Sigma_{j=1}^{N} r_{ij}^* + U_i$ holds for all distributions of investments, not just the distribution arising from a particular theory of the supply behavior of individuals. Furthermore, the rates of return are not assumed to depend on any characteristics of the economy, such as the capital intensity or the distribution of capital among jobs or the state of technology. Also, in taking variances on both sides of the earnings function the rates of return are not treated as a function of the distribution of investments in individuals. Using an individual with no human capital investments as the standard person, individual i's labor earns $E_{N,i}/E_0$ times as much as the standard person's labor per time period. Assuming earnings are proportional to contributions to production, individual i's labor is therefore equivalent to $E_{N,i}/E_0$ units of the standard person's labor, i.e. individual i's labor is equivalent to $E_{N,i}/E_0$ efficiency units. The ratio $E_{N,i}/E_0$ depends only on the characteristics of individual i, his rates of return and his investments in human capital. The Becker–Chiswick analysis therefore incorporates the efficiency units assumption. (In reaching this conclusion, I have undoubtedly misrepresented Becker and Chiswick's presentation of the theory. But I have at least misrepresented their version of the theory in a clear and consistent manner.)

Besides the reduction of heterogeneous labor to homogeneous efficiency units, the assumption leads to several other very strong conclusions. First, it is possible to construct microeconomic or macroeconomic production functions which depend only on the sum of efficiency units and not on their distribution among individuals. The marginal product of an efficiency unit is then well defined and is the same for all individuals independent of how many efficiency units their labor is equivalent to. The distribution of efficiency units is then the same shape as the distribution of marginal productivities, and this in turn is presumably the same shape as the distribution of productive abilities. Secondly (and this follows almost immediately from the first conclusion), it does not matter who does which job. If one hundred efficiency units are required, an employer could use one hundred people of one efficiency unit apiece, fifty people of two units apiece, or twenty-five people of four units apiece. The cost in wages paid would be the same. Another way of putting this result is to say that there is no economic reason, other than that some individuals have already received differentiated training for the jobs, to allocate particular individuals or individuals with particular levels of productivity to particular jobs. Thirdly (and the point most relevant to any theory relating the earnings distribution solely to individual characteristics), the number of efficiency units that an individual's labor is equivalent to is a property of the individual himself, since it is invariant under any change of the economic system. It is then entirely appropriate to relate the distribution of earnings, via the distribution of efficiency units, to the distribution of individual characteristics.

It is understandable why the Mincer model and the Becker–Chiswick model have coexisted for so long. It is easy to switch from interpreting r as the discount rate to interpreting it as a rate of return. In Mincer's model in equilibrium, the discount rate equals the rate of return from the point of view of an individual. Nevertheless, the two models are inconsistent. The horizontal supply curves of the Mincer model do not in general meet the horizontal demand curves of the Becker–Chiswick model. The human capital school of thought cannot claim that both models are simultaneously valid. A choice must be made between explaining the earnings function (and assuming present values of lifetime earnings are equalized) and explaining the distribution of earnings (and adopting the efficiency units assumption).

4. Marshall's objections

Marshall's discussion (1964, pp. 454–459) of the efficiency units assumption indicates the conditions under which the assumption does not hold (see Taubman, 1976; Rosen, 1977a, 1977b; and Sattinger, 1977a) for other presentations). Marshall, in explaining why earnings could differ within an occupation, argued that competition tended to make earnings in occupations of equal difficulty correspond to the efficiency of the workers. While Marshall was certainly being vague about the notion of individual efficiency, he has definitely identified a limitation of the efficiency units assumption. The relative efficiency of two workers depends in general on the difficulty of the occupation and is not independent of the job performed. This limitation is closely related to comparative advantage. If there exists comparative advantage in the performance of two jobs by two workers, then the ratio of one worker's contributions to production divided by the other worker's contributions to production depends on which job is used to compare the two. Whenever there is comparative advantage, then, the efficiency units assumption does not hold.

Marshall also argued that the efficiency units assumption does not hold when there is expensive fixed capital. When labor is combined with capital, employers would pay the more efficient workers more than in proportion to their production. Contrary to the efficiency units assumption, an employer is not indifferent between hiring two workers producing, say, fifty units apiece per time period and one worker producing one hundred units per time period if the employer must provide a machine for each worker. He would pay the worker producing one hundred units more than twice what he would pay the other workers because he would be required to provide less capital. In contrast, the efficiency units assumption requires that any number of workers can be combined with a given amount of the cooperating factor, in this case capital. That is to say, there are no diminishing marginal returns to the addition of more bodies as long as the sum of efficiency units remains the same. There are only diminishing marginal returns to the addition of more efficiency units to a given amount of capital.

Neither the assumption simplifying the supply side nor the assumption simplifying the demand side is reasonable. Neither is desirable. They rule out the most interesting questions concerning the earnings distribution. How do capital accumulation, technological change and improvements in labor quality affect wage differentials and earnings inequality? The human capital approaches cannot answer these questions; they do not even pose them. With their tremendous normative and ideological implications, these questions can only be answered in a general multimarket equilibrium framework.

Chapter 3

SOME OF THE LITERATURE

1. Introduction

This chapter does not summarize the literature concerning the size distribution of labor earnings. There have been several attempts to do so (Reder, 1968, 1969; Lydall, 1968; Mincer, 1970; Pen, 1971; Bronfenbrenner, 1971; Johnson, 1973; Atkinson, 1975; Blinder, 1977; Brown, 1978; Sahota, 1978; and Wood, 1978). But the distribution of earnings has a rich internal structure. It allows for a large variety of approaches and for the application of completely unrelated methodologies. For this reason it has been possible to pursue one line of inquiry without building on or even being aware of foregoing work on the distribution of earnings. The consequence has been that while the chance, human capital, dualistic growth and path analysis models have been developed, other valid and interesting approaches have been neglected. This chapter discusses in depth the literature that has largely been ignored or slighted in other surveys of the literature.

Although Tinbergen's work on income distribution is widely known and regarded in Europe, American economists have only recently begun to take notice of his contributions. As a result of his recent book (Tinbergen, 1975a), there has been some discussion of his approach (Haveman, 1977; Osberg, 1976a, 1976b; Atkinson, 1975; Chiswick, 1976; Kuipers, 1976; Wood, 1975; Sahota, 1977; see also the general reply by Tinbergen, 1977). Despite the recent discussion, many US economists working on the distribution of earnings are unfamiliar with the ideas which lie behind Tinbergen's book and are similarly unaware of the long period of time (three decades) over which those ideas have been developed. The next section therefore concentrates on Tinbergen's early contributions.

In an independent contribution, Roy (1951) developed a model of the market assignment of individuals to jobs. This paper has, however, been overshadowed by an earlier paper attempting to show that abilities combine multiplicatively instead of additively. Roy's model of the assignment of individuals to jobs will be discussed in section 3.

Tuck's development of the theory of rank (1954) raises the possibility that the rank an individual has in a hierarchy and the number of subordinates under his control are related to his income. Tuck develops the rudiments of a multi-market equilibrium model of the assignment of employees to level of control, in which the size distribution of firms adjusts to reconcile the supplies and demands for employees of different managerial abilities. Tuck's contribution, along with those of Mayer and Reder, are discussed in section 4.

2. Tinbergen's theory of the distribution of earnings

Tinbergen's theory of the earnings distribution has come to be known as a "supply and demand" model. This terminology is something of a misnomer. It is certainly true that supply and demand are behind the workings of the model. But the term is too rigidly associated with supply and demand curves and an equilibrium price to suggest the way in which the distribution of earnings is determined. The process by which supply and demand operate in a continuum of markets is unlike anything one would expect from the everyday supply and demand analysis.

In Tinbergen's original treatment of the problem, published in Dutch in 1947 and translated into English in 1951, he discusses the way in which he views the earnings distribution question. It is useful to distinguish three elements of the theory. The first is the characterization of jobs that are available in an economy. These jobs or occupations can be described by one or more parameters. The second element in the model is the characterization of the individuals seeking jobs. Again, one or more parameters are used to describe (perhaps ordinally) the individuals. The third element is the principle which guides the assignment of individuals to jobs. This principle obviously depends on the way in which jobs and individuals are characterized.

In the special case that is worked out by Tinbergen, jobs differ by effort required, represented by the parameter s, and individuals differ by what is called ability, represented by the parameter t. The terminology here is perhaps inappropriate: effort and ability are not related to production in the model. Instead, the principle which guides individuals into jobs arises from their preferences. Their indifference curves between income and job choices depend upon the parameter t. In particular, along a single indifference curve the wage an individual would be just willing to accept is a positive function of the square of the difference between the individual's value of t and the value of s for the job chosen. The indifference or wage offer curve can be written

$$w = w_0 + a(s - t)^2,$$

where w is the wage, w_0 is a parameter for the level of utility and a is a constant which is the same for all individuals. In a later article, Tinbergen refers to the difference between s and t as the "tension". For a job with a relatively high value of s, individuals with higher values of t are willing to accept lower wages. In equilibrium, individuals are almost automatically assigned to jobs so that, comparing two individuals, the one with the lower value of t will end up in the job with the lower value of s. The equilibrium wage function (the wage as a function of the job parameter s) occurs when the distribution of jobs that the people seek exactly conforms to the distribution of jobs available. (It should be emphasized that the particular form of the indifference curve is not essential to Tinbergen's theory, and he has later (1975a) experimented with other forms.)

The way in which individuals are led to select jobs is presented graphically in fig. 3.1. For values of s which are greater than an individual's value of t, the individual's indifference curve is upward-sloping; for values of s less than his value of t, the indifference curve is downward-sloping. For example, in fig. 3.1 the individual with the parameter t_3 has all his indifference curves horizontal at the value of the job parameter equal to t_3.

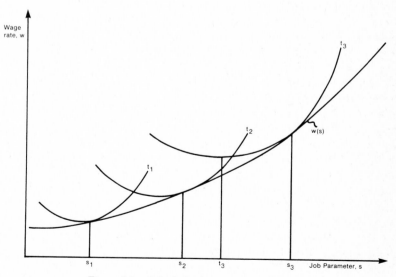

Figure 3.1. Job choice in Tinbergen's model.

The upward-sloping wage function $w(s)$ shown in this graph occurs when the individual parameters, e.g. t_1, t_2 and t_3, are always greater than the values of the jobs they choose, s_1, s_2 and s_3. If the parameters for individuals were greater than the job parameters, the wage function would be downward-sloping.

Individuals choose the jobs which place them on the highest indifference curves. For individual 1, with parameter t_1, the highest attainable indifference curve is the one which is just tangent to the wage function $w(s)$; hence, he is led to select the job with parameter s_1. Individual 2, with a higher parameter t_2, would not select job s_1. To see this, consider the point where individual 1's indifference curve is tangent to the wage function $w(s)$. At this point, the slope of individual 2's indifference curve is less, since the difference between t_2 and s_1 is greater than the difference between t_1 and s_1. Hence, individual 2 chooses a higher value of s; his highest indifference curve is tangent at s_2.

Figure 3.1 shows only how individuals select jobs for a given wage function $w(s)$; it does not show whether $w(s)$ is in fact an equilibrium wage function. For $w(s)$ to be consistent with equilibrium, it is necessary that the density function of jobs offered conforms to the density function of jobs available. In terms of fig. 3.1 this means that the number of individuals seeking jobs in any given interval, say s_1 to s_2, is equal to the number of jobs that are available in that interval. In this sense the model is certainly a supply and demand one. But clearly, the determination of the wage function $w(s)$ is far removed from the intersection of the supply and demand curves.

Instead, the equilibrium wage function is determined by individuals' trade-offs between jobs with different parameters and wages. Figure 3.1 suggests the way in which the equilibrium wage function might be determined. Suppose we could establish, on some *a priori* basis, that in equilibrium individual 1, with parameter t_1, would end up in the job with parameter s_1, and similarly individuals with parameters t_2 and t_3 would end up with jobs with parameters s_2 and s_3. The wage function that would bring this about would be such that its slope at s_1 would be the same as the slope of individual 1's indifference curve at s_1, and similarly for points s_2 and s_3. Going further, suppose we knew the value of t that would be associated with each value of s in equilibrium. Then for each value of s, we could calculate the slope of each indifference curve that is tangent to the wage function at that value of s. Then we would have the slope of the wage function at each value of s, i.e. a differential equation. Solving this differential equation yields the wage function, but the solution involves an arbitrary constant. This constant is then determined by a boundary condition, so-called because it refers to the marginal jobs or the marginal workers. Briefly, this boundary condition sets the absolute level of the wage for the "last" workers employed, i.e. the employed workers with the lowest values of the parameter t.

These workers have the alternative of not working, and the amount which they must be paid so that they are just willing to work (their "reserve price") determines the arbitrary constant in the wage function. (The determination of the arbitrary constant through the boundary condition will be discussed in Chapter 6.)

The determination of the wage function in the above case was made easy by the assumption that we could figure out who would do which job without knowing what the wage function was. This requires that the distribution of jobs not depend on the wage costs of filling them. Tinbergen describes this case as one in which the frequency distribution of the demand for labor is rigid. In general, however, the distribution of jobs will depend on the wage function, even in a short-run equilibrium. There may still exist an equilibrium wage function, but it is not so easy to uncover. The assignment of workers to jobs and the equilibrium wage function must now be determined simultaneously instead of one at a time. Nevertheless, it is possible to solve for both the equilibrium assignment and the equilibrium wage function using iterative numerical techniques.

The foregoing discussion should make clear the connection between Tinbergen's theory of the distribution of earnings and Ricardo's differential rents. In both cases the rate of change of a price (the rent in one case and the wage in the other) equals in equilibrium the rate of change of the objective function (agricultural output or individual utility) with respect to its argument (fertility of the soil or the job parameter s). The result in both cases is a differential equation relating a slope to a partial derivative.

The conceptual accomplishments of Tinbergen's first paper are as follows:

(a) Tinbergen recognized the existence of an assignment problem. Not only are workers heterogeneous in their skills and preferences, but jobs are heterogeneous in various ways. One must therefore study how the economic system assigns individuals to jobs.

(b) The earnings received by individuals operate to assign individuals to different jobs; they are not simply rewards for different levels of productivity.

(c) The relative earnings for two individuals are determined by their trade-offs in the jobs they perform, i.e. by the extent of substitution.

(d) The distribution of earnings is not a simple reflection of the distribution of individual characteristics but also depends on the distribution of jobs in the economy.

The most important conclusion arising from Tinbergen's analysis is that the distribution of labor earnings "depends in a complicated manner on the frequency distribution of employments offered and of the personal abilities of the individuals, as well as on their psychological preferences". Two conclusions flow from this result. First, the distribution of earnings cannot be explained solely in terms of distributions of individual characteristics, contrary to much of the course of economic inquiry in the thirty years subsequent to the publication of Tinbergen's original article. Secondly, it is possible to develop public policies which influence the distribution of earnings through the distribution of jobs. In contrast, most public policies aimed at reducing earnings inequality operate through the manipulation of individual characteristics, e.g. eduation, training and experience.

The wage function in Tinbergen's simple model is an early example of an hedonic price function. The individual parameter in the model may be viewed as a quality variable. The wage function then provides a "price" for differences in this quality variable. An important aspect of Tinbergen's model is that by deriving an explicit wage function, he was able to relate the function to the underlying distributions of the job parameter and the individual parameter. Following an early contribution by Houthakker (1952), Rosen (1974) described the determination of an hedonic price function in the context of product differentiation.

Another rediscoverer of Tinbergen's approach is Thurow (1975). In Thurow's model there is a job queue and a labor queue. Both jobs and workers can be described by ordinal rankings. Based on screening and training costs, higher ranking workers are put into higher ranking starting jobs, where they develop their employment-relevant abilities on the job. Unlike Tinbergen, however, Thurow does not develop an explicit economic theory underlying the assignment of workers to jobs. The determination of the wages for different workers is therefore somewhat arbitrary. Nevertheless, Thurow has grasped the essential point that the distribution of earnings depends on the distribution of jobs.

Tinbergen expands upon his conceptual framework in a later article (1956). There, he abandons his expression of the problem in terms of continuous parameters and density functions and presents the problem in terms of "compartments" defined by small differences in the attributes used to describe jobs and individuals. Furthermore, he generalizes the problem by assuming, in the model that is worked out, that jobs are characterized by two attributes and that individuals are characterized by two attributes. The assignment mechanism is the same: personal preferences. These are assumed to depend on the attributes of jobs and individuals only through the tension between them. That is to say, if an individual with attributes t_1 and t_2 takes a job which has attributes s_1 and s_2, then his utility depends on the wage and on $s_1 - t_2$ and $s_2 - t_2$. The distribution of earnings, via a function relating the wage to the job attributes, then performs the assignment role of deforming the distribution of jobs that individuals seek until it conforms to the distribution of jobs available. This brings about equality between quantity supplied and quantity demanded within each compartment.

The multidimensional aspect of individual abilities or employment-relevant characteristics has been developed further by others (Mandelbrot, 1962; Welch, 1969; Houthakker, 1974; and Hartog, 1976a, 1976b, 1977, 1978). Consider, for example, the simple model proposed by Houthakker. Each individual has a vector of aptitudes, representing the performances of the individual in different occupations. Each individual chooses an occupation on the basis of income maximization. For a given set of wage rates per unit of output in each of the professions, how is the distribution of incomes related to the underlying distribution of aptitudes in each of the professions? The incomes, being a kind of order statistic, will be distributed differently from the distributions of underlying aptitudes. In a more complex model, Mandelbrot applies factor analysis to the question of the distribution of offers made to individuals for employment at a given occupation, and to the question of which individuals will choose a given occupation. Welch applies factor analysis to the problem of reducing the dimensionality of the skill distribution. Applying the procedure to data on schooling, he finds that eight Census schooling classes can be reduced to three. Hartog has developed a multicapability theory to an advanced level. In his doctoral thesis he presents an analysis which incorporates both the supplies of individuals according to their multidimensional capacities and the demands for individuals. The model is then applied to questions of tax incidence. (There are many other elements to Hartog's analysis which are too extensive to discuss here.)

Much of Tinbergen's later work follows logically from the points made in his original paper. Because the offer curves which determine the equilibrium wage function are derived from individual utility functions, the model can be developed into a normative theory of the distribution of earnings (Tinbergen, 1970). In more general versions of the model, the relative wages between two levels of education depend not only on individual preferences but on the degrees of substitution in production. This has led to an investigation of the substitution between academically trained and other manpower (1974, 1975c).

3. Comparative advantage

In "The distribution of earnings and of individual output" (1950), Roy conducts an empirical investigation of the proposition that abilities combine multiplicatively to yield an individual's productivity. If this proposition were correct, individual outputs would be distributed lognormally instead of normally and would therefore be skewed to the right. To examine the proposition, Roy collected data on individual outputs in a number of jobs, such as chocolate packing, spring manufacture, and armature winding. He then tested whether the observed distributions were normal or lognormal.

An objection to this procedure is that individuals in a particular job or occupation are not a random selection from the whole population. There exists a certain amount of self-selection, either on the part of employees or on the part of employers. If an individual were relatively poor at a certain job, he might find that his relative performance and earnings were better in another job. He would then select that other job, or else perhaps his employer would refuse to continue employing him. As a result, the individuals in a particular occupation or job tend to be those individuals in the population who can earn more money at that job than they can in any other job; therefore, their performances do not reflect the performances in that occupation of the population as a whole.

Following up on this consideration, Roy in "Some thoughts on the distribution of earnings" (1951) considers the consequences of this self-selection for the distribution of earnings within occupations and for the economy as a whole. The context of his basic model is a primitive village in which there are two occupations: hunting rabbits and fishing for trout. The rabbits are easy to catch, so even the less-skilled villagers can catch a moderate number and the more skilled hunters cannot catch many more. The trout, however, are "wily" and difficult to catch, and the number of trout caught by the villagers in a year would vary greatly from villager to villager. Supply and demand for meat and fish determines the price of a trout in terms of rabbits. Individuals "self-select" their occupations by choosing to hunt or fish on the basis of which pursuit gives them the highest income.

Consider the case in which the better fishermen are the better rabbit hunters. The villagers who are more skilled at both hunting and fishing will find that their potential incomes are higher at fishing, and will opt for that occupation. The unskilled villagers will find that their income disadvantage is relatively less as rabbit hunters, and will choose that occupation. Every fisherman will earn more than every rabbit hunter, with the best rabbit hunter earning slightly less than the worst fisherman. The upper tail of the earnings distribution will be the upper tail of the distribution of fishing abilities for the population as a whole, and the lower tail will be the distribution of rabbit hunting abilities for the population as a whole. Since the distribution of fishing abilities is more dispersed than the distribution of rabbit hunting abilities, the distribution of earnings will tend to be skewed to the right.

In further elaborations of the model, Roy considers the consequences for the distribution of earnings of a negative correlation or a zero correlation between abilities in catching trout and abilities in snaring rabbits. He also extends the model to more than two occupations.

From the point of view of later work, the major contributions of Roy's analysis are as follows.

(a) Roy recognized the existence of a self-selection process, so that the individuals within an occupation do not represent the population as a whole.

(b) Comparative advantage in the performances of different jobs by different individuals acts to guide the assignment of individuals to jobs.

(c) Occupations vary according to difficulty, and this difficulty is reflected in the amount of dispersion of performances in the occupation for the population as a whole. In a difficult occupation, performances are spread out, whereas in an easy occupation performances are concentrated.

Roy's theoretical results are not expressed in terms of comparative advantage, although Roy recognized the relevance of the concept. My paper on comparative advantage and the distribution of earnings and abilities is essentially an introduction of the principle of comparative advantage into Tinbergen's analytical apparatus (Sattinger, 1975). As in Tinbergen's paper, jobs are characterized by one parameter, called the difficulty, and workers are characterized by another parameter, called their grade of labor. In equilibrium, a wage function is determined which allocates workers to jobs. Unlike Tinbergen's model, the economic principle guiding the assignment is not preferences but the comparative advantage different individuals have at different jobs.

One conclusion of the paper is that a minimum condition for the distribution of earnings to differ in shape from the distribution of abilities is that there exist comparative advantage in the performance of tasks or jobs by individuals. In turn, such comparative advantage will arise if and only if the time taken to perform a task is not a multiplicatively separable function of the worker's grade and the difficulty of the task. Whenever there is comparative advantage, the distribution of earnings will be skewed to the right relative to the distribution of abilities.

A later paper (Sattinger, 1978) investigates the existence of comparative advantage in individuals, using data on mechanical aptitude tests. Both parametric and nonparametric tests indicate that there is indeed comparative advantage in the performance of tasks by individuals. The parametric test for comparative advantage in that paper is based on the observation that comparative advantage will arise if and only if there is some interaction between the ability of the worker (taken from his performance on another test) and the difficulty of the task being performed. The estimates of these interactions then lead to a measure of difficulty of a task. This measure is interpretable in terms of the comparative advantage that arises between two individuals at two jobs.

The performances on the tasks of the subjects in the mechanical aptitudes tests yield a simple way of revealing the self-selectivity biases discussed by Roy.

Suppose we regard the different aptitude tests as occupations. First, the performances on the tests can be standardized by dividing by the mean population performance. Then a wage of one dollar is "offered" for each task performed in the time period. Following a mechanism developed by Houthakker (1974), an occupation is selected for each individual so as to maximize his income. The occupation chosen for an individual is the one in which his standardized performance is greatest. It is then possible to examine the distribution of earnings for the population as a whole and compare it to the population's distribution of abilities in each occupation. These distributions can then be compared to the distribution of earnings and abilities for the individuals selected for a given occupation.

A number of phenomena are revealed by these artificial economies. The distribution of earnings within an occupation tends to be more highly skewed to the right than the whole population's distribution of abilities. The average intelligence quotient tends to be higher in more difficult occupations, but the overlap is substantial. After the selection process, the distribution of earnings in a particular occupation tends to be more equal than the whole population's distribution of abilities in that occupation. Finally, the distribution of earnings for the whole population is significantly skewed to the right relative to a normal distribution.

The theory of comparative advantage in individuals has been developed further by Rosen (1977a, 1977b, 1978). He applies the concept to several interesting subjects, including labor aggregation, the definition of occupations and optimum job assignments. Roy's theory and comparative advantage in individuals have elsewhere been discussed by Westergaard-Nielsen (1975, pp. 11–28).

4. The scale of resources effect

One of the possible influences on the distribution of labor earnings is the presence of cooperating factors. The question of the manner in which such cooperating factors could affect the distribution of earnings is large and complicated; this book is in some senses only a beginning. There have nevertheless been several previous discussions of this topic.

Tuck (1954) provided an early and seminal contribution. Tuck's declared interest is in the way in which an economic system performs the task of "assigning each individual member of the economy to work of an appropriate level of responsibility, and of doing this in such a way that the best possible use is made of the available human talent and experience".

There are many aspects to Tuck's analysis. The content relevant to the subject matter of this book is as follows. In an economy there is an underlying, exogenously determined distribution of employees by managerial ability or talent. On the demand side, firms have fairly well-defined hierarchies required for the control of production. These hierarchies in turn lead to demands for employees at different levels of control or rank. The hierarchies differ within a given industry according to the size of the firm. Larger firms require hierarchies with more levels of control. The distribution of employee requirements for a given distribution of firms does not automatically equal the distribution of employees that are available. What reconciles the two distributions is the size distribution of firms. If there are too many employees capable of operating at the lower levels of control, some of these employees will quit as a result of not being advanced and will start their own firms. The excess numbers of employees capable of operating at the lower levels of control will therefore be soaked up by the new, smaller firms. In this way the size distribution of firms adjusts the demands for employees to match the supplies of employees.

The differentials in salaries between employees of different managerial talent are determined by two opposing economic forces. The first is the existence of economies of scale in production, assumed to be present to a greater or lesser extent in all firms. Secondly, there are diseconomies of scale in the control of productive enterprises. The larger the firm, the more top-heavy and expensive the hierarchy. The resulting differences in profit rates of firms of different sizes lead to differences in the earnings of employees of different managerial talent.

One of the assumptions used by Tuck in deriving the implied distribution of earnings is that the logarithm of income of an employee is proportional to the logarithm of the number of units of basic productive work under his control (1954, p. 39). Two mechanisms could generate this positive association. First, owners of capital could entrust more resources to entrepreneurs with greater evidence of managerial talent. The supply schedules of capital are therefore different for different entrepreneurs (p. 6). Secondly, in filling a given job, employers will choose more competent employees for jobs controlling more resources.

The implications of hierarchies for the distribution of labor earnings have been pursued elsewhere by Simon (1957) and Lydall (1959). In a related development, Osberg (1975, 1976b) has investigated the influence of industrial structures on the distribution of earnings via the work roles they generate. Näslund (1977) has investigated further the relation between the distributions of firm sizes and incomes.

In an independent development Mayazawa (1964, 1976) attributes the inequality in wages to the inequality in the availability of capital funds to firms of different sizes. The context of the model is an economy with a "dual structure", such as Japan's, in which large modern enterprises and medium and small traditional enterprises coexist in the same branches of industry. Mayazawa demonstrates that larger firms in Japan have been able to borrow more funds per employee (1976, p. 112), have greater productivity and pay higher wages (p. 106) than small and medium enterprises. The inequality in the distribution of capital among jobs therefore results in greater wage inequality. This result is similar to the conclusion reached in Chapter 6, although the reasoning is substantially different.

In an analysis along the lines of Tuck's inquiry, Mayer (1960) applies the scale of operations effect to explain the proportional shock mechanisms used in statistical explanations of the size distribution of earnings. Mayer assumes that there will be a positive correlation between the ability of a worker and his scale of operations. Like Tuck, Mayer did not derive this relation from underlying principles of production. Because of the positive correlation between ability and the scale of operations, the distribution of earnings will be skewed (relative to the distribution of abilities) because differences in ability are reinforced by differences in the scale of operations or resources.

One of the models that Mayer discusses is the following. Let

N = the number of units in the process of production;
V = the value of each unit;
P = the probability of a given worker completing a unit succesfully;
I = the cost of inputs per unit of production; and
W = the earnings of the individual.

The probability P is considered a measure of the individual's ability. The worker's earnings are then $W = N(VP - I)$. There are two phenomena relevant to the distribution of earnings among workers. First, $VP - I$ has the same shape as the distribution of the probabilities P but differs from that distribution by a scale shift. That is, $VP - I$ is a linear transformation of ability, P. The second phenomenon is that the number of units, N, and ability, P, are positively correlated, i.e. N is higher when P is higher. This second phenomenon results in skewness.

Mayer evidently regarded the second point as more interesting and cited a number of examples of the positive correlation of scale of operations and ability. However, the first point also merits close attention. The distribution of the values of output, given by $VP - I$, is more unequal than the distribution of abilities, given by P. What happens as the value of a unit of production increases? Both V and I would increase; if they do not increase by the same proportion, then the inequality for a given distribution of probabilities P will change. The investigation of this possibility would lead to an analysis similar to that in Chapter 4.

Another interesting aspect of Mayer's paper is a model in which entrepreneurs can pass on their abilities to subordinates in a hierarchy, presumably by supervising them.

Reder (1968, 1969), in two papers surveying the theory of the size distribution of earnings, applies the scale of operations effect to the question of why earnings vary more in some occupations than in others. Although other authors had discussed the scale of operations effect as applying only to the number of subordinates of an individual, Reder extends the argument to include the value of resources that are utilized in a job. He gives a more rigorous (although not mathematical) statement of the scale of operations effect. Everything else the same, the greater the value of complementary resources used in a job, the greater will be the range of outcomes (net value products) of alternative employees in the job. When this range is greater, the employer is willing to offer a greater premium for employees with superior performance. Furthermore, average compensation will be greater in occupations using more complementary resources.

In addition to complementary resources, Reder discusses the sensitivity of a job as a cause of a greater range of outcomes. Sensitivity and the range of outcomes are clearly related to the concept of difficulty.

There are two distinct issues connected with the scale of operations effect. The first is the question of how individuals, differing in managerial talent or ability, will be assigned to jobs, differing in the responsibility, number of subordinates or complementary resources. More simply, who will take which job? Secondly, how do the responsibility of a job, the number of subordinates or complementary resources connected to a job affect the earnings of the individual who happens to have that job? The distinction between these two questions has not always been maintained in the literature. The necessity of answering them in the context of a multimarket equilibrium model has also not generally been recognized. Chapters 5 and 6 develop, respectively, theories of the assignment of individuals to jobs and the effect of the distribution of resources among jobs on the distribution of earnings. But these developments treat capital as the only resource with which labor is combined. In particular, they ignore the hierarchical aspects of organizations. There are therefore more implications of the scale of operations effect to be explored.

5. Capital models

The attempt to relate the distribution of earnings to the capital intensity of the economy is not without precedent. Allen established the foundations for such a relation in his development of multifactor production theory (1938, pp. 503–509). Griliches made the theory relevant to the distribution of earnings by supposing that the three factors were capital, raw labor and skilled labor (1969, 1970). A reduction in the price of capital will affect the quantities demanded of raw labor and of skilled labor. If in response to this reduction the demand for skilled labor increases relative to the demand for raw labor, then the condition of capital-skill complementarity holds. This condition depends on the relative values of partial elasticities of substitution, parameters that had been defined by Allen. The dual concepts of partial elasticities of complementarity have been developed and applied to income distribution by Hicks (1970), Sato and Koizumi (1973a, 1973b) and Fallon and Layard (1975). These concepts are very relevant to the aggregate analysis undertaken in Chapter 4 and will be discussed more extensively as they arise.

The shortcoming of the literature on capital-skill complementarity as it now stands is that it is only relevant to homogeneous factors of production, although there are two types of labor, raw and skilled. To draw conclusions about the distribution of earnings, one must suppose that individuals providing labor own different amounts of the two types of labor, and that their earnings are a linear combination of the earnings from the provision of the two types of labor. Essentially, Chapter 4 demonstrates how the production theory that has been developed can be applied to an economy in which capital is homogeneous and labor is heterogeneous.

An alternative approach, closer in spirit to the analysis undertaken in Chapters 5 and 6, has been developed by Akerlof (1969). The intention of Akerlof's article is to explain how structural unemployment can arise in a neoclassical framework. Solow had previously demonstrated that in a model with heterogeneous capital, differing in vintage, and homogeneous labor, capital scrappage could occur, i.e. capital would be removed from productive use. Akerlof turns Solow "on his head" by presenting a model with heterogeneous labor, differing in grade, and homogeneous putty-type capital. The economy then allocates capital among workers so as to maximize production. Just as Solow obtains capital scrappage, Akerlof obtains labor scrappage, which is interpreted as unemployment. Akerlof concludes that an increased supply of capital will result in a reduction in structural unemployment. Akerlof's model could easily be extended to produce a theory of the distribution of earnings. His conclusions concerning structural unemployment are also relevant to the theory of poverty developed in Chapter 4.

There have also been attempts to place the study of the distribution of earnings within the context of a general equilibrium model. Yndgaard (1975, 1976a) surveys theories of the distribution of personal incomes and describes the determination of the distribution using an Arrow-Hahn general equilibrium framework. Yndgaard (1976b, 1978) then develops a computerized general dis-equilibrium model in which the course of macroeconomic events are determined by preset policy parameters and individual household and firm decision-making, i.e. without relying on aggregate relations. As part of the output of a computer run, the model generates the distribution of incomes by source and the distribution of wealth. The advantage of such an approach is that complex relations between macroeconomic policies and the distribution of income can be discovered experimentally, and the relation between capital markets and the distribution of income can be brought out. Of course there have been other attempts to use microsimulation in the study of aspects of the distribution of earnings, notably Blinder (1977), Ritzen (1977), and Adelman et al. (1979).

6. Conclusions

The distribution of income is not a standard undergraduate course. The reason is that it does not have a well-defined and established subject matter which can be presented using a common methodology. Instead, since nearly everything affects the distribution of income, nearly all of economics would have to be included in a comprehensive course. Also, the distribution of income borrows analysis from many professions, e.g. statistics for the stochastic theories, psychology for the study of inherited and environmental effects, as well as from many parts of economics.

The consequence for the literature is that it is disconnected, lumpy and discrete, not to mention partitioned. Well-intentioned attempts to provide synthesis often lead to the academic equivalent of a bowl of cold porridge. Rather than attempt such a synthesis, this chapter has presented some literature, much of it neglected, which deserves to be kept in mind when thinking about the distribution of earnings.

Chapter 4

THE INEQUALITY MULTIPLIER: AN AGGREGATE ANALYSIS

1. Introduction

This chapter develops a theory relating the amount of inequality in the size distribution of labor earnings in an economy to the capital intensity of the economy. Using an aggregate production function, the distribution of the marginal products of individuals providing labor services can be inferred. The conditions under which capital intensity affects earnings inequality are discussed and related to output coefficients, factor shares, wage differentials and capital-skill complementarity. The chapter establishes that only in very special cases will the production function be such that capital intensity does not affect earnings inequality.

There are two major questions concerning the distribution of earnings. First, what determines the shape of the distribution of earnings? In particular, what determines the functional form of the distribution, and what phenomena could explain the amount of skewness and perhaps kurtosis in the distribution?

The second question concerns simply the amount of inequality in the distribution of earnings. What is the relation between inequality in earnings and inequality in productive abilities at one point in time, and what causes changes in the amount of earnings inequality over time?

For the first question, a disaggregated approach is appropriate. One must explain the supplies of individuals with various productive abilities, the demands for individuals with those abilities, and the multimarket equilibrium that arises from the market (and nonmarket) allocation of individuals to jobs. This approach will be taken in Chapters 5 and 6. The second question allows a more aggregative approach. The assumption of an aggregate production function, properly specified, is useful in explaining what may be regarded as an aggregate phenomenon, the level of earnings inequality, but it is not very revealing about the shape of the size distribution of earnings.

The approach taken in this chapter is essentially neoclassical but not strictly so. What will be explained is the size distribution of marginal products of laborers. This theory of the distribution of marginal products can be combined with the neoclassical assumption (that factors and individual units of those factors are paid their marginal products) to yield a theory of the distribution of earnings. But clearly, one can reject the neoclassical assumption and retain the theory of the distribution of marginal products presented in this chapter. Nevertheless, the neoclassical assumption will be made. At appropriate points in the discussion it will be assumed that workers are paid their marginal products and also that capital receives its marginal product.

2. Assumptions of the model

Let us begin by specifying the differences among workers that result in differences in earnings. Suppose for simplicity that these differences can be represented by a single variable. Let g_j be the value of the variable for worker j. The variable g_j can be interpreted as the productive ability, human capital or skill of worker j. The particular interpretation is not important; instead, what matters is how the g_j enter the production function.

Suppose there are n workers and let

$$\gamma = \frac{\sum_{j=1}^{n} g_j}{n},$$

so that γ is the average productive ability. Suppose k is the amount of capital in the economy, and let $\rho = k/n$ be the capital to labor ratio.

Suppose that output per worker, or the average product of labor, depends on the capital intensity ρ and on the average productive ability γ. Let $f(\rho,\gamma)$ be output per worker, and let us assume that the function f has continuous first- and second-order partial derivatives. Write $f_1 = \partial f/\partial \rho$, $f_2 = \partial f/\partial \gamma$, $f_{12} = \partial^2 f/\partial \rho \partial \gamma$, $f_{11} = \partial^2 f/\partial \rho^2$ and $f_{22} = \partial^2 f/\partial \gamma^2$. Aggregate production Q is then given by

$$Q = nf(\rho\ \gamma).$$

Suppose that the price per unit of output is one, so that the value of a marginal product is the marginal product itself.

Under a simple restriction, aggregate production is a linearly homogeneous function of labor and capital no matter what functional form $f(\rho,\gamma)$ takes. The simple restriction is that additions to or subtractions from the labor supply have the same average productive ability as the original labor supply, so that the average productive ability does not change. Then if, say, k and n are doubled, both ρ and γ and hence $f(\rho,\gamma)$ would remain the same but aggregate production would double. Of course, $f(\rho,\gamma)$ need not be linearly homogeneous in ρ and γ for this result to hold.

Consider now the marginal product of worker j with productive ability g_j. The total differential of Q is

$$dQ = f(\rho,\gamma)dn + nf_1 \, d\rho + nf_2 \, d\gamma. \tag{4.1}$$

For worker j,

$$dn = 1,$$

$$d\rho = \frac{k}{n} - \frac{k}{n-1} = \frac{(n-1)k - nk}{n(n-1)} = -\frac{k}{n(n-1)},$$

and

$$d\gamma = \frac{\sum\limits_{i=1}^{n} g_i}{n} - \frac{\sum\limits_{i=1}^{n} g_i - g_j}{n-1}$$

$$= \frac{\sum\limits_{j=1}^{n} g_i}{n}(n-1-n) + \frac{g_j}{n-1}$$

$$= \frac{\sum\limits_{i=1}^{n} g_i}{n(n-1)} + \frac{g_j}{n-1} = \frac{1}{n-1}(g_j - \gamma).$$

If n is very large then there is almost no error in using the approximations

$$d\rho = -\frac{k}{n^2}$$

and

$$d\gamma = \frac{1}{n}(g_j - \gamma).$$

For worker j, the total differential of Q is then

$$dQ_j = f(\rho,\gamma)dn + nf_1\left(-\frac{k}{n^2}\right) + nf_2\frac{1}{n}(g_j - \gamma)$$

$$= f(\rho,\gamma) - f_1\,\rho + f_2\,(g_j - \gamma). \tag{4.2}$$

From (4.2), the marginal product of worker j consists of three terms. The first term, $f(\rho,\gamma) = Q/n$, is merely the average product of labor for the economy as a whole. From this average product is subtracted the term $f_1\rho$. This term arises because the addition of one more worker to a fixed amount of capital reduces the capital available to other laborers to work with. If f_1 happens to equal the market cost of capital, then $f_1\rho$ is the average cost of capital per worker. Then $f(\rho,\gamma) - f_1\rho$ would be the average product of labor net of capital costs. The third term, $f_2\,(g_j-\gamma)$, arises because worker j may differ from the average productive ability, either raising or lowering the average and thereby affecting aggregate production.

3. The inequality multiplier

Consider now the distribution of marginal products among the work force. The average value of dQ_j is

$$\frac{\sum\limits_{j=1}^{n} dQ_j}{n} = \frac{nf(\rho,\gamma) - f_1\rho}{n}$$

$$+ f_2\frac{\sum\limits_{j=1}^{n} g_j}{n} - f_2\gamma$$

$$= f(\rho,\gamma) - f_1\rho. \tag{4.3}$$

The variance of dQ_j is simply f_2 times the variance of g_j. Writing $\sigma(g_j)$ as the standard deviation of the productive abilities g_j, the standard deviation of the marginal product is

$$f_2\sigma(g_j).$$

Let us choose to use the coefficient of variation (the standard deviation divided by the mean) as the measure of inequality. This measure has the advantage that it is derived from common statistical concepts and does not depend on the units used to measure productivity. There are also many other measures of inequality, each with its own advantages. The coefficient of variation of the marginal products is

$$\frac{f_2 \sigma(g_j)}{f(\rho,\gamma) - f_1 \rho} = \frac{f_2 \gamma}{f(\rho,\gamma) - f_1 \rho} \; \frac{\sigma(g_j)}{\gamma} \; ,$$

where

$$\frac{\sigma(g_j)}{\gamma}$$

is the coefficient of variation of workers' productive abilities. Let us agree to call

$$\frac{f_2 \gamma}{f(\rho,\gamma) - f_1 \rho}$$

the inequality multiplier and represent it by the symbol π. If workers are paid their marginal products, then the inequality in earnings, as measured by the coefficient of variation, is π times the inequality in the productive abilities of workers. The question of what determines the level of inequality in earnings can thus be broken into two parts. In this model the source of all earnings inequality is differences in the productive abilities of workers. However, the inequality in productive abilities is multiplied by π (which may be less than or greater than one) to yield the inequality in earnings. Hence, earnings inequality can be less than or greater than the inequality in productive abilities. The determinants of inequality in productive abilities are essentially those individual characteristics, such as schooling, job experience and measures of intelligence, that have been investigated by economists using the human capital approach. But the determinants of the inequality multiplier have not been considered.

The important questions at this point are immediately clear. Under what circumstances is the inequality multiplier π identically one; under what circumstances is it some constant unequal to one; and under what circumstances does it depend on capital intensity ρ and average productive ability γ?

The first question may be answered by setting π equal to one. This yields

$$f(\rho,\gamma) = f_1 \rho + f_2 \gamma$$

for all positive values of ρ and γ. By Euler's relation, this is a necessary and sufficient condition for $f(\rho,\gamma)$ to be linearly homogeneous. Hence, the inequality in marginal products (and, adopting the neoclassical assumption, in earnings) will be the same as the inequality in productive abilities if and only if $f(\rho,\gamma)$ is linearly homogeneous in ρ and γ.

Suppose now that π, the inequality multiplier, equals some constant C unequal to one. Then

$$Cf(\rho,\gamma) = C\rho f_1 + \gamma f_2. \tag{4.4}$$

Several classes of functions satisfy this condition. First, if one restricts attention to functions with a constant degree of homogeneity (i.e. a constant function coefficient) then $f(\rho,\gamma)$ can be shown to be of the general Cobb-Douglas form. For instance, if $f(\rho,\gamma) = A\,\rho^\alpha\gamma^\beta$, then the inequality multiplier is

$$\pi = \frac{\beta A\,\rho^\alpha\gamma^{\beta-1}\gamma}{A\,\rho^\alpha\gamma^\beta - \alpha A\rho^{\alpha-1}\gamma^\beta\rho} = \frac{\beta}{1-\alpha}.$$

If $\alpha + \beta$ is less than one, $f(\rho,\gamma)$ will have decreasing returns to scale in ρ and γ and the inequality multiplier will be less than one. If $\alpha + \beta$ exceeds one, $f(\rho,\gamma)$ will have increasing returns to scale in ρ and γ and the inequality multiplier will exceed one (this is a specific case of a more general result that will be discussed later).

A more general class of functions satisfying (4.4) is given by a subclass of Sato's almost-homogeneous function (1977, p. 564). The function $f(\rho,\gamma)$ would be almost-homogeneous if an increase in ρ by α_1 percent and an increase in γ by α_2 percent results in an increase in f of α_3 percent, where α_1, α_2 and α_3 are constants. Then it can be shown that

$$\alpha_3 f(\rho,\gamma) = \alpha_1\rho f_1 + \alpha_2\gamma f_2.$$

If in addition $\alpha_1 = \alpha_3$, then (4.4) is satisfied. A specific example of such a function is

$$f(\rho,\gamma) = (\alpha_1\rho^{1/\alpha_1} + \alpha_2\gamma^{1/\alpha_2})^{\alpha_1}.$$

Then $\pi = 1/\alpha_1\alpha_2$.

In general, however, there is no *a priori* reason to believe either that $f(\rho,\gamma)$ is linearly homogeneous in ρ and γ or that it satisfies the condition in (4.4). Under the restriction discussed previously (that changes in the number of workers not affect the average level of productivity), aggregate production will be linearly homogeneous in labor and capital no matter what the functional form of $f(\rho,\gamma)$

is, i.e. the assumption of constant returns to scale imposes no restrictions on $f(\rho,\gamma)$. Thus, the inequality multiplier will in general depend on capital intensity and average productive ability.

The inequality multiplier can be regarded as a measure of the difficulty of work, discussed in Chapter 3. In Roy's discussion of the distribution of earnings (1951), the difficulty of an occupation or task is reflected in how sensitive the performance of the task is to the ability of the worker. An easy task is one in which the performances of the very able and the inept are similar (rabbit hunting); a difficult task is one in which small differences in abilities result in large differences in performances (trout fishing). The dispersion of performances for a given population is therefore greater for a more difficult task than for an easier task. Similarly, the inequality multiplier relates dispersion in performances (as measured by marginal products) to dispersion in the underlying abilities of individuals. In terms of the dispersion of performances, the work is more difficult when the inequality multiplier is greater.

4. Effects of capital intensity on earnings inequality

So far, this chapter has established the logical possibility of capital intensity affecting the amount of earnings inequality. But no indication has yet been given of the conditions under which increased capital intensity will lead to greater earnings inequality instead of less. The problem now is to express those conditions in economically meaningful terms.

The inequality multiplier may be rewritten as

$$\pi = \frac{f_2\gamma}{f(\rho,\gamma) - f_1\rho} = \frac{f_2\ (\gamma/f(\rho,\gamma))}{1 - f_1\ (\rho/f(\rho,\gamma))} = \frac{\epsilon_\gamma}{1 - \epsilon_\rho}, \tag{4.5}$$

where ϵ_γ and ϵ_ρ are the output elasticities (the elasticities of output with respect to changes in the inputs) for γ and ρ, respectively (Ferguson, 1969, p. 76). The sum of the output elasticities is the function coefficient, ϵ, the elasticity of output with respect to a proportional change in all inputs:

$$\epsilon = \epsilon_\gamma + \epsilon_\rho.$$

If $\epsilon = 1$, then $\epsilon_\gamma = 1 - \epsilon_\rho$ and $\pi = 1$. If $\epsilon > 1$, then $\epsilon_\gamma < 1 - \epsilon_\rho$ and π is greater than one. If $\epsilon < 1$, then $\epsilon_\gamma < 1 - \epsilon_\rho$ and $\pi < 1$. Thus, earnings inequality will be greater or less than inequality in productive abilities depending upon whether $f(\rho,\gamma)$ has increasing or decreasing returns to scale in ρ and γ.

It can also be shown that $1 - \epsilon_\rho$ is the negative of the elasticity of output per unit of capital with respect to capital intensity. The inequality multiplier is thus the ratio of two elasticities, the elasticity of output per worker with respect to average labor productive ability and the elasticity of output per unit of capital with respect to capital intensity.

Using (4.5), several special cases can be developed.

4.1. Multiplicatively separable form

Suppose $f(\rho,\gamma)$ takes the multiplicatively separable form $f_a(\rho) f_b(\gamma)$. Then

$$\epsilon_\rho = \frac{\partial(f_a(\rho) f_b(\gamma))/\partial\gamma}{f_a(\rho) f_b(\gamma)/\gamma} = \frac{\partial f_a(\rho)/\partial\rho}{f_a(\rho)/\rho}$$

and similarly

$$\epsilon_\gamma = \frac{\partial f_b(\gamma)/\partial\gamma}{f_b(\gamma)/\gamma} \ .$$

It follows that $\partial\epsilon_\gamma/\partial\rho = 0$, i.e. the output elasticity for one variable does not depend on the other. In particular, if ρ increases, then the inequality multiplier increases if and only if ϵ_ρ increases. If capital is paid its marginal product, ϵ_ρ is capital's factor share and $1 - \epsilon_\rho$ is labor's factor share. Thus, if $f(\rho,\gamma)$ is multiplicatively separable, the inequality multiplier increases as capital intensity increases if and only if capital's share goes up as capital intensity increases. Similarly, the effect of increases in the average productive ability on earnings inequality depends on how γ affects ϵ_γ. If ϵ_γ goes down as γ increases, then greater average productive ability on the part of workers reduces earnings inequality.

4.2. Constant function coefficient

Further conclusions may be drawn by differentiating the inequality multiplier with respect to capital intensity:

$$\frac{\partial\pi}{\partial\rho} = \frac{\partial(\epsilon_\gamma/(1 - \epsilon_\rho))}{\partial\rho} = \frac{\partial}{\partial\rho} \left(\frac{1 - \epsilon_\rho}{1 - \epsilon_\rho} + \frac{\epsilon_\gamma + \epsilon_\rho - 1}{1 - \epsilon_\rho} \right)$$

$$= \frac{\partial}{\partial\rho} \left(\frac{\epsilon - 1}{1 - \epsilon_\rho} \right) = \frac{1}{(1 - \epsilon_\rho)^2} \left[(1 - \epsilon_\rho) \frac{\partial\epsilon}{\partial\rho} + (\epsilon - 1) \frac{\partial\epsilon_\rho}{\partial\rho} \right] \ . \quad (4.6)$$

Now suppose the function coefficient is constant so that $\partial \epsilon / \partial \rho$ is zero. This occurs if and only if $f(\rho,\gamma)$ is homogeneous of degree ϵ. From (4.6), the sign of $\partial \pi / \partial \rho$ depends only on the sign of $(\epsilon - 1)\partial \epsilon_\rho / \partial \rho$. Two subcases arise. If ϵ is greater than one (so that the inequality multiplier is also greater than one), then $\partial \pi / \partial \rho$ is positive if and only if ϵ_ρ increases as ρ increases. If ϵ is less than one, then $\partial \pi / \partial \rho$ is positive if and only if ϵ_ρ decreases as ρ increases.

4.3. Labor and capital factor shares independent of capital intensity

Assuming capital is paid its marginal product ϵ_ρ will be capital's factor share and $1 - \epsilon_\rho$ will be labor's factor share. Suppose now that these factor shares do not depend on the capital intensity ρ, so that $\partial \epsilon_\rho / \partial \rho = 0$. Then the sign of $\partial \pi / \partial \rho$ depends only on whether the function coefficient increases or decreases as ρ increases. From (4.6), if ϵ increases as ρ increases, then the inequality multiplier increases as capital intensity increases. In terms of the original formulation of π, the inequality multiplier will increase as ρ increases if and only if ϵ_γ increases as ρ increases.

4.4. Almost-homothetic output per unit of capital

Suppose output per worker $f(\rho,\gamma)$ takes the form

$$\rho h (a_1 \rho^{\alpha_1} + a_2 \gamma^{\alpha_2}), \qquad (4.7)$$

where a_1, a_2, α_1 and α_2 are parameters. The function h is output per worker divided by the capital to labor ratio, i.e. it is output per unit of capital. Assume that h is continuous and has a continuous derivative and assume further that h is either a monotone increasing or a monotone decreasing function of its argument. The function h in (4.7) satisfies Sato's condition for an almost-homothetic function (1977) if h is monotone increasing. However, the following derivations also hold if h is monotone decreasing. Then

$$\epsilon_\gamma = \frac{\partial f / \partial \gamma}{f / \gamma} = \frac{\rho h' a_2 \alpha_2 \gamma^{\alpha_2 - 1}}{\rho h / \gamma} = \frac{h'}{h} a_2 \alpha_2 \gamma^{\alpha_2}$$

and

$$\epsilon_\rho = \frac{\partial f / \partial \rho}{f / \rho} = \frac{h + \rho h' a_1 \alpha_1 \rho^{\alpha_1 - 1}}{\rho h / \rho} = 1 + \frac{h'}{h} a_1 \alpha_1 \rho^{\alpha_1}.$$

Hence, the inequality multiplier is

$$\pi = \frac{(h'/h)a_2\alpha_2\gamma^{\alpha_2}}{1 - (1 + (h'/h)a_1\alpha_1\rho^{\alpha_1})} = -\frac{a_2\alpha_2}{a_1\alpha_1}\gamma^{\alpha_2}\rho^{-\alpha_1}.$$

Thus, if output per worker takes the general form given in (4.7), the inequality multiplier will be a loglinear function of capital intensity and labor average productive ability. Furthermore, it is not necessary to specify the form of the function h to estimate the inequality multiplier.

There are four distinct cases consistent with output per unit of capital being an increasing function of average labor productive ability and a decreasing function of capital intensity:

(1) $h' > 0, a_1 > 0, a_2 > 0, \alpha_1 < 0$, and $\alpha_2 > 0$, so that $\partial\pi/\partial\rho > 0$ and $\partial\pi/\partial\gamma > 0$;

(2) $h' > 0, a_1 < 0, a_2 > 0, \alpha_1 > 0$ and $\alpha_2 > 0$, so that $\partial\pi/\partial\rho < 0$ and $\partial\pi/\partial\gamma > 0$;

(3) $h' < 0, a_1 < 0, a_2 > 0, \alpha_1 < 0$, and $\alpha_2 < 0$, so that $\partial\pi/\partial\rho < 0$ and $\partial\pi/\partial\gamma < 0$; and

(4) $h' < 0, a_1 < 0, a_2 > 0, \alpha_1 < 0$ and $\alpha_2 < 0$, so that $\partial\pi/\partial\rho < 0$ and $\partial\pi/\partial\gamma < 0$.

4.5.   General case

In general, all three of the elasticities ϵ_ρ, ϵ_γ and ϵ, will vary as capital intensity varies. The ultimate effect on the inequality multiplier depends on the proportional effect of changes in ρ on ϵ_γ compared to the proportional effect on $(1 - \epsilon_\rho)$. If

$$\frac{\partial\epsilon_\gamma/\partial\rho}{\epsilon_\gamma} > \frac{\partial(1 - \epsilon_\rho)/\partial\rho}{1 - \epsilon_\rho},$$

then the inequality multiplier increases as capital intensity increases.

5.   Wage differentials

To relate earnings inequality to wage differentials, rewrite (4.2) to yield a linear relation between the productive ability of a worker and his wage:

$$dQ_j = (f(\rho,\gamma) - f_1\rho - f_2\gamma) + f_2 g_j. \tag{4.8}$$

Let

$$a = f(\rho,\gamma) - f_1\rho - f_2\gamma$$

and

$$b = f_2.$$

Then $dQ_j = a + b\, g_j$, and a is the y-intercept and b is the slope of the linear relation. If $f(\rho,\gamma)$ is linearly homogeneous, the y-intercept a is identically zero and marginal products and earnings are proportional to productive ability.

Consider two individuals in an economy with productive abilities g_1 and g_2, where g_1 is greater than g_2. Then the relative marginal products of the individuals is given by $(a + b\, g_1)/(a + b\, g_2)$. In general, the coefficients a and b depend on the capital intensity, ρ. Let us write a_1 and b_1 for the coefficients when capital intensity is ρ_1 and a_2 and b_2 for the coefficients when capital intensity is ρ_2. Suppose that ρ_1 is greater than ρ_2. The matrix of marginal products or earnings is then

Capital intensity

		ρ_1	ρ_2
Productive ability	g_1	$a_1 + b_1 g_1$	$a_2 + b_2 g_1$
	g_2	$a_1 + b_1 g_2$	$a_2 + b_2 g_2$

Now consider the following question. Under what circumstances will the relative earnings of the more productive worker be greater in the more capital intensive state of the economy? That is, under what circumstances will the following inequality hold:

$$\frac{a_1 + b_1 g_1}{a_1 + b_1 g_2} > \frac{a_2 + b_2 g_1}{a_2 + b_2 g_2} \,?$$

Performing identical operations on both sides of the inequality yields

$$(a_1 + b_1 g_1)(a_2 + b_2 g_2) > (a_1 + b_1 g_2)(a_2 + b_2 g_1)$$

or

$$a_1 a_2 + a_1 b_2 g_2 + a_2 b_1 g_1 + b_1 b_2 g_1 g_2 > a_1 a_2 + a_2 b_1 g_2 + a_1 b_2 g_1 + b_1 b_2 g_1 g_2$$

or

$$a_2 b_1 (g_1 - g_2) > a_1 b_2 (g_1 - g_2)$$

or

$$a_2 b_1 > a_1 b_2 \text{ (since } g_1 - g_2 \text{ is positive)}$$

or

$$\frac{a_2}{b_2} > \frac{a_1}{b_1} \, .$$

This inequality can be expressed in its original terms as

$$\frac{f(\rho_2, \gamma) - \dfrac{\partial f}{\partial \rho} \rho_2 - \dfrac{\partial f}{\partial \gamma} \gamma}{\partial f / \partial \gamma} > \frac{f(\rho_1, \gamma) - \dfrac{\partial f}{\partial \rho} \rho_1 - \dfrac{\partial f}{\partial \gamma} \gamma}{\partial f / \partial \gamma}$$

or

$$\frac{\gamma}{\pi_2} - \gamma > \frac{\gamma}{\pi_1} - \gamma$$

or

$$\pi_1 > \pi_2 ,$$

where π_1 and π_2 are the inequality multipliers for the economy when capital intensity is ρ_1 and ρ_2, respectively.

The conclusion of the foregoing analysis may be stated as follows. The relative earnings of more productive workers will be greater in more capital intensive economies (everything else the same) if the inequality multiplier increases as capital intensity increases.

The reverse conclusion can also be drawn, so that the conditions under which relative earnings of more productive earners will be greater in more capital intensive economies are identical with the conditions under which the inequality multiplier will be an increasing function of capital intensity. Thus, to conclude that $\partial \pi / \partial \rho$ is positive, it is sufficient to demonstrate that the marginal products of more productive workers increase more rapidly than those of less productive workers as capital intensity increases, everything else the same.

6. Relation to partial elasticities of complementarity

The conditions under which $\partial\pi/\partial\rho$ and $\partial\pi/\partial\gamma$ are positive or negative can be related to elasticities of complementarity by writing the aggregate production function as $Q = F(k,n,g)$, where k is total capital, n is the number of labor units (raw labor), and g is the sum of the productive abilities of the n workers, so that $g = \Sigma_{j=1}^{n} g_j = \gamma n$. Assume F has constant returns to scale in k, n, and g. Let

$$F_1 = \partial F/\partial k; \quad F_2 = \partial F/\partial n \quad \text{and} \quad F_3 = \partial F/\partial g.$$

Then, the marginal product of worker j is $MP_j = \mathrm{d}F_j = F_2 + F_3 g_j$. For all workers, the mean marginal product is $F_2 + F_3\gamma = F_2 + F_3 g/n$ and the standard deviation of marginal products is $F_3 \sigma(g_j)$. The inequality multiplier is then given variously by

$$\pi = \frac{F_3 g/n}{F_2 + F_3 g/n} = \frac{gF_3}{nF_2 + gF_3} = \frac{gF_3}{F - kF_1} = \frac{1}{nF_2/gF_3 + 1}.$$

From these expressions it is clear that π is identically one whenever F_2 is identically zero, i.e. the marginal product of raw labor n is zero. Aggregate production is thus a function of the two variables k and g. The efficiency units assumption then holds, with a worker's productive ability g_j proportional to the number of efficiency units his labor is equivalent to. The inequality in marginal products equals the inequality in productive abilities, which in turn equals the inequality in efficiency units.

Consider now the effect of an increase in capital on the inequality multiplier, holding n and g constant. Then $\rho = k/n$ increases but $\gamma = g/n$ remains the same. Write $\pi = gF_3/(nF_2 + gF_3)$. Then

$$\frac{\partial\pi}{\partial k} = \frac{1}{(nF_2 + gF_3)^2} \left[\frac{gF_{13}}{nF_2 + gF_3} - gF_3(nF_{12} + gF_{13}) \right]$$

$$= \frac{1}{(nF_2 + gF_3)^2} [n\,gF_2 F_{13} - n\,gF_3 F_{12}]$$

$$= \frac{n\,gF_1 F_2 F_3}{F(nF_2 + gF_3)^2} \left(\frac{F\,F_{13}}{F_1\,F_3} - \frac{F\,F_{12}}{F_1\,F_2} \right).$$

Let $c_{13} = FF_{13}/F_1 F_3$ and $c_{12} = F F_{12}/F_1 F_2$. The quantities c_{13} and c_{12} are partial elasticities of complementarity (Hicks, 1970; Sato and Koizumi 1973a, 1973b). A partial elasticity of complementarity is intended to measure the effect on the price (or marginal product) of one factor arising from a change in the quantity of another factor, holding the quantities of the other factors of production and marginal cost constant. If c_{ij} is greater than one, an increase in the quantity of factor j will raise the relative share of factor i, holding the quantities of the other factors fixed. As demonstrated by Sato and Koizumi, the concept is dual to the partial elasticity of substitution, developed previously by Allen (1938, p. 504). The latter elasticity measures the effect of a change in the price of one factor on the quantity demanded of another factor, holding the other prices and output constant.

The conditions under which $\partial\pi/\partial k$ is positive can be divided into two cases. First, suppose F_2, the marginal product of raw labor, is positive, so that π is less than one. Then $\partial\pi/\partial k$ is positive if and only if $c_{13} > c_{12}$, i.e. if and only if the partial elasticity of complementarity between capital and productive ability is greater than the partial elasticity of complementarity between capital and raw labor. This condition is closely related to the capital-skill complementarity hypothesis developed by Griliches (1969, 1970). Griliches's hypothesis is expressed in terms of partial elasticities of substitution, following the traditional development by Allen. However, Fallon and Layard (1975) later expressed the capital-skill complementarity hypothesis in terms of the partial elasticities of complementarity.

In the second case, suppose F_2 is negative. Then the condition for $\partial\pi/\partial k$ to be positive is that $c_{13} < c_{12}$. In a three-factor production function it is possible for one of the partial elasticities of complementarity to be negative. However, the three partial elasticities of complementarity, c_{11}, c_{12} and c_{13}, must satisfy $\kappa_1 c_{11} + \kappa_2 c_{12} + \kappa_3 c_{13} = 0$, where κ_1, κ_2 and κ_3 are the relative shares of the three "factors" (Sato and Koizumi, 1973b, p. 47). Since $c_{11} < 0$, if c_{12} is also negative, then c_{13} cannot be negative. It follows that if F_2 is negative and c_{12} is negative, then $\partial\pi/\partial k$ must also be negative. If the inequality multiplier is to be an increasing function of k when F_2 is negative, c_{12} must be positive and F_{12} must be negative. That is to say, an increase in capital must reduce the marginal product of raw labor.

Now let us investigate the effect of an increase in average productive ability on the inequality multiplier. Suppose g increases, while k and n remain constant. Then $\rho = k/n$ remains the same but $\gamma = g/n$ goes up:

$$\frac{\partial\pi}{\partial g} = \frac{1}{nF_2 + gF_3} \left[(nF_2 + gF_3)(F_3 + gF_{33} - gF_3(nF_{23} + F_3 + gF_{33})\right]$$

$$= \frac{1}{(nF_2 + gF_3)^2} \left[nF_2(F_3 + gF_{33}) - n gF_3 F_{23}\right]$$

$$= \frac{n\,gF_2F_3^2}{(nF_2 + gF_3)^2 F} \left[\frac{F}{gF_3} + \frac{FF_{33}}{F_3F_3} - \frac{FF_{23}}{F_2F_3} \right]$$

$$= \frac{nF_2\,F_3}{(nF_2 + gF_3)^2} \,(1 + \kappa_3 c_{33} - \kappa_3 c_{23}),$$

where $\kappa_3 = gF_3/F$ is the relative "share" of the factor g in aggregate production. One of the conditions imposed by the assumption that F is homogeneous of degree one is that $\kappa_1 c_{31} + \kappa_2 c_{32} + \kappa_3 c_{33} = 0$. Since $\kappa_1 + \kappa_2 + \kappa_3 = 1$ and $c_{32} = c_{23}$, $1 + \kappa_3 c_{33} - \kappa_3 c_{23} = \kappa_1 + \kappa_2 + \kappa_3 - \kappa_1 c_{31} - \kappa_2 c_{32} + \kappa_3 c_{32}$
$= \kappa_1 (1 - c_{31}) + (\kappa_2 + \kappa_3)(1 - c_{32}).$

The quantity κ_1 is capital's relative factor share and $\kappa_2 + \kappa_3$, the sum of the relative shares of raw labor and productive ability, is labor's relative factor share. Thus, the expression in (4.9) is a weighted average of the deviations from unity of the partial elasticities of complementarity between capital and productive ability and raw labor and productive ability. Assuming that F_2 is positive, $\partial\pi/\partial\gamma$ will be negative whenever the expression in (4.9) is negative. A similar result holds when F_2 is negative.

More specific results can be obtained under the assumption that output per worker,

$$f(\rho,\gamma) = F\left(\frac{k}{n}, 1, \frac{g}{n}\right),$$

is a homogeneous function of degree $\epsilon < 1$. Suppose further that $f_{12} = \partial^2 f/\partial\rho\partial\gamma$ is positive. By Euler's theorem,

$$\epsilon f = \rho f_1 + \gamma f_2.$$

Then the inequality multiplier may be represented as

$$\pi = \frac{\gamma f_2}{f - \rho f_1} = \frac{\gamma f_2}{f - \rho f_1 - \gamma f_2 + \gamma f_2} = \frac{\gamma f_2}{(1-\epsilon)f + \gamma f_2}.$$

Thus,

$$\frac{\partial\pi}{\partial\rho} = \frac{\gamma f_{12}}{(1-\epsilon)f + \gamma f_2} - \frac{\gamma f_2}{((1-\epsilon)f + \gamma f_2)^2}\,((1-\epsilon)f_1 + \gamma f_{12})$$

$$= \frac{\gamma}{((1-\epsilon)f + \gamma f_2)^2}\,[(1-\epsilon)f f_{12} + \gamma f_2 f_{12} - (1-\epsilon)f_1 f_2 - \gamma f_2 f_{12}]$$

$$= \frac{(1-\epsilon)\gamma f f_{12}}{((1-\epsilon)f + \gamma f_2)^2} \left[1 - \frac{f_1 f_2}{f f_{12}} \right].$$

Similarly,

$$\frac{\partial \pi}{\partial \gamma} = \frac{\partial}{\partial \gamma} \left[\frac{\gamma f_2}{(1-\epsilon)f + \gamma f_2)} \right]$$

$$= \frac{f_2 + \gamma f_{22}}{((1-\epsilon)f + \gamma f_2)} - \frac{\gamma f_2}{((1-\epsilon)f + \gamma f_2)^2} \left[(1-\epsilon)f_2 + f_2 + \gamma f_{22} \right]$$

$$= \frac{1}{((1-\epsilon)f + \gamma f_2)^2} \left[(1-\epsilon)f f_2 + \gamma f f_{22} (1-\epsilon) - (1-\epsilon)\gamma f_2^2 \right].$$

By use of Euler's theorem,

$$f_{22} = \frac{(\epsilon - 1)f_2}{\gamma} - \frac{\rho}{\gamma} f_{12}.$$

Therefore

$$\frac{\partial \pi}{\partial \gamma} = \frac{1}{((1-\epsilon)f + \gamma f_2)^2} \left[(1-\epsilon)f f_2 - (1-\epsilon)(1-\epsilon)f f_2 - (1-\epsilon)\rho f f_{12} \right.$$

$$\left. - (1-\epsilon)\gamma f_2^2 \right]$$

$$= \frac{1}{((1-\epsilon)f + \gamma f_2)^2} \left[(1-\epsilon)(\rho f_1 + \gamma f_2) - (1-\epsilon)\rho f f_{12} - (1-\epsilon)\gamma f_2^2 \right]$$

$$= \frac{(1-\epsilon)\rho f f_{12}}{((1-\epsilon)f + \gamma f_2)^2} \left[\frac{f_1 f_2}{f f_{12}} - 1 \right].$$

The signs of $\partial \pi/\partial \rho$ and $\partial \pi/\partial \gamma$ therefore both depend on $f_1 f_2/f f_{12}$. If f had been linearly homogeneous, this quantity would be the elasticity of substitution between capital per worker and average productive ability. However, the degree of homogeneity is ϵ, assumed to be less than one. By substitution into the general expression for the elasticity of substitution (Ferguson, 1969, p. 91), it can be shown that the elasticity of substitution for a function homogeneous of degree ϵ is

$$\sigma = \frac{1}{\epsilon \dfrac{f f_{12}}{f_1 f_2} + 1 - \epsilon}.$$

It can be seen that as ϵ approaches one, σ approaches the familiar expression $f_1 f_2 / f f_{12}$. Rearranging yields

$$\frac{f_1 f_2}{f f_{12}} = \frac{1}{\dfrac{1}{\epsilon} \left(\dfrac{1 - \sigma}{\sigma} \right) + 1} .$$

It is clear that $f_1 f_2 / f f_{12}$ will be less than one whenever the elasticity of substitution, σ, is less than one. This yields the following result.

Under the assumption that output per worker, f, is homogeneous of degree $\epsilon < 1$ in ρ and γ and that f_{12} is positive, $\partial \pi / \partial \rho > 0$ and $\partial \pi / \partial \gamma < 0$ whenever the elasticity of substitution between capital per worker and average productive ability is less than one. Similarly, if the elasticity of substitution is greater than one, then $\partial \pi / \partial \rho < 0$ and $\partial \pi / \partial \gamma > 0$.

Analogous results can be obtained in the case $\epsilon > 1$ and for the less likely condition that f_{12} is negative.

7. Technological progress

The intention of this section is to extend the Hicks-Harrod taxonomy to describe the effects of technological progress on earnings inequality. The Hicks and Harrod concepts of neutral technological progress describe conditions under which the relative factor shares of labor and capital do not change as technology changes. Writing the inequality multiplier as $\pi = \epsilon_\gamma / (1 - \epsilon_\rho)$, the denominator is labor's relative factor share if capital is paid its marginal product. The concepts of neutral technological progress are clearly relevant to earnings inequality, but they are not the whole story: one must also take account of the numerator in this expression for the inequality multiplier.

The focus here is on the amount of inequality in earnings that would result for a given workforce. Therefore, in analyzing the effects of technological progress, the distribution of skills or productive ability among workers will be assumed to be held constant.

Consider first the Hicks terminology for technological progress, which describes the effects for a fixed capital to labor ratio. This corresponds to the short run, before the quantity of capital can be adjusted (Ferguson, 1969, ch. 11). Technological progress is Hicks-neutral if the marginal rate of technical substitution between capital and labor remains the same. Then, $1 - \epsilon_\rho$ stays the same; earnings inequality for a given workforce goes up or down depending on whether ϵ_γ, the elasticity of output with respect to the average productive ability, goes up or down.

In analogy to Hicks' definition, let us define Hicks earnings-neutral technological progress as occurring whenever the inequality multiplier remains the same, holding the amounts of capital, labor and labor's average productive ability constant. Similarly, Hicks difficult-biased technological progress occurs when π goes up as a result of the technological progress, and Hicks easy-biased technological progress occurs when π goes down. The point of these definitions is that technological progress affects earnings inequality via its effect on the ease or difficulty of work, as discussed in section 3.

A two-factor production function of the form $A(t)F(K,L)$, where t is the technology parameter or time, K is total capital and L is total labor, will exhibit Hicks-neutral technological progress. The relative factor shares will not change as t changes. The three-factor analogue to this production function is $A(t)F(k,n,g)$, where the three factors are now capital, raw labor (or total number of labor units) and total productive ability. The relative factor shares of capital and labor (combining returns to raw labor and productive ability) will also be constant. In particular, capital's relative factor share will be $kA(t)F_1/A(t)F(k,n,g) = kF_1/F$, an amount unaffected by t. The production function $A(t)F(k,n,g)$ will also exhibit Hicks earnings-neutral technological progress. The inequality multiplier is given by

$$\pi = \frac{gA(t)F_3}{nA(t)F_2 + gA(t)F_3} = \frac{gF_3}{nF_2 + gF_3} ,$$

which does not depend on t.

An example of a production function that is Hicks earnings-neutral but not Hicks-neutral is $F(k,A(t)n,A(t)g)$. Then the inequality multiplier is again given by the above expression and hence is unaffected by the technology parameter t. However, capital's factor share is $kF_1/F = kF_1/(kF_1 + nA(t)F_2 + gA(t)F_3)$. In general, if F is not a Cobb-Douglas type production function, it will not yield Hicks-neutral technological progress.

Let us now examine the more complicated Harrod terminology. The Harrod treatment is intended to describe the behavior of factor shares in the long run, after the economy has adjusted to technological progress. The interest rate is assumed to be fixed. In the long run the quantity of capital goes up or down for a fixed quantity of labor until the marginal product returns to its former value. The question then is whether, considering both the technological progress and the adjustment in capital, production has increased by a greater or smaller proportion than the amount of capital. If the ratio of production to capital remains the same, then the technological progress is Harrod-neutral and the relative factor shares of capital and labor will stay the same.

An ambiguity arises in trying to extend this definition to describe what happens to earnings inequality. After the technological progress, both the amount of capital and the distribution of productive abilities (which are substantially affected by the investments individuals have made in their education or training) will adjust to the new economic circumstances. However, our interest is in the amount of inequality for a given population; let us therefore continue to assume that the distribution of productive abilities in the work force remains unchanged and recognize that this is not a true long run. The consequences of an additional change in the distribution of productive abilities could be considered separately.

Now suppose that technological progress is Harrod-neutral, so that F/k and F_1 are the same after the adjustment of capital. Write the inequality multiplier as

$$\pi = \frac{g\,F_3}{F - kF_1} = \frac{(g/k)F_3}{F/k - F_1}\,.$$

Assuming g is held constant, the change in the inequality multiplier is in the same direction as the change in the ratio F_3/k.

In analogy to the extension of the Hicks terminology, define technological progress as Harrod earnings-neutral if π stays the same, Harrod difficult-biased if π goes up and Harrod easy-biased if π goes down, the above changes in π to be measured after equilibrium has again been reached, with the marginal product of capital equal to the former interest rate.

As in the case of the Hicks terminology, Harrod earnings-neutral technological progress is not necessarily Harrod-neutral technological progress.

By and large, exercises in the taxonomy of technological progress are not intellectually satisfying. There are too few theorems ruling out categories of possibilities. The major questions are empirical. Given the taxonomy, what has been the nature of technological progress over a period of years? The real challenges lie in isolating the effects of technological progress.

8. Graphical analysis

The economic problem that has been discussed in previous sections can be presented in more general terms and given graphical interpretation. (See Hartog, 1978, p. 99, for a similar discussion.) One variable, x, has values distributed along the positive part of the horizontal axis. A second variable, y, is related to x by a linear relation, $y = a + bx$, where it is assumed that b is positive. In this chapter, x has been productive ability and y has been the marginal product or earnings. The relation between the coefficient of variation of y and the coefficient of variation of x can be derived in a straightforward manner. Let $\bar{x}$ be the mean of x and $\bar{y} = a + b\bar{x}$ be the mean of y. Then

$$\text{var}(y) = b^2 \, \text{var}(x) \quad \text{and} \quad \frac{\sqrt{[\text{var}(y)]}}{\bar{y}} = \frac{b\bar{x}}{a + b\bar{x}} \frac{\sqrt{[\text{var}(x)]}}{\bar{x}} \;.$$

Hence, the coefficient of variation of y is $b\bar{x}/(a + b\bar{x})$ times the coefficient of variation of x. The term $b\bar{x}/(a + b\bar{x})$ corresponds to the inequality multiplier in previous sections. This inequality multiplier will be greater than one, equal to one, or less than one, depending on whether a is negative, zero, or positive. In graphical terms the inequality or dispersion in y will be greater, equal to or less than the inequality or dispersion in x if the straight line $a + bx$ (with positive

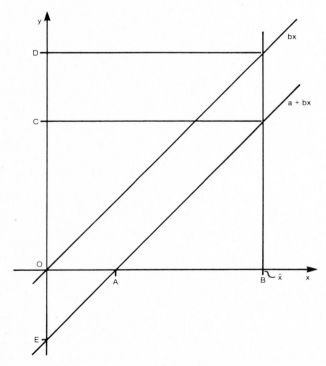

Figure 4.1. Inequality multiplier greater than one.

slope b and y-intercept a) intersects the x-axis to the right of the origin, at the origin, or to the left of the origin. The inequality multiplier may also be represented graphically. In fig. 4.1, the linear relation $a + bx$ has a negative y-intercept OE and intersects the x-axis to the right of the origin, so that the inequality multiplier is greater than one. Suppose OB equals the average value of x. Consider a line parallel to $a + bx$ drawn through the origin. This intersects a vertical line drawn through $x = \bar{x}$ at a height of OD or $b\bar{x}$. The original line $a + bx$ intersects the vertical line through $x = \bar{x}$ at a height OC or $a + b\bar{x}$. The inequality multiplier is $b\bar{x}/(a + b\bar{x})$, or OD divided by OC. By similar triangles, this is equal to OB divided by AB (or $\bar{x}$ divided by $\bar{x} + a/b$).

The case of an inequality multiplier less than one is illustrated in fig. 4.2. In analogy to the derivation of the inequality multiplier for fig. 4.1, the inequality multiplier is given by OB divided by AB.

Now suppose the linear relation changes, and consider the effect of the change on the inequality in y. Either the line may rotate (a change in the slope b) or the line may shift (a change in the y-intercept) or both. This question may

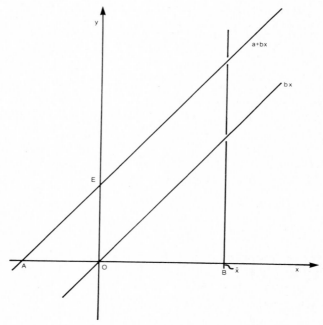

Figure 4.2. Inequality multiplier less than one.

be answered very simply using the preceding analysis. If the point of intersection of the line $a + bx$ with the x-axis moves to the right, inequality increases; if the point of intersection moves to the left, inequality decreases; if it stays the same, inequality stays the same.

In turn, the movement of the point of intersection of $a + bx$ with the x-axis is determined entirely by the point of rotation of the line $a + bx$. Assume that the slope b increases as the change takes place. If the point of rotation is above the x-axis, the point of intersection of $a + bx$ with the x-axis will move to the right, and the inequality multiplier will increase. This is illustrated in fig. 4.3, in the case where the inequality multiplier is greater than one. The line changes from $a + bx$ to $a' + b'x$. The point around which the line rotates is above the x-axis, so the point of intersection of the line with the x-axis moves to the right, from A to A'. The inequality multiplier increases from OB/AB to $OB/A'B$. The corresponding case in which the inequality multiplier is less than one is illustrated in fig. 4.4.

In the efficiency units case, the inequality multiplier is identically one and y is proportional to x. The linear relation then goes through the origin and any change in it consists in a rotation around the origin, which leaves the inequality multiplier unaffected.

If the inequality multiplier is a constant unequal to one, then the linear relation rotates around a point on the x-axis. If this point is to the left of the origin, the inequality multiplier is less than one. If the point of rotation is on the x-axis to the right of the origin, then the inequality multiplier is a constant greater than one.

The value of x at which the line rotates, labeled $\hat{g}$ in Figs. 4.3 and 4.4, is the value of x such that the value of y does not change as the linear relation changes. When the point of rotation is above the x-axis, $\hat{g}$ is greater than OA, and inequality increases.

The value of $\hat{g}$ may be related to the question of what happens to individuals with particular levels of productive ability as capital intensity increases, as will be discussed in the following section.

9. A theory of poverty

An increase in capital intensity generally raises the marginal product of labor, treating labor as a homogeneous factor of production. However, if labor is heterogeneous, it is possible that the marginal products of some units are increased while the marginal products of other labor units are decreased by a rise in the capital to labor ratio.

The foregoing section provides a means of analyzing this possibility, and leads

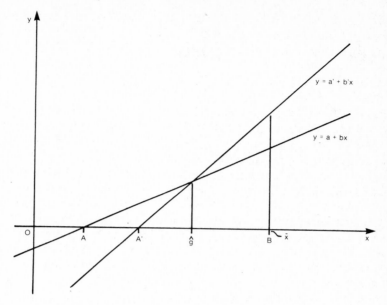

Figure 4.3. Rotation, inequality multiplier greater than one.

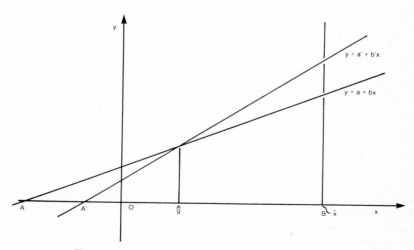

Figure 4.4. Rotation, inequality multiplier less than one.

directly to a theory of poverty or, more accurately, a theory of the effect of progress on the low-income working population.

Consider the expression for the marginal product of worker j:

$$dQ_j = f - \rho f_1 - \gamma f_2 + f_2 g_j. \tag{4.10}$$

As discussed in the previous section, this is a linear relation between productive ability g_j and the marginal product dQ_j. The vertical intercept is $f - \rho f_1 - \gamma f_2$ and the slope is f_2. Suppose now that ρ increases. The slope f_2 will increase whenever f_{12} is positive. A positive value of this mixed partial derivative is not in general necessary for the isoquant (between the inputs capital per worker and average productive ability) to be concave from above. However, a negative value of f_{12} is an exceptional case (Ferguson, 1969, p. 89). Generally, an increase in capital intensity will raise f_2, the marginal product of average productive ability in the function output per worker.

The effect of an increase in ρ is therefore to rotate the linear relation (4.10) in a counterclockwise direction. The point of rotation can be found by taking $\partial(dQ_j)/\partial\rho$, setting it equal to zero and solving for the value of g_j such that dQ_j does not change. Represent this value of g_j by $\hat{g}$:

$$\frac{\partial(dQ_j)}{\partial\rho} = f_1 - f_1 - \rho f_{11} - \gamma f_{12} + \hat{g} f_{12} = 0.$$

Thus,

$$\hat{g} = \frac{\rho f_{11} + \gamma f_{12}}{f_{12}} = \gamma + \rho \frac{f_{11}}{f_{12}}. \tag{4.11}$$

Since f_{11} is negative and f_{12} is assumed to be positive, $\hat{g}$ will be less than γ, the average value of g_j. The linear relation in (4.10) rotates around the point $(\hat{g}, f - \rho f_1 - \gamma f_2 + \hat{g} f_2)$. The economic meaning of $\hat{g}$ is that a worker with this level of productive ability will find that his marginal product and earnings do not change as ρ changes. Anyone with a greater level of productive ability will find that this marginal product and earnings go up as ρ increases.

However, anyone with a level of productive ability less than g will find that his marginal product and earnings are reduced by the increase in the capital to labor ratio. The process of capital accumulation worsens absolutely as well as relatively the economic status of these individuals. Economic progress does not inevitably raise the absolute economic well-being of all workers. For some workers, economic progress is an enemy, bringing about a loss in earning power for which they are not compensated.

It is quite possible that there are no workers with productive ability less than $\hat{g}$, so that all workers would be made better off by capital accumulation. For example, if the inequality multiplier is identically one, then $\hat{g}$ is zero, and presumably no workers have negative productive ability.

Whether or not the inequality multiplier π increases as ρ increases can be related to how close $\hat{g}$ is to γ. Writing

$$\pi = \gamma f_2 / (f - \rho f_1),$$

$$\frac{\partial \pi}{\partial \rho} = \frac{\gamma}{f - \rho f_1} \, f_{12} \left(1 + \pi \, \frac{\rho f_{11}}{\gamma f_{12}}\right).$$

Substituting $(\hat{g} - \gamma)/\gamma$ for $\rho f_{11}/\gamma f_{12}$ from (4.11),

$$\frac{\partial \pi}{\partial \rho} = \frac{\gamma}{f - f_1} \, f_{12} \left(1 + \pi \left(\frac{\hat{g} - \gamma}{\gamma}\right)\right).$$

Assuming $f_{12} > 0$, $\partial \pi / \partial \rho$ will be positive if and only if

$$\frac{\hat{g}}{\gamma} > 1 - \frac{1}{\pi} = \frac{\pi - 1}{\pi} \, .$$

In particular, if π is less than one, $\hat{g}$ need only be positive for $\partial \pi / \partial \rho$ to be positive.

Another potential economic phenomenon is that there may be no positive wage at which a worker can be employed. If the inequality multiplier is greater than one, the linear relation for the marginal product intersects the x-axis at a positive value of productive ability, as indicated in fig. 4.3. Then the marginal product will be zero for an individual with positive productive ability. Any individual with a smaller level of productive ability would have a negative marginal product and would be unemployable. Very simply, individuals with low productive abilities do not contribute enough to production to cover the costs of the capital their labor is combined with.

Let us now investigate the effects of an increase in average productive ability. Since f_{22} must be negative, the effect of an increase in γ must be to reduce the slope of the linear relation between productive ability and the marginal product. Let $\tilde{g}$ be the value of productive ability such that the marginal product does not change as γ increases. This value can be found by setting $\partial (dQ_j)/\partial \gamma$ equal to zero and solving for $\tilde{g}$:

$$\frac{\partial(dQ_j)}{\partial\gamma} = f_2 - \rho f_{12} - f_2 - \gamma f_{22} + \tilde{g} f_{22} = 0.$$

Thus

$$\tilde{g} = \frac{\rho f_{12} + \gamma f_{22}}{f_{22}} = \gamma + \rho \frac{f_{12}}{f_{22}} .$$

If f_{12} is positive, $\tilde{g}$ must be less than γ.

As γ increases, all individuals with productive ability less than $\tilde{g}$ find that their marginal products and earnings increase. For the low-income population, it is not necessary to increase their productive abilities to increase their economic well-being. It is sufficient to increase the average productive ability. Similarly, individuals with a productive ability greater than $\tilde{g}$ find that their earnings go down as γ increases.

10. Unobserved sources of variation in earnings

One of the major explanations of the distributions of earnings is that the regular shapes of these distributions arise from underlying statistical laws, such as the ergodic properties of stochastic processes (Champernowne, 1953, 1973). While these theories can explain the shape of the distribution of earnings, they give no explanation for the amount of inequality and suggest no variables that would affect it.

More recently, Jencks et al. (1972) and Taubman (1976a, 1977b) among others have attempted to estimate the proportion of the variance in earnings attributable to genetic inheritance, home or early environment and schooling. The residual is attributable to luck or after-home environment. The small amount of inequality in earnings attributable to cognitive inequality and the distribution of schooling resources leads Jencks to the conclusion that policies to affect inequality in cognitive skills and schooling resources will not do much to reduce earnings inequality. For example, Jencks argues that reducing the inequality in schooling will not reduce the inequality in earnings: for a given level of schooling, the inequality in earnings is about equal to the inequality in earnings for the population as a whole (as measured by the coefficient of variation).

This argument would be valid if redistributing or changing school resources only changed the distribution of the population according to their schooling and left the residual variation in earnings unaffected. But redistributing schooling resources can also act to reduce earnings inequality by changing the valuations that the economy places both on education and on the unobserved sources of variation in earnings.

This possibility can be investigated in the following manner. Suppose now that an individual's productive ability g_j is itself a function of two variables, years of schooling s_j and an unobserved variable t_j. Let g_s be the average level of productive ability and let $\sigma(g_s)$ be the standard deviation of productive ability for all individuals with level of schooling s. The mean earnings for individuals with s years of schooling is $f - \rho f_1 - \gamma f_2 + g_s f_2$ and the standard deviation of earnings is $f_2 \, \sigma(g_s)$. The inequality of earnings for individuals with s years of schooling is therefore

$$\frac{f_2 \, \sigma(g_s)}{f - \rho f_1 - \gamma f_2 + g_s f_2} = \frac{g_s f_2}{f - \rho f_1 - \gamma f_2 + g_s f_2} \, \frac{\sigma(g_s)}{g_s} = \pi_s \frac{\sigma(g_s)}{g_s} \, .$$

The quotient $\sigma(g_s)/g_s$ is the inequality in productive abilities among individuals with s years of schooling and π_s is the inequality multiplier applied to $\sigma(g_s)/g_s$ to yield the inequality in earnings for that group.

Let us now investigate whether π_s increases or decreases as ρ and γ change. Because of its form, it is easier to work with $1/\pi_s$:

$$\frac{1}{\pi_s} = \frac{f - \rho f_1 - f_2(\gamma - g_s)}{g_s f_2} = \frac{f - \rho f_1}{g_s f_2} - \frac{\gamma}{g_s} + 1$$

$$= \frac{\gamma}{g_s} \frac{1}{\pi} - \frac{\gamma}{g_s} + 1,$$

where π is the inequality multiplier for the whole labor force. Then

$$\frac{\partial(1/\pi_s)}{\partial \rho} = \frac{\gamma}{g_s} \frac{\partial(1/\pi)}{\partial \rho} \, .$$

If π increases as ρ increases, then π_s is an increasing function of capital intensity. Similarly, if increases in γ do not affect g_s and $\sigma(g_s)$,

$$\frac{(1/\pi_s)}{\partial \gamma} = \frac{1}{g_s} \left(\frac{1}{\pi} - 1 \right) - \frac{\gamma}{g_s} \left(\frac{\partial \pi/\partial \gamma}{\pi^2} \right) \, .$$

If $\pi < 1$ and $\partial \pi/\partial \gamma < 0$, then π_s unambiguously decreases as γ increases.

The above analysis indicates that the residual "unexplained" variance in earnings for given levels of observed variables can be affected by public policy. Changes in capital intensity and average productive ability can change the amount of earnings inequality for a given level of schooling.

11. Implications for growth accounting

Whether the inequality multiplier π is identically one (and the efficiency units
assumption holds) can be related to the question of whether the methods of
growth accounting are valid. Growth accounting is the procedure of using rates
of growth of factors of production and factor shares to determine the sources of
growth in aggregate output over time. Typically, the contribution of technological progress is regarded as a residual after other contributions are calculated.
The intention of this section is to examine the conditions under which current
practice leads to an accurate revelation of the sources of growth. The concern
here is with the growth attributable to factors of production; hence, for purposes of exposition, it will be assumed that there is no technological progress.

Suppose aggregate production is given by $Q = n\,f(\rho,\gamma)$. By the chain rule,

$$dQ/dt = f\,dn/dt + n\,f_1\,d\rho/dt + n\,f_2\,d\gamma/dt$$

or

$$\frac{dQ/dt}{Q} = \frac{f\,dn/dt}{n\,f} + \frac{n\,f_1\,d\rho/dt}{n\,f} + \frac{n\,f_2\,d\gamma/dt}{n\,f}$$

$$= \frac{dn/dt}{n} + \frac{f_1}{f/\rho}\,\frac{d\rho/dt}{\rho} + \frac{f_2}{f/\gamma}\,\frac{d\gamma/dt}{\gamma}$$

$$= \dot{n} + \dot{\rho}\epsilon_\rho + \dot{\gamma}\epsilon_\gamma,$$

where $\dot{n}$, $\dot{\rho}$ and $\dot{\gamma}$ are the proportional rates of change in n, ρ and γ over time,
and ϵ_ρ and ϵ_γ are the elasticities of output per worker with respect to capital
intensity and average productive ability, respectively. In the absence of technological progress, there are three sources of growth: increases in the labor force,
increases in capital per worker and increases in average productive ability.

Suppose now that we wish to discover the relative contributions of each of
these sources. There is no problem with n because it is directly observable.
Similarly, the contribution of increases in capital intensity can be observed
because ϵ_ρ is simply capital's share of total output. However, ϵ_γ is not directly
observable. The practice in growth accounting has been to use labor's factor
share for ϵ_γ (see for example Denison, 1974, pp. 103–106). Labor's factor share
is given by $1 - \epsilon_\rho$.

The practice of using labor's factor share as the weight for skill or education's
contribution to growth arises from the assumption that the production function
takes the form $F(k,en)$, where F is a linearly homogeneous function of its two

arguments, k and en, and e is an index of labor quality analogous to γ. This index is a weighted average of different educational levels and different labor groups. That is to say, increases in education or skill are treated as augmenting the quantity of labor. Then the output coefficient for e is identical to the output coefficient for n Hence, the use of labor's factor share for the output coefficient of the labor quality index would be appropriate.

If the aggregate production function takes the form $F(k,en)$, the inequality multiplier is identically one. By Euler's relation, since F is linearly homogeneous,

$$\pi = \frac{\rho F_2}{F - k F_1} = \frac{\rho F_2}{\rho F_2} = 1.$$

Suppose instead that the aggregate production function takes the general form $n\, f(\rho,\gamma)$. Suppose, further, that π is not identically one. This occurs if the function f is not linearly homogeneous. Then, the returns to scale, given by the function coefficient $\epsilon_f = \epsilon_\rho + \epsilon_\gamma$, is unequal to one. The consequence is that ϵ_γ is no longer given by labor's factor share:

$$\epsilon_\gamma = \epsilon_f - \epsilon_p \neq 1 - \epsilon_\rho.$$

The difference between labor's factor share and ϵ_γ is given by

$$1 - \epsilon_\rho - \epsilon_\gamma = 1 - \epsilon_f.$$

If ϵ_f is less than one, labor's factor share overestimates the output elasticity of average productive ability. Consequently, the contribution of increases in skill per worker to growth in aggregate output is overestimated. If technological progress is calculated as a residual, then it would be underestimated by the foregoing procedure.

It should be emphasized that the conclusion regarding the validity of growth accounting does not depend on π being a function of either ρ or γ. This inequality multiplier could be a constant unequal to one and growth accounting would still be invalid.

The efficiency units assumption creeps into some other theoretical nooks. Despite its sophisticated methodology, the optimal income tax literature is based on a crude assumption concerning potential incomes (Mirrlees, 1971, p. 176). Similarly, in a model generating the size distribution of income from both labor and capital sources, Conlisk (1977, p. 347) assumes that individuals' potential labor earnings are proportional to an individual characteristic. The point of this chapter is that the distribution of earnings cannot be specified *a priori* in terms of some individual characteristic. The distribution of earnings is determined as the outcome of the particular equilibrium of the economy.

12. Summary and limitations of the analysis

The major contribution of this chapter has been the distinction introduced between the distribution of characteristics among the population and the valuations placed on those characteristics by the economy. The inequality in earnings depends both on the inequality in productive abilities and on the inequality multiplier, which summarizes the effects on earnings inequality of the valuations that the economy places on the individual productive abilities. The problem of explaining earnings inequality then divides into two parts which can be analyzed separately. This chapter has concentrated on the inequality multiplier.

The inequality multiplier is determined by the production function and its partial derivatives. It has therefore been possible to relate the inequality multiplier to traditional production theory, integrating the theory of the distribution of earnings with the theory of factor shares and technological progress.

With the formal development of the inequality multiplier, it has been possible to specify the conditions under which previous analysis, employing implicitly the efficiency units assumption, is valid. These conditions are very restrictive and require that output per worker be a linearly homogeneous function of capital intensity and the average productive ability. It has also been possible to describe the conditions under which the inequality multiplier is an increasing function of capital intensity and a decreasing function of average productive ability.

Despite the extensive investigation of these conditions, the effect of capital intensity and average productive ability on earnings inequality is theoretically ambiguous. There is no theorem in this chapter saying that under all circumstances $\partial \pi / \partial \rho > 0$ and $\partial \pi / \partial \gamma < 0$. The effect of ρ and γ on the inequality multiplier depends on the nature of the production function and cannot be specified *a priori*. This question is an empirical one and cannot be settled in this chapter.

The limitations of the analysis should be kept in mind. The development of the inequality multiplier ignores the question of how individuals will be assigned to jobs in the economy. This is inevitable in an aggregate analysis. Another shortcoming is that the analysis relies on aggregate measures of capital, raw labor and productive ability. Probably many economists reject out of hand any analysis which depends to such an extent on aggregates. From their point of view, it would be preferable to develop a disaggregated analysis with heterogeneous capital units, heterogeneous labor units and microeconomic production functions. Such an analysis is developed in the next two chapters.

Chapter 5

THE ASSIGNMENT OF WORKERS TO JOBS

1. Introduction

Ricardo's analysis of differential rents is an early model of the determination of factor payments to a heterogeneous factor of production (1953, ch. II). This model of an agricultural economy is characterized by heterogeneous land, differing by fertility and homogeneous labor. With only land being heterogeneous, there is no question of which worker should work with which tract of land, since the workers are all identical in the labor they provide. However, if the workers are also heterogeneous, differing in their productivities, an assignment question arises: which worker will be assigned to which tract of land in equilibrium?

There are some precursors to the assignment problem discussed in this chapter. Marx (1967, vol. I, part VI) discusses the application of different amounts of capital to similar-sized tracts differing in fertility, in the context of Ricardo's differential rents model. Marx considers a number of alternative hypothetical cases to investigate whether the resulting differences in agricultural output are attributable to the different amount of capital or to underlying differences in fertility or location. Buchanan (1947) discusses the relevance of the "third" margin to the determination of land rents (the first two margins being the intensive and extensive). The third margin arises because different types of agricultural commodities can be raised on a given tract of land. There is therefore another assignment problem: which commodity will be raised on which tract of land? Clearly, changes in the demands for some commodities versus others can affect the relative rents if the commodities differ in their suitability for cultivation on different tracts of land.

The assignment problem can be divided into two separate questions. First, what is the principle which determines the equilibrium assignment of labor units to tracts of land? Secondly, what mechanism guides labor units to the appropriate tracts of land?

Workers may have imperfect information concerning their own productive abilities or may not be able to calculate the tracts on which they should be working. New entrants and the changing productive characteristics of existing workers may lead to a system continuously out of equilibrium. Costs of changing assignments may result in rigidities in which nonoptimal assignments are not eliminated. The consequence of the above consideration is that the mechanisms by which labor units get assigned to tracts is also important.

The distinction between the two questions is best brought out by reference to Arrow's paper on higher education as a filter, or screening (1973). In the two-factor model that he develops, the principle determining the optimal assignment of individuals to jobs is clearly comparative advantage: the ratio of the productivities for individuals from the two classes is different for the two types of jobs. However, because of the lack of information concerning the classes of a particular individual, the assignment mechanism is a screening procedure. The question of how individuals find jobs more properly belongs in the job search literature and will not be pursued in this chapter. (See for example recent work by Jovanovic, 1978a–d, and Mortensen, 1978.)

The factors of land and labor have been retained in the foregoing introductory discussion to provide an intuitive understanding of the questions that will be addressed here. But the theory that will be developed holds for arbitrary heterogeneous factors of production. The two factors chosen for presenting the theory are labor and capital, since these are the two factors most relevent to our present economic environment.

Before considering specific assignment principles, let us first investigate the nature of the assignment problem from the point of view of general equilibrium. A competitive equilibrium in a production and exchange economy consists of a set of quantities and a set of prices. The quantities completely describe the allocation of resources, i.e. the factors of production provided by household units and used by producing units, and on the output side the quantities of goods produced and their distribution among household units. The prices and quantities are such that each household unit maximizes its utility function and each producing unit maximizes its profit, and the markets for all goods with positive prices are exactly cleared.

As in the analysis of competitive equilibrium, the analysis of the distribution of earnings requires that we find a set of quantities, the amounts of labor of each type supplied by individuals and the amounts used by producing units, and a corresponding set of prices. In a competitive equilibrium the prices and quantities will be such that the suppliers of heterogeneous labor services will be maximizing their utilities and will not seek to change jobs or the quantities of labor provided. Similarly, the users of labor services will be maximizing profit (or minimizing cost) and will not seek to change the types or quantities of labor used.

Left in this general form, very little can be said about any resulting distribution of earnings. The topological and activity analysis developments of competitive equilibrium are intended to be used to investigate the Pareto optimality of the competitive equilibrium solution, the existence and uniqueness of such an equilibrium, and the stability of the competitive equilibrium solution. But these questions are of little interest in studying the distribution of earnings. Instead, the important problem is to describe the distribution of earnings. In turn, this distribution can only be described by exploiting underlying regularities in the economy. These regularities reduce the problem to a point where it is actually possible to solve explicitly for the distribution of earnings.

The first stage in the reduction of the problem is to restrict attention to factor markets. It is of course conceivable that equilibrium in the goods markets can influence the distribution of earnings, but such influences can be considered separately. Next, the demand side of the labor market can be represented in terms of the potential jobs that are available. Similarly, the supply side can be represented by the labor units or workers that are available for employment. As a result of this representation of the supply and demand sides, the problem of finding a competitive equilibrium no longer requires the application of marginal analysis and the determination of the quantities of each type of heterogeneous labor. Instead, the problem reduces to the following: in a competitive equilibrium, which worker will be employed at which job, and what will the distribution of earnings be such that no worker seeks to change jobs and no employer seeks to change the worker holding a particular job?

This is a version of the "assignment problem" which has been developed in operations research (Dantzig, 1963, ch. 15). Given an arbitrary matrix of outcomes, the problem is to assign one set of objects to another set of objects so as to maximize or minimize the sum of the outcomes. There exist techniques for solving the assignment problem in the general case. However, the assignment problem being considered in this chapter is one of considerably reduced dimensionality. One set of objects, the individuals or workers, differ by only a single parameter. The other set of objects, either the jobs or the units of the cooperating factor, differ by another parameter. The entries in the resulting matrix of outcomes are entirely determined by these two parameters. Once the functional form of the relation between the outcome and the values of the parameters is specified, it becomes possible in general to solve explicitly for the competitive equilibrium. The questions of Pareto optimality, existence, uniqueness and stability become nearly trivial.

In the model discussed in the next section the jobs will differ by level of

satisfaction and individuals will differ by level of productivity or potential income. The outcomes which guide the assignment of individuals to jobs are the
utilities received by individuals for different combinations of job satisfaction and
earnings. In section 3 jobs differ by difficulty and individuals differ by ability.
The outcome is the production obtained. Comparative advantage then arises in
the performance of jobs by individuals. The underlying assignment principle
arises from the requirement for technical efficiency. In sections 4 and 5 the jobs
are defined implicitly in terms of the distribution of cooperating factors of
production, called machines, and individuals again differ by ability. The outcome is again production obtained. The underlying assignment principle arises
from the requirement that the total value of production be maximized.

In the models discussed in this chapter it is possible to determine the assignment of individuals to jobs without solving at the same time for the relative
earnings of workers or the relative rents of machines, in the case of sections 4
and 5. This is because, with jobs described by only one parameter and individuals described by only one parameter, the kth individual in order of the declining
value of the individual parameter will be assigned to the kth job in order of the
value of the job parameter. The assignment principle merely determines the
direction of the assignment. That is to say, the assignment principle determines
whether individuals with higher values of the individual parameter get assigned
to jobs with higher values of the job parameter or to jobs with lower values of
the job parameter.

As a result of this simplification, it is possible to solve for the competitive
equilibrium in two stages. First, as discussed above, one can determine the
assignment of individuals to jobs that is consistent with competitive equilibrium.
Secondly, one can determine the relative earnings and machine rents that will
lead individuals and employers to choose that particular assignment. This two-
stage solution for the competitive equilibrium is apparent in Tinbergen's model,
discussed in Chapter 3. First, one determines who will work at which job in
equilibrium. Then from the individual wage offer curves, the wage function
(relating the wage to the individual parameter) bringing about this assignment
can be determined. The rest of this chapter discusses the principles underlying
the assignment of individuals to jobs and some of the implications for relative
wages. The next chapter develops the implications for the distribution of earnings.

2. Preferences

The assignment principle in the specific model developed by Tinbergen (discussed in Chapter 3, section 2) arises from individual preferences. These preferences are represented by a wage offer curve for different jobs. The wage at which an individual would be willing to work at a given job depends on the square of the difference between the individual's parameter and the job parameter. The consequence of that particular form for the wage offer curves is that individuals with higher values of the individual parameter almost automatically get assigned in equilibrium to jobs with higher job parameters.

An alternative preference-based assignment principle is developed in papers on compensating wage differences (Sattinger, 1976a, 1977b). In that model the more-productive individuals could end up in more or less satisfying jobs in equilibrium, depending on the elasticity of substitution between job satisfaction and earnings in the utility function.

Consider an economy in which jobs differ according to the satisfaction received by workers. Suppose the amount of satisfaction can be measured by a parameter s and suppose that the satisfaction is the same for all workers.

To eliminate the effects of comparative advantage and cooperating factors, let us adopt the efficiency units assumption. Suppose that a worker's productivity can be represented by a single parameter, n. The amount of the worker's earnings will be proportional to this productivity n. We may regard n as the amount of labor input to which a worker's labor is equivalent. The wage rate per unit of labor input will clearly depend on the level of job satisfaction. The more-satisfying jobs will pay less per unit of labor input. Let $w(s)$ be the wage rate corresponding in equilibrium to a job with satisfaction level s.

Each individual works at one job and receives earnings $w(s)n$. The problem facing the individual is to choose the optimal combination of earnings and job satisfaction that makes him best off. Suppose the utility function for individuals is as follows:

$$u = (\delta s^{-\rho} + (1 - \delta)(w(s)n)^{-\rho})^{-1/\rho}.$$

This utility function has a constant elasticity of substitution between job satisfaction and earnings of $\sigma = 1/(\rho + 1)$.

Three cases arise. First, suppose $\rho < 0$ so that the elasticity of substitution between satisfaction and earnings is less than one. Then it can be shown in equilibrium, the more-productive workers will be employed at the more-satisfying jobs. The equilibrium wage function, $w(s)$, which yields this assignment is an envelope of the individual offer curves obtained from the utility function by expressing the wage as a function of u, s, and n. This is illustrated in fig. 5.1, where $n_1 > n_2 > n_3$. The interpretation of this case is that the more-productive individuals 'spend' part of their higher incomes by performing more-satisfying but lower paying (per unit of labor input) jobs.

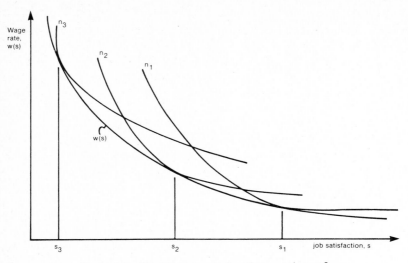

Figure 5.1. Equilibrium wage function, $\sigma < 1, \rho < 0$.

In the second case suppose $\rho > 0$ so that the elasticity of substitution between satisfaction and earnings is greater than one. In equilibrium, more-productive workers will be found at less-satisfying jobs, and less-productive workers will be employed at more-satisfying jobs. This unlikely case arises because less-productive workers are able to substitute higher job satisfaction for lower earnings. For the more-productive workers the greater earnings from higher paying jobs more than make up for the lower job satisfaction. This case is illustrated in fig. 5.2. The equilibrium wage function $w(s)$ is again determined as an envelope of individual offer curves.

The borderline case arises when the utility function takes the simple Cobb-Douglas form

$$u = s^\delta \, (w(s)n)^{1-\delta}.$$

Then $\rho = 0$ and the elasticity of substitution between job satisfaction and earnings is one. In this case individuals' trade-offs between job satisfaction and earnings do not depend on their level of productivity. The offer curves are therefore identical for all individuals, and the equilibrium wage function is congruent with these offer curves. This case is illustrated in fig. 5.3. The wage function $w(s)$ is such that individuals are indifferent as to which job they take. The compensating wage differences needed for an individual to be willing to take a particular job are the same for all individuals.

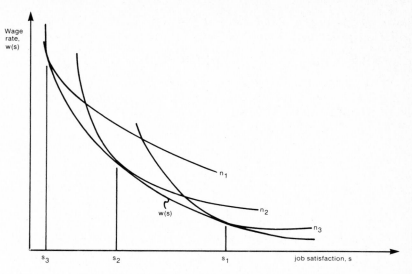

Figure 5.2. Equilibrium wage function, $\sigma > 1$, $\rho > 0$.

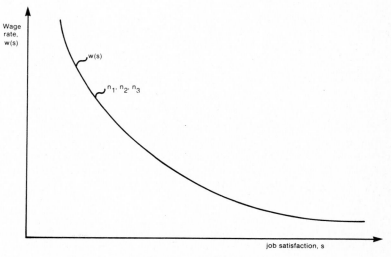

Figure 5.3. Equilibrium wage function, $\sigma = 1$, $\rho = 0$.

It is now possible to discuss some of the implications of the existence of an assignment problem in the distribution of earnings. First, unless the utility function takes a special form, the wage function $w(s)$ is not determined solely by the utility function. When the utility function takes the multiplicatively separable Cobb-Douglas form, the wage function depends only on the parameters of the utility function. But if the elasticity of substitution between job satisfaction and earnings is unequal to one, the wage function depends both on the utility function and on the distributions of individuals and jobs.

Secondly, even with the efficiency units assumption, the distribution of earnings is different from the distribution of productive abilities. This is because in equilibrium there is in general a systematic association between the characteristics of individuals and the characteristics of the jobs at which they work. In the case where $\sigma < 1$, the more-productive individuals earn less per unit of labor input because the jobs at which they work are more satisfying.

Thirdly, suppose we had attempted to observe the relationship between an individual's characteristics and his earnings. To take a specific case, suppose $\sigma < 1$. Because the more-productive individuals will be found at more-satisfying jobs, part of the differences in individuals' earnings will be explained by the differences in the satisfaction levels of the jobs they take. The estimated relationship between individual characteristics and earnings will therefore be biased. This problem is analogous to the self-selectivity bias in the attempt to estimate the relation between earnings and ability and schooling. The more-able individuals may select more years of schooling, so that the observed relation between schooling and earnings also reflects differences in abilities.

Fourthly, the amount of inequality in productive abilities directly affects the economic well-being of the low-income population in the general case where $\sigma \neq 1$. Consider fig. 5.1. Because of the assignment problem, individuals with low productive abilities compete for the less-satisfying jobs, bidding down their wage rates relative to the wage rates for the moderately satisfying jobs. In fig. 5.1. the wage rate for the job with satisfaction level s_3 is less than it would be if everyone had the productivity n_2. A similar result holds in fig. 5.2.

The major consequence of the assignment problem is that in attempting to develop a disaggregated model of the distribution of earnings, one must describe the distribution of jobs as well as the distribution of individuals and one must describe the principles guiding the assignment of individuals to jobs in equilibrium.

3. Comparative advantage

Comparative advantage as an assignment principle has by now been extensively discussed in the literature and will be only briefly presented here (see Chapter 3, section 3).

Suppose there are two individuals and two jobs which involve different types of tasks. For each individual we have the number of tasks of each type that he can perform within a given time period.

		Tasks	
		1	2
Individuals	1	a_{11}	a_{12}
	2	a_{21}	a_{22} ,

where a_{ij} is the number of tasks of type j performed by individual i within a given time period. Comparative advantage arises if a_{11}/a_{21} is unequal to a_{12}/a_{22}. For instance, suppose a_{11}/a_{21} is greater than a_{12}/a_{22}. It is then said that the first individual has a comparative advantage at the first task while the second individual has a comparative advantage at the second task.

Three major conclusions can be drawn from the existence of comparative advantage. First, giving the first individual the first task and the second individual the second task (hereafter referred to as assignment α) would be an efficient assignment. It would be impossible, by reallocating individuals' time between the two tasks, to get more tasks of one type done without getting fewer of the other type done. Also, giving the first individual the second task and the second individual the first task (hereafter referred to as assignment β) must be an inefficient assignment in the above sense.

Secondly, it is possible to draw some conclusions for the existence of equilibrium. Suppose in equilibrium we observe assignment α. It is then possible to determine the boundaries within which relative wages must fall.

The third conclusion that can be obtained results from the extension of the above two-individual, two-task analysis to the whole economy. Suppose, as before, that individuals differ according to their productive ability, g, and that the values of g cover an interval. Suppose, furthermore, that the tasks which employers seek to have performed can be completely described by the parameter h for the difficulty of the task. The values of this parameter also cover an interval. Finally, suppose that, comparing any two individuals and any two tasks, the individual with the greater ability has a comparative advantage at the more-difficult task. Then, in equilibrium, individuals with greater productive ability will be found working at the more difficult jobs. Thus, the principle of comparative advantage determines the order in which individuals, characterized by the parameter g, are assigned to tasks, characterized by the parameter h. This principle also determines what the equilibrium wage function must be, up to a multiplicative constant.

Comparative advantage can be related to the assignment of individuals to jobs according to capital intensity by supposing that the number of tasks of a given type that an individual can perform depends on a production function. Suppose $a_{ij} = f(g_i, k_j)$, where g_i is a cardinal measure of the productive ability of individual i and k_j is the capital intensity of job j. Then if $f(g_i, k_j)$ is multiplicatively separable, as in the Cobb-Douglas production function, no comparative advantage will arise. However, suppose $f(g_i, k_j)$ takes the constant elasticity of substitution form

$$(\delta g_i^{-\rho} + (1 - \delta)k_j^{-\rho})^{-1/\rho}.$$

If ρ is positive and $g_1 > g_2$ and $k_1 > k_2$, then

$$\frac{(\delta g_1^{-\rho} + (1 - \delta)k_1^{-\rho})^{-1/\rho}}{(\delta g_2^{-\rho} + (1 - \delta)k_1^{-\rho})^{-1/\rho}} > \frac{(\delta g_1^{-\rho} + (1 - \delta)k_2^{-\rho})^{-1/\rho}}{(\delta g_2^{-\rho} + (1 - \delta)k_2^{-\rho})^{-1/\rho}}$$

because

$$\frac{\delta g_1^{-\rho} + (1 - \delta)k_1^{-\rho}}{\delta g_2^{-\rho} + (1 - \delta)k_1^{-\rho}} < \frac{\delta g_1^{-\rho} + (1 - \delta)k_2^{-\rho}}{\delta g_2^{-\rho} + (1 - \delta)k_2^{-\rho}}$$

or

$$\delta g_1^{-\rho}(1 - \delta)k_2^{-\rho} + \delta g_2^{-\rho}(1 - \delta)k_1^{-\rho} > \delta g_2^{-\rho}(1 - \delta)k_2^{-\rho} + \delta g_1^{-\rho}(1 - \delta)k_1^{-\rho}$$

or

$$g_1^{-\rho}(k_2^{-\rho} - k_1^{-\rho}) > g_2^{-\rho}(k_2^{-\rho} - k_1^{-\rho})$$

or

$$g_1^{-\rho} < g_2^{-\rho} \quad \text{or} \quad g_1 > g_2.$$

Thus, if ρ is positive, the more-productive workers have a comparative advantage (in the sense that the ratio of outputs is greater) at the more capital-intensive job. Similarly, if ρ is negative, the more-productive workers have a comparative advantage at less capital-intensive jobs. The borderline case arises when the elasticity of substitution is one. This is the Cobb-Douglas case where no comparative advantage arises.

4. Scale-of-resources effect

As in international trade the principle of comparative advantage depends only on the productivity of individuals in different tasks; specifically, it does not depend in any way upon the market prices of cooperating factors or upon the extra revenues that employers can obtain by having more tasks performed. In fact, cooperating factors do not even enter the analysis.

There is, however, another principle based on production which influences the assignment of individuals to jobs. This principle operates even in the absence of comparative advantage and depends on the presence and cost of cooperating factors. This is the scale-of-resources effect. The genesis of this principle has been discussed in Chapter 3, section 4. Essentially, the argument is that the greater the resources (including subordinates) with which labor is combined, the greater will be the value of any differences in the productive abilities of individuals. The more-productive individuals would then be assigned to jobs requiring greater resources or more cooperating factors. The scale-of-resources effect has been used to explain the distribution of executive incomes, which have been found to depend primarily on the size of firms and not on their profits. Except in certain applications, however, the theory behind the scale-of-resources effect has not been presented formally and rigorously.

Consider a large economy in which many individuals work with many separate capital units to produce different types of goods. Suppose that this economy is characterized by perfect competitition. A competitive equilibrium in the context of this model is a combination of an assignment of workers to capital units and rent and wage functions such that no worker seeks to change his employment and no capital owner seeks to change the employment of his capital unit. Competitive equilibrium therefore implies that no entrepreneur can hire factors at their market factor prices and so organize production in a way that he is able to make a profit without supplying any factor himself. This in turn means that neither individuals supplying labor nor owners of capital can, by taking the price of the other factor as given, make more than its own market factor price. An individual's wage must therefore equal the maximum he could obtain from renting a capital unit, combining it with his labor, and keeping the residual. Also, the rental price for a capital unit must equal the maximum the owner of the capital unit could obtain by hiring labor to work with his capital and keeping the residual.

Let us isolate two capital units and two individuals for further consideration. Suppose that only one individual can work with a capital unit at a time. It is convenient to refer to these capital units as machines. Let r_1 and r_2 be the rental costs for the two machines; their determination will be discussed shortly.

The prices of output produced by the two machines are p_1 and p_2 (it is assumed that the machines produce different types of output). Let a_{ij} be the amount of output produced by individual i, using machine j. To distinguish the effect of cooperating factors from the effect of comparative advantage, let us rule out the latter by assuming that

$$\frac{a_{11}}{a_{21}} = \frac{a_{12}}{a_{22}}. \tag{5.1}$$

In general, it can be shown that there will be no comparative advantage if the production function relating outputs to inputs is multiplicatively separable.

Now consider the earnings that individuals can achieve by renting machines and selling the product of their labor:

		Machine	
		1	2
Individual	1	$p_1 a_{11} - r_1$	$p_2 a_{12} - r_2$
	2	$p_1 a_{21} - r_1$	$p_2 a_{22} - r_2$

Without loss of generality, let us assume that individual 1 is more productive than individual 2, so that

$$a_{11} > a_{21} \quad \text{and} \quad a_{12} > a_{22}. \tag{5.2}$$

Without making any assumption about which machine is more costly or more productive, let us now investigate the circumstances under which individual 1, the more-productive individual, will choose to use the first machine and individual 2 will choose the second machine. This particular assignment can be referred to as assignment α. Similarly, let β represent the assignment where individual 1 chooses the second machine and individual 2 chooses the first machine. The analysis will proceed by deriving the necessary conditions for assignment α to occur.

If individual 1 chooses the first machine, then his earnings in doing so must be at least as great as if he chose the second machine:

$$p_1 a_{11} - r_1 \geq p_2 a_{12} - r_2. \tag{5.3}$$

Similarly, for individual 2 choose the second machine, we must have

$$p_2 a_{22} - r_2 \geq p_1 a_{21} - r_1. \tag{5.4}$$

Adding the left-hand side of (5.3) to the left-hand side of (5.4), and similarly for the right-hand sides, yields the following inequality:

$$p_1 a_{11} + p_2 a_{22} - r_1 - r_2 \geq p_2 a_{12} + p_1 a_{21} - r_1 - r_2$$

or

$$p_1(a_{11} - a_{21}) \geq p_2(a_{12} - a_{22})$$

or

$$p_1 a_{21} \left(\frac{a_{11}}{a_{21}} - 1 \right) \geq p_2 a_{22} \left(\frac{a_{12}}{a_{22}} \right) - 1$$

By virtue of (5.1) and (5.2) this becomes

$$p_1 a_{21} \geq p_2 a_{22}. \tag{5.5}$$

Thus, a necessary condition for assignment α is that the value of output be greater using the first machine than using the second. (It does not matter which individual we use to compare the values of output since (5.5) is equivalent to $p_1 a_{11} \geq p_2 a_{12}$.)

This conclusion can be strengthened as follows. By analogous reasoning, a necessary condition for assignment β is that the value of output be greater with the second machine than with the first, i.e. the inequality in (5.5) is reversed. It follows that if the value of output is strictly greater using the first machine, i.e. if

$$p_1 a_{21} > p_2 a_{22},$$

then it is impossible in equilibrium for assignment β to occur. The only possible assignment in which the two individuals choose different machines is for the first individual to select the first machine and the second individual to select the second machine, i.e. assignment α.

Let us now examine the relative costs of the two machines. Multiplying the left-hand side in (5.3) by the left-hand side in (5.4), and similarly for the right-hand sides, yields

$$(p_1 a_{11} - r_1)(p_2 a_{22} - r) \geq (p_2 a_{12} - r_2)(p_1 a_{21} - r_1)$$

or

$$p_1 p_2 a_{11} a_{22} - r_1 p_2 a_{22} - r_2 p_1 a_{11} + r_1 r_2 \geq p_1 p_2 a_{12} a_{21} - r_1 p_2 a_{12}$$
$$- r_2 p_1 a_{21} + r_1 r_2.$$

By virtue of (5.1) this yields

$$-r_1 p_2 a_{22} - r_2 p_1 a_{11} \geq r_1 p_2 a_{12} - r_2 p_1 a_{21}.$$

Rearranging and using (5.1), (5.2), and (5.3), this yields

$$\frac{r_1}{r_2} \geq \frac{p_1 a_{21}}{p_2 a_{22}} = \frac{p_1 a_{11}}{p_2 a_{12}} \geq 1. \tag{5.6}$$

Thus, another necessary condition for assignment α is that the rental cost of the first machine must be greater than the rental cost of the second. By analogous reasoning a necessary condition for the opposite assignment, β, is that the rental cost of the second machine be greater than the rental cost of the first. It follows that if the first machine has the greater rental cost, it is impossible for assignment β to occur. The only consistent assignment is for the more productive individual to work with the more costly machine.

The result in (5.6) can be rearranged to provide yet another necessary condition:

$$\frac{r_1}{p_1 a_{21}} \geq \frac{r_2}{p_2 a_{22}}. \tag{5.7}$$

That is to say, if assignment α occurs, then the ratio of capital costs to value of output for the first machine will be greater than or equal to the ratio of capital costs to output for the second machine. (Again, either individual may be used to make this comparison.)

This assignment principle can also be viewed from the point of view of the owners of the machines. Let w_1 be the market wage for individual 1 and let w_2 be the wage for individual 2. Treating the returns to capital owners as residuals after payment of wage costs, one obtains the following matrix of potential returns to capital:

Machine

		1	2
	1	$p_1 a_{11} - w_1$	$p_2 a_{12} - w_1$
Individual			
	2	$p_1 a_{21} - w_2$	$p_2 a_{22} - w_2$

If the owner of the first machine chooses to hire the first individual, then

$$p_1 a_{11} - w_1 \geq p_1 a_{21} - w_2. \qquad (5.8)$$

Similarly, if the owner of the second machine chooses the second individual, then

$$p_2 a_{22} - w_2 \geq p_2 a_{12} - w_1. \qquad (5.9)$$

The inequalities (5.8) and (5.9) can then be used to derive (5.5) and another inequality corresponding to (5.6):

$$\frac{w_1}{w_2} \geq \frac{a_{12}}{a_{22}} = \frac{a_{11}}{a_{21}} > 1.$$

Thus, the ratio of the more-productive individual's wage to the less-productive individual's wage must equal or exceed the ratio of productivities on either machine. This inequality could also have been derived from (5.3) and (5.4) by making the substitutions $r_1 = p_1 a_{11} - w_1$ and $r_2 = p_2 a_{22} - w_2$.

It is useful at this point briefly to discuss in alternative terms the reasons why individuals should be assigned to particular machines even when there is no comparative advantage. All the assignments that have been considered above are technically efficient, whether or not they could occur in equilibrium. That is, if individual 1 worked with machine 2 and individual 2 worked with machine 1, and conditions (5.1), (5.2) and (5.5) held, no reallocation of the individuals' time would allow us to produce more of one of the goods without producing less of the other. However, because the goods produced with the two machines carry prices, it is possible to calculate opportunity costs of using one machine instead of another, or of using one individual instead of another.

What is the opportunity cost of using machine 1 with individual 1 instead of machine 2? The answer is $p_2 a_{12} - w_1$. Similarly, the opportunity cost of using machine 2 with individual 1 is $p_1 a_{11} - w_1$. The difference in these opportunity costs is $p_1 a_{11} - p_2 a_{12}$. The wage rate for the first individual does not effect the difference in opportunity costs. Individual 1, in deciding whether to use machine

1 or machine 2, will compare the difference in rental cost with the difference in the values of output, which is given by the difference in opportunity costs. Individual 1 will prefer machine 1 whenever the difference in rental costs, $r_1 - r_2$, falls below the difference in opportunity costs, $p_1 a_{11} - p_2 a_{12}$.

Similarly, individual 2 compares the difference in rental costs with the difference in opportunity costs. However, the difference in opportunity costs is now given by $p_1 a_{21} - p_2 a_{22}$. Individual 2 will select machine 2 when the difference in opportunity costs is less than the difference in machine rents.

For assignment α to occur, then, it is necessary for the difference in machine rents to lie between the difference in opportunity costs using individual 1 and the difference in opportunity costs using individual 2: $p_1 a_{11} - p_2 a_{12} \geq r_1 - r_2 \geq p_1 a_{21} - p_2 a_{22}$. This same condition arises from (5.3) and (5.4). Assignment α, instead of assignment β, arises because the individual for whom the difference in opportunity costs (or production) is greater gets assigned to the machine which produces the greater output.

Similarly, the difference between the wage for individual 1 and the wage for individual 2 will lie between the difference in opportunity costs for the two workers using machine 1 and the difference using machine 2. The resulting inequalities may also be derived from (5.8) and (5.9): $p_1 a_{11} - p_1 a_{21} \geq w_1 - w_2 \geq p_2 a_{12} - p_2 a_{22}$.

A consequence of assigning individuals to machines according to opportunity costs is that the total value of output will be maximized. From either of the above two sets of inequalities, $p_1 a_{11} + p_2 a_{22} \geq p_1 a_{21} + p_2 a_{12}$. The amount on the left-hand side is the value of output with assignment α, and the amount on the right-hand side is the value of output with assignment β. Therefore the equilibrium assignment must be the one which maximizes the value of output. Even in the absence of comparative advantage, the difference in opportunity costs for individual 1, comparing two machines, will not be the same as for individual 2. Although both assignments will be technically efficient, they will yield different total values of output. Opportunity costs will then guide the assignment of individuals to machines. It is only natural to refer to this assignment principle as the opportunity cost principle.

Suppose now that we observe an equilibrium in the factor markets. That is, no individuals can make higher earnings by working with different machines (taking machine rental costs as given to them) and no machine owners can receive greater incomes by hiring different workers (taking wages as given). Consider now any two individuals and the machines they are observed to work with in equilibrium. The necessary conditions that have been derived above must hold for these two individuals and the two machines with which they work. We may therefore draw the following conclusions concerning the assignment in the absence of comparative advantage.

(1) The more-productive individual will always be found working with a machine that has at least as high a rental cost as the machine used by the less-productive individual.

(2) Using either individual for purposes of comparison, the value of output obtained with the more productive individual's machine will exceed the value of output obtained with the less-productive individual's machine.

(3) Again, using either individual for purposes of comparison, the ratio of capital costs to value of output will be greater for the more-productive individual's machine than for the less-productive individual's machine.

A simple argument is sufficient to establish the efficiency of the equilibrium solution of assigning more productive workers to larger machines. Suppose there exists an alternative assignment that yielded a greater total value of production (using the same output prices). To be different, this alternative assignment must have two workers such that the worker with the greater productive ability is employed at the smaller machine. Then it is possible to increase the total value of production by switching the machines at which the two individuals work. The alternative assignment is therefore inefficient.

It would be nice to conclude directly from the established results that more productive individuals work with more capital-intensive production processes. But we have not assumed any objective measurement of quantities of capital. The relative rental costs of two machines depend on the prices of output, as well as the quantities produced. Then, it is impossible to deduce which of two machines constitutes more capital without reference to arbitrary output prices.

However, if the concept of capital is well defined and if there is an objective measure of capital, then in equilibrium capital costs will certainly be proportional to the amount of capital. The more-productive individuals, being employed at production processes which have greater ratios of capital costs to value added, will also therefore be employed at more capital-intensive processes.

5. Scale-of-resources effect with comparative advantage present

Now let us abandon the assumption that there is no comparative advantage and investigate the necessary and sufficient conditions for the more-productive workers to be assigned to larger machines. Suppose that equilibrium holds and consider two workers and the machines they are observed to work with in equilibrium. Without loss of generality, suppose that individual 1 is the more productive, so that $a_{11} > a_{21}$ and $a_{12} > a_{22}$, where a_{ij} is the output of worker i, using machine j. The assumption of equilibrium yields conditions (5.3) and (5.4); these can be rearranged to yield

$$p_1 a_{11} - p_2 a_{12} \geq r_1 - r_2 \geq p_1 a_{21} - p_2 a_{22}.$$

From this inequality can be derived the necessary and sufficient conditions for r_1 to be greater than r_2, i.e. for the more productive individual to work with the more costly machine. The necessary condition for $r_1 - r_2$ to be positive is that $p_1 a_{11} - p_2 a_{12}$ be positive, i.e. individual 1 must produce a higher value of output using the first machine than using the second machine. Similarly, a sufficient condition for $r_1 - r_2$ to be positive is that $p_1 a_{21} - p_2 a_{22}$ be positive, i.e. the second worker must produce a higher output using the first machine than using the second machine.

The conditions under which the more-productive worker is assigned to the smaller machine can also be stated. The necessary condition for $r_1 - r_2$ to be negative is that $p_1 a_{21} - p_2 a_{22} < 0$, and the sufficient condition is that $p_1 a_{11} - p_2 a_{12} < 0$. It is therefore certainly possible for the more-productive workers to be assigned to smaller machines.

These results can also be related to comparative advantage. The first case, where the more-productive worker is assigned to the larger machine, can occur either when the first worker has a comparative advantage with the smaller or with the larger machine. For example, suppose the matrix of output values in a time period is as follows:

		Machine	
		1	2
	1	$12	$9
Worker			
	2	$ 3	$2

In this case the equilibrium assignment is with the first individual working with the first (larger) machine. The difference in machine rents then lies in the range $12–$9 = $3 \geq r_1 - r_2 \geq $3–$2 = $1. However, the first individual has a comparative advantage at the smaller machine in the sense that $9/2$ is greater than $12/3$.

In contrast, the more-productive worker will be assigned to the smaller machine only if he has a comparative advantage at the smaller machine. The proof runs as follows. We assume that the first worker is unambiguously more productive, so that $a_{11} > a_{21}$ and $a_{12} > a_{22}$. We assume that the first worker is assigned to the first machine, so that by (5.3) and (5.4)

$$p_1 a_{11} + p_2 a_{22} \geq p_2 a_{12} + p_1 a_{21}$$

or

$$p_1 a_{11} \left(1 - \frac{a_{21}}{a_{11}}\right) \geq p_2 a_{12} \left(1 - \frac{a_{22}}{a_{12}}\right).$$

Finally, we assume that the second machine has the higher rent. The necessary condition for this to occur is that $p_1 a_{11} < p_2 a_{12}$. It follows that

$$1 - \frac{a_{21}}{a_{11}} > 1 - \frac{a_{22}}{a_{12}} \quad \text{or} \quad \frac{a_{11}}{a_{21}} > \frac{a_{12}}{a_{22}},$$

i.e. the first worker has a comparative advantage at the first or less productive machine.

As a numerical example, consider the following matrix of output values:

		Machine	
		1	2
Worker	1	$10	$14
	2	$ 8	$13

Then the only equilibrium assignment in which each worker chooses a different machine is with the first worker to be assigned to the first machine and the second worker to the second, more-productive machine. The machine rents fall in the range $-4 \geq r_1 - r_2 \geq -5$, and the first worker has a comparative advantage using the first machine.

The foregoing analysis demonstrates that a sufficient condition for the more-productive worker to be assigned to the larger (most costly) machine in equilibrium is that he must have a comparative advantage at that machine. But this condition is not at all necessary.

More specific results can be obtained by assuming that output is homogeneous in the economy and that $p_1 = p_2 = 1$. Then the necessary condition for the more-productive worker to be assigned to the less costly first machine is that $a_{11} - a_{21} \geq a_{12} - a_{22}$, i.e. the difference in outputs between the two individuals must be greater on the smaller machine. Suppose now that the output a_{ij} can be represented parametrically as a function of some measure of the productive ability of workers, g, and the size of the machine, k. Specifically, let $a_{ij} = f(g_i, k_j)$. Then a sufficient condition for the more-productive workers to be assigned to the larger machines in equilibrium is that $\partial^2 f / \partial g \, \partial k > 0$. Then if $g_1 > g_2$ and $k_1 > k_2$,

$$f(g_1,k_1) - f(g_2,k_1) > f(g_1,k_2) - f(g_2,k_2). \tag{5.13}$$

Now the second machine is the smaller or less costly, and the more-productive worker can only be found using the larger machine in equilibrium. That is to say, comparing any two workers and the two machines they work with in equilibrium, the condition $\partial^2 f/\partial g \, \partial k > 0$ implies that we will never observe the more productive worker using the smaller machine.

If $f(g, k)$ is linearly homogeneous, the condition $\partial^2 f/\partial g \, \partial k$ is equivalent to a decreasing marginal rate of technical substitution. If $f(g, k)$ is not linearly homogeneous, then the two conditions are not equivalent (see Ferguson, 1969, p. 89).

The condition $\partial^2 f/\partial g \, \partial k > 0$ is not, however, necessary for more-productive workers to be assigned to more costly or larger machines. The condition implies that (5.13) holds for every g_1 and g_2 and every k_1 and k_2 such that $g_1 > g_2$ and $k_1 > k_2$. Instead, we only need the condition to hold for any two workers and the machines they work with in equilibrium.

6. Scale-of-resources effect with Cobb-Douglas production function

This section demonstrates that the foregoing results on the scale-of-resources effect can be extended to a standard neoclassical production function allowing substitution of one factor for another. This case is more difficult analytically because the capital to labor ratio is determined endogenously and the wage function cannot be eliminated from the optimal conditions for equilibrium.

Suppose each firm in the economy has a production function of the general Cobb-Douglas form $n\rho^\theta \gamma^b$, where n is the number of workers, ρ is the capital to labor ratio and γ is the average productive ability of the workers. Suppose the values of the parameter θ cover an interval between zero and one. That is, production in the economy is undertaken by a continuum of industries, with a different value of θ for each industry. The price of a unit of output in each industry will be different and will be determined by the perfectly competitive condition that maximum profits are zero.

Let r be the return to capital, assumed to be constant for all capital to labor ratios in this model. Let $w(\gamma)$ be the wage rate for labor of productive ability γ, where the values of γ are assumed to cover an interval. If $w(\gamma)$ is a concave function (so that the slope of $w'(\gamma)$ increases as γ increases), then only one level of productive ability will be used in an industry. The case where $w(\gamma)$ is convex could not arise, since then firms would hire workers at extreme high and low levels of productive ability and would avoid workers with inbetween levels. For example, if γ were convex it would be cheaper to hire one worker with, say, productive ability ten and one with productive ability two, than to hire two workers with productive ability six apiece, for the average productive ability and output would be the same. A convex wage function $w(\gamma)$ is therefore inconsistent with equilibrium in the labor market and can be ruled out.

Regardless of the price of output, each firm will choose values of n, ρ, and γ that will maximize production subject to a cost constraint. Using a Lagrangian multiplier the problem facing the firm is to maximize

$$V = n\rho^\theta \gamma^b - \lambda(n\rho r + nw(\gamma) - 1).$$

The first order conditions are

$$V_n = \rho^\theta \gamma^b - \lambda(\rho r + w(\gamma)) = 0, \tag{5.10}$$

$$V_\rho = \theta n \rho^{\theta-1} \gamma^b - \lambda nr = 0, \tag{5.11}$$

$$V_\gamma = bn\rho^\theta \gamma^{b-1} - \lambda nw'(\gamma) = 0, \tag{5.12}$$

$$V_\lambda = n\rho r + nw(\gamma) - 1 = 0. \tag{5.13}$$

Eliminating λ and n from (5.11) and (5.12) and rearranging yields the following two conditions that must hold for firms to be maximizing profits:

$$\theta(\rho r + w(\gamma)) - \rho r = 0 \tag{5.14}$$

and

$$b(\rho r + w(\gamma)) - \gamma w'(\gamma) = 0. \tag{5.15}$$

Differentiating these two conditions totally with respect to θ yields the system

$$\begin{pmatrix} (\theta - 1)r & \theta w'(\gamma) \\ br & (b-1) w'(\gamma) \end{pmatrix} \begin{pmatrix} \partial\rho/\partial\theta \\ \partial\gamma/\partial\theta \end{pmatrix} = \begin{pmatrix} -(\rho r + w(\gamma)) \\ 0 \end{pmatrix}. \tag{5.16}$$

Let M equal the determinant

$$\begin{vmatrix} (\theta - 1)r & \theta w'(\gamma) \\ nr & (b-1) w'(\gamma) - w'(\gamma) \end{vmatrix}$$

$$= rw'(\gamma)(1 - \theta - b + \frac{(1-\theta)\gamma w''(\gamma)}{r\, w'(\gamma)}).$$

It can be shown that the second order conditions for profit maximization on the part of the firm imply that the determinant M is positive.

Solution of the system in (5.16) yields

$$\frac{\partial \rho}{\partial \theta} = \frac{1}{M} \left[(\rho r + w(\gamma)) ((1 - b) w'(\gamma) + \gamma w''(\gamma)) \right] \tag{5.17}$$

and

$$\frac{\partial \gamma}{\partial \theta} = \frac{1}{M} \left[br(\rho r + w(\gamma)) \right]. \tag{5.18}$$

Examination of the terms of (5.17) and (5.18) reveals that $\partial \rho / \partial \theta > 0$ and $\partial \gamma / \partial \theta > 0$. As the parameter θ increases, both the capital to labor ratio and the average productive ability increase. Industries with higher capital to labor ratios will employ workers with greater productive ability. This establishes the scale-of-resources effect in a case where substitution between factors of production is possible.

7. Relation to capital-skill complementarity

At this point it is appropriate to distinguish the hypothesis that the more-productive workers will be assigned to more capital-intensive jobs from the hypothesis of capital-skill complementarity (previously discussed in Chapter 4, section 6). The latter hypothesis, proposed and tested by Griliches, asserts that the (Allen-Uzawa) partial elasticity of substitution between raw labor and capital is greater than the partial elasticity of substitution between skill (considered as a factor) and capital. Then a reduction in the price of capital would, roughly, raise the amount of capital used to produce a given quantity. Also, it would reduce the ratio of raw labor to capital relative to the ratio of skill to labor, thus increasing the skill to raw labor ratio. Expressed in terms of partial elasticities of complementarity, the hypothesis states that an increase in the quantity of capital would reduce the ratio of the marginal products of raw labor and capital relative to the ratio of the marginal products of skill and capital. Then the ratio of the marginal product of skill to the marginal product of raw labor would increase. The net effect of the capital-skill complementarity hypothesis is that the demand for skill increases relative to the demand for raw labor as capital accumulation proceeds.

It seems reasonable to ask whether the capital-skill complementarity hypothesis implies that in equilibrium more-productive workers will be employed at more capital-intensive jobs. This is in fact the wrong question. The two hypotheses are not comparable.

For example, consider the economy described in the previous section. Each industry, characterized by a value of θ, has a Cobb-Douglas production function. The partial elasticities of substitution between any two of the factors are therefore identically equal to one. The capital-skill complementarity hypothesis does not hold for any of the industries. But, as demonstrated, more-productive workers will be employed in more capital-intensive industries, so the scale-of-resources effect holds.

The capital-skill complementarity hypothesis concerns the response of a firm or an economy with a fixed production function to a change in factor prices or factor supplies. In contrast, the scale-of-resources effect concerns the response of firms with different production functions to common factor prices. In other words, the capital-skill complementarity hypothesis deals with intertemporal differences in factor use, whereas the scale of resources effect concerns interindustry differences at one point in time. An immediate consequence is that the capital-skill complementarity hypothesis cannot be tested using cross-section data by industry, because the capital costs will be the same for all firms with similar risk structures.

8. Some observations on the assignment problem

The importance and relevance of the assignment problem can now be assessed. The assignment of individuals to jobs is of course an interesting economic phenomenon in itself. But it is also a phenomenon that occurs in any real economy. The existence of job preferences, comparative advantage or cooperating factors of production, as demonstrated in this chapter, results in an assignment problem. Only trivial models lack preferences, comparative advantage and cooperating factors.

The jobs at which individuals end up working are not the capricious result of chance. Instead, even before specific training is received, individuals are led to choose particular jobs.

The major consequence of the assignment problem is that the distribution of earnings cannot be explained solely by a theory of individual behavior. One must also know which job the individual will be working at in alternative states of the economy.

The existence of the assignment problem means that the extensive collections of longitudinal data on individual workers and households cannot be used to reveal either the effects of the supplies or of the demands for workers on the distribution of earnings. The reason is that one cannot make the *ceteris paribus* assumption. Suppose that a social scientist, attempting to discover the effects of supplies and demands on the distribution of earnings, regresses the earnings of an individual not only on the individual's employment-relevant characteristics but also on the characteristics of the job at which the individual was employed. Suppose our social scientist wishes to infer the effects of a change in the distribution of one of the individual characteristics, say schooling. The problem is that when the distribution of schooling changes, individuals are reassigned to jobs. One must have a model of the entire factor market before one can determine what the new correspondence between individual characteristics and job characteristics is. This result can be put differently as follows. Suppose again that we are considering the effects of a change in the distribution of individual characteristics, and we make the *ceteris paribus* assumption that the correspondence between individual characteristics and job characteristics remains the same. Then along with the change in individual characteristics will be a simultaneous change in the distribution of the job characteristics.

These ideas may be formalized as follows. Suppose that we have estimated the earnings function $y_i = as_i + bh_i$, where y_i is individual i's earnings, s_i is his years of schooling, and h_i is the characteristic of the job at which individual i works and a and b are estimated coefficients. Suppose further that we have estimated the correspondence between the individual characteristic and the job characteristic and that this correspondence is given by $h(s)$. Let $S(s)$ be the cumulative density function for schooling and let $H(h)$ be the cumulative density function for the job characteristic. Then the two are related as follows:

$$H(h(s_0)) = \int_0^{s_0} h(x)\, S(x)\, \mathrm{d}x. \tag{5.19}$$

The cumulative density function for earnings, $F(y)$, is given by

$$F(as_0 + bh(s_0)) = \int_0^{s_0} (ax + bh(x))\, S(x)\, \mathrm{d}x. \tag{5.20}$$

Now suppose we wish to investigate the effects on the distribution of earnings of a change in the distribution of schooling from $S(s)$ to $\hat{S}(s)$. One cannot merely substitute $\hat{S}(s)$ into (5.20) and make the *ceteris paribus* assumption that a, b, and $h(s)$ stay the same. If a, b, and $h(s)$ stay the same, then the distribution of job characteristics, given in (5.19), must also have changed by the substitution of $\hat{S}(s)$ for $S(s)$. It follows that we are not estimating the effects of a change in the distribution of schooling alone but a simultaneous change in the distributions of schooling and job characteristics. One can therefore not isolate the effects of a change in the distribution of schooling using this procedure. If $S(s)$ changes and

$H(h)$ stays the same, then $h(s)$ and the estimated coefficients a and b also change, so that the estimated earnings function is useless.

By and large, the assignment problem has been ignored by economists studying the distributions of earnings. In the simple models that have been studied, no assignment problem arises. This is inevitably the case in models implicitly using the efficiency units assumption. The failure to recognize the existence of an assignment problem arises because wages have generally been treated as mere rewards for the provision of labor services. Instead, wages like all prices play an allocative role. They are the mechanism by which a market economy assigns individuals to jobs. Recognition of the assignment problem leads inevitably to a recognition of the allocative role of wages.

This chapter has dealt with the assignment of individuals to jobs that the equilibrium set of wages must bring about. The discussion has led to some elementary conclusions concerning the limits within which relative wages must fall to be consistent with equilibrium assignments. The next chapter develops explicitly the equilibrium wage and rent functions.

Chapter 6

DIFFERENTIAL RENTS

1. Introduction

The previous chapter established the result that more-productive workers will in general be employed at more capital-intensive jobs in equilibrium. This chapter investigates the wage and capital rent functions that would bring about the equilibrium assignment of individuals to jobs.[1] The major conclusion is that the distribution of earnings depends on the distribution of capital among jobs.

The methodology of this chapter is similar in nature to the approach taken by Ricardo in analyzing differential rents arising from differences in fertility. The faults of Ricardo's analysis or presentation need not concern us here. The relevant aspects of differential rents are as follows. The rent function (rent as a function of the land's fertility) is determined in two parts. First, the difference in rents for two equal-sized tracts of close but unequal fertility is roughly determined by the difference in the outputs obtained, holding the amount of labor used constant. Secondly, the amount which land owners must receive to be willing to use the land in the production of grain determines the last tract of land that will be cultivated and the absolute level of the rents of all land.

In mathematical terms, the slope of the rent function is determined by the rate of change of output (on equal-sized tracts) with respect to fertility, considered as a continuous variable. This differential equation can then be solved to yield the rent function itself. However, the solution includes an arbitrary constant of integration. The rent on the marginal land employed provides a "boundary condition" which determines the value of this arbitrary constant of integration.

With the introduction of a second heterogeneous factor of production, there

---

1 Some of the results of this chapter appeared previously in Sattinger (1976b, 1979).

arise factor payment functions for both factors of production. The slopes of these functions are determined by partial derivatives.

Chapter 3, Section 2, established the connection between Tinbergen's model and differential rents. In both cases the factor payment function is determined as the integral of a differential equation. In Tinbergen's model the slope of the wage function equals the derivative of the wage offer curve with respect to the individual parameter. Tinbergen then obtains the wage function by integration. The methodology of this chapter is therefore fundamentally the same as Tinbergen's.

The theory that is constructed in the first sections is essentially a short-run theory. The distributions of individuals with respect to productive ability and of machines or units of capital with respect to size are assumed to be determined exogenously, perhaps as a result of previous investment decisions.

The underlying necessary conditions which will determine the wage and capital rent functions have already appeared in Chapter 5. From (5.3) and (5.4) the assumption of equilibrium on the part of individuals implies that

$$p_1 a_{11} - p_2 a_{12} \geq r_1 - r_2 \geq p_1 a_{21} - p_2 a_{22}.$$

That is to say, the difference in machine rents must be less than the difference in value of outputs between the two machines for the first individual and greater than the difference in value of outputs for the second individual. Similarly, using (5.8) and (5.9), the assumption of equilibrium implies that

$$p_1 a_{11} - p_2 a_{21} \geq w_1 - w_2 \geq p_2 a_{12} - p_2 a_{22}.$$

The differences in wages for the two individuals must therefore lie between the differences in values of outputs for the first and second machine.

Taking individuals in decreasing order of productivity, it would therefore be possible, by looking at consecutive individuals and the machines they work with, to establish a double sequence of intervals into which differences in wages and differences in capital rental costs must fall.

Instead of dealing with inequalities, however, let us develop the model in continuous form, thereby eliminating indeterminacy. One other change must also be made. The generality of a model with heterogeneous outputs must be abandoned. The reason is that otherwise changes in the distributions of individuals or machines would affect the wage and capital rental cost functions not only through relative productivities but also through changes in the prices of goods being produced. Although empirical models can easily be developed which involve industries with heterogeneous goods, it does not seem practicable to do so in an abstract model.

2. Assumptions

Consider a large economy in which workers differ according to productive ability. The productive ability for a worker is assumed to be determined exogenously, perhaps in a period prior to the one under consideration. Suppose there are a sufficiently large number of workers that the distribution of workers according to productive ability can be described by a continuous density function. Let g be the measure of productive ability and suppose the values of g cover an interval. Let $G(g)$ be the density function of workers with respect to productive ability, so that $\int_{g_1}^{g_2} G(x)dx$ is the number of workers with productive ability between g_1 and g_2.

Suppose capital is the factor with which labor is combined to produce output. Suppose that this capital takes the form of separate units such that one worker can only be combined with one unit of capital. It is convenient to refer to these units of capital as machines. Suppose there exists an objective measure of the amount of capital contained in each machine. Let k be the amount of capital contained in a machine and suppose the values of k cover an interval. It is convenient to refer to k as the size of a machine. Let $K(k)$ be the density function of machines with respect to size, so that $\int_{k_1}^{k_2} K(x)dx$ is the number of machines with size between k_1 and k_2. The density function $K(k)$ describes the distribution of capital among jobs.

Consider now the behavior of workers. Workers can obtain income in two ways. First, a worker can offer his or her labor services at the market wage corresponding to his or her productive ability. Secondly, a worker can rent a machine, combine it with his or her labor and keep the value of output net of the machine rent as his or her income. Workers choose among employment opportunities on the basis of income maximization, subject to the following qualification. There exists a reserve price of labor that must be received by a worker in order for the worker to be willing to work at all. If his potential income does not exceed this reserve price, then a worker will not provide labor services. Let $\hat{w}$ be the reserve price for labor, assumed to be same for all workers.

Consider now the behavior of owners of machines. These owners can obtain income in two ways. First, an owner can rent his machine out at the market-determined rate corresponding to the machine size. Secondly, he can hire labor, combine the labor with his machine and keep as his income the value of output net of the cost of the labor. As with labor, assume that owners of capital have a reserve price and that they will not rent a machine out or use it in production unless the income obtained exceeds this reserve price. Let $\hat{r}$ be the reserve price, assumed to be the same for all machines.

Assume that the output obtained in the production process is homogeneous.

Let $f(g,k)$ be the output produced by a worker of productive ability g using a machine of size k. Assume that the function f has continuous first- and second-order partial derivatives and that $\partial f/\partial g > 0$, $\partial f/\partial k > 0$, $\partial^2 f/\partial g^2 < 0$, and $\partial^2 f/\partial k^2 < 0$. Thus, the production function has positive marginal products and obeys the law of diminishing marginal returns.

Finally, suppose that the economy under consideration is characterized by perfect competition. In the context of the model, this means that no entrepreneur, by renting a machine and hiring a worker, can realize a positive profit from the sale of output after paying off the factors. No worker can, by renting a machine and obtaining his income from the value of output net of the machine rental cost, earn more than he could by working at the going market wage. Similarly, no owner of a machine can, by hiring labor, earn more from the residual than he could by renting his machine out at the rent corresponding to the machine size. In other words, in perfect competition it is immaterial whether workers or the owners of capital act as the organizers of production. It is further assumed that the economy is sufficiently large that no worker can, by withholding his labor from the market, influence the wage rates paid to workers in any interval of productive ability. Similarly, no owner of capital can, by withholding his machine from the market, influence the machine rents for machines in a given size interval.

The assumption that only one worker can be combined with a machine essentially eliminates the intensive margin of labor. That is, no extra output is gained by adding one more worker to a machine where another worker is already employed.

3. Wage and rent functions

Let $w(g)$ be the wage function for individuals and let $r(k)$ be the rental cost function for machines. The objective of the following analysis is to derive these functions from the assumption of equilibrium, the production function $f(g,k)$ and the density functions $G(g)$ and $K(k)$.

The derivation proceeds in several steps. First, it is necessary to make a tentative assumption concerning the assignment of individuals to machines in equilibrium. This assumption is used to derive the implied wage and rental cost functions. Whether these functions are consistent with equilibrium depends on whether the second-order conditions are satisfied. These conditions will be investigated later, and the class of production functions for which the tentative assumption is valid will be specified.

For purposes of deriving $w(g)$ and $r(k)$ it is therefore assumed (following

Chapter 5) that the more-productive individuals will work with larger machines. It follows that the nth individual, in order of decreasing productive ability, will be found working with the nth machine, in order of decreasing size. The number of machines with size greater than a given level k is $\int_k^{\overline{k}} K(x)\mathrm{d}x$, where $\overline{k}$ is the largest size of a machine. Similarly, the number of individuals with productive ability above a given level g is $\int_g^{\overline{g}} G(x)\mathrm{d}x$, where again $\overline{g}$ is the greatest productive ability. For k to be the size of machine used by the individual with productive ability g, the following equality must hold: $\int_k^{\overline{k}} K(x)\mathrm{d}x = \int_g^{\overline{g}} G(x)\mathrm{d}x$. Using this equality it is possible to solve for the size of machine used by an individual with productive ability g in equilibrium, if the tentative assumption is valid. Provided the numbers of machines and workers are different, there will inevitably be some unemployment of one or the other. This unemployment will be discussed when reserve prices are introduced in the next section.

Unless there are intermediate intervals over which $G(g)$ and $K(k)$ are zero, the size of machine will be a strictly increasing function of productive ability. This relation may be written as $k(g)$ or, in its inverse form, as $g(k)$.

The next step is to derive expressions for the derivatives $r'(k)$ and $w'(g)$ from earnings and rent maximizing considerations. Consider the earnings that an individual with productive ability g^* could get in equilibrium. From his point of view the market rental costs for different sizes of machines can be taken as given by the function $r(k)$. The earnings for alternative levels of k are given by $f(g^*,k)-r(k)$. Earnings maximization requires that the derivative of earnings with respect to machine size be zero:

$$\frac{\partial f(g^*,k)}{\partial k} - r'(k) = 0 \quad \text{or} \quad r'(k) = \frac{\partial f(g^*,k)}{\partial k}. \tag{6.1}$$

This is a first-order condition and does not hold for arbitrary values of k. It holds only for the value of k which maximizes the earnings of the individual with productive ability g^*. However, it does hold for all values of g^* and k such that $g^* = g(k)$. Thus, the first-order condition (6.1) can be used to derive the slope or derivative of the rent function for every size of machine. This derivative is

$$r'(k) = \left(\frac{\partial f(g^*,k)}{\partial k} \right)_{g^* = g(k)}. \tag{6.2}$$

Thus, to find the derivative of the rent function at k, one obtains the partial derivative of the production function with respect to its second argument (that is, one treats the first argument, g^*, as a constant and not as a function of k);

this partial derivative is then evaluated at the value of g corresponding to k in equilibrium.

Similarly, consider the rent that an owner of a machine of size k^* can obtain using individuals with different productive abilities. This rent is $f(g,k^*)-w(g)$. Rent maximization requires that

$$w'(g) = \frac{\partial f(g,k^*)}{\partial g} \, . \tag{6.3}$$

Again, eq. (6.3) does not hold for arbitrary values of g but only for $g = g(k^*)$. As with the rent function, the derivative of the wage function is obtained by evaluating the partial derivative at the value of k that corresponds to g in equilibrium:

$$w'(g) = \left(\frac{\partial f(g,k^*)}{\partial g} \right)_{k^* = k(g)} . \tag{6.4}$$

The next step is to investigate whether the tentative assumption which yielded the equilibrium assignment given by $k(g)$, and which was used to derive (6.2) and (6.4), is valid. For this assumption to be valid the second-order conditions for earnings maximization by individuals and for rent maximization by owners of capital must be satisfied.

These second-order conditions are:

$$\frac{\partial^2 f(g^*,k)}{\partial k^2} - r''(k) \leq 0, \quad \text{for} \quad k = k(g^*), \tag{6.5}$$

and

$$\frac{\partial^2 f(g,k^*)}{\partial g^2} - w''(g) \leq 0, \quad \text{for} \quad g = g(k^*), \tag{6.6}$$

where $r''(k) = \mathrm{d}^2 r/\mathrm{d}k^2$ and $w''(g) = \mathrm{d}^2 w/\mathrm{d}g^2$.

We can now derive conditions under which the tentative assumption that more productive individuals work with larger machines is valid. From (6.2),

$$r''(k) = \left(\frac{\partial^2 f(g^*,k)}{\partial k^2} \right)_{g^* = g(k)}$$

$$+ \left(\frac{\partial^2 f(g^*,k)}{\partial g^* \partial k} \right)_{g^* = g(k)} \left(\frac{\mathrm{d}g^*}{\mathrm{d}k} \right) .$$

Thus, in (6.5)

$$\left(\frac{\partial^2 f(g^*,k)}{\partial k^2}\right)_{g^*=g(k)} - r''(k) = - \left(\frac{\partial^2 f(g^*,k)}{\partial g^*\partial k}\right)_{g^*=g(k)} \left(\frac{dg^*}{dk}\right)$$

It follows that the second-order condition in (6.5) holds if and only if

$$\left(\frac{\partial^2 f(g^*,k)}{\partial g^*\partial k}\right)_{g^*=g(k)} \quad \text{and} \quad \left(\frac{dg^*}{dk}\right)$$

are of the same sign. If the first term is positive, then dg^*/dk must also be positive in equilibrium, i.e. the more-productive workers will be employed at larger machines. A sufficient (but not necessary) condition for the above term on the left to be positive is that $\partial^2 f/\partial g \partial k$ be positive for all values of g and k. The same conditions could have been derived from (6.6).

Once the wage function $w(g)$ is determined, the size distribution of earnings can be constructed using the worker density function $G(g)$. Because the wage will be a strictly increasing function of productive ability, the inverse function $g(w)$ can be defined. The number of workers with productive ability between g_1 and g_2 is $\int_{g_1}^{g_2} G(g)dg$. Now let us treat g as a function of w and perform a transformation of variables on the integral. Then

$$dg = g'(w)dw \quad \text{and} \quad \int_{w(g_1)}^{w(g_2)} G(g(w))g'(w)dw$$

is the number of individuals with wages between $w(g_1)$ and $w(g_2)$. Thus, the density function of individuals with respect to earnings is given by $G(g(w))g'(w)$.

4. Reserve prices and the unemployment of labor and machines

The differential equations in (6.2) and (6.4), if solved, yield the machine rent function $r(k)$ and the wage function $w(g)$; these functions would, however, involve constants of integration. These constants are arbitrary in the sense that any values are consistent with the differential equations (6.2) and (6.4). In fact, they are completely determined by the division of output between the marginally employed labor and the marginally employed machine. Furthermore, if we know the value of one of the constants, we can immediately determine the value of the other from the condition that factor payments exhaust the product. The determination of these constants of integration is the subject of this section.

The traditional way in which the output is divided among the marginally employed factors is to specify reserve prices, i.e. prices at which the owners of factors are indifferent between providing them for use in production and withholding them from the market. In section 2 we assumed that the reserve price of labor is $\hat{w}$. An individual will agree to work as long as his earnings are at least $\hat{w}$, the same for all individuals. Similarly, $\hat{r}$ is the reserve price for owners of capital (this reserve price may be zero).

Two principles guide the determination of the constants of integration. The first is that the existence of any unemployed workers will bid down the wage of the marginally employed worker to the reserve price $\hat{w}$. The second principle is that the existence of any unemployed machines will bid the rent on the marginally employed machine down to the reserve price $\hat{r}$. Three possible cases arise.

4.1. Unemployed workers

The number of workers exceeds the number of machines, and the production obtained from the last machine and worker employed is sufficient to pay for the reserve prices (i.e. the value of production exceeds $\hat{w} + \hat{r}$). Suppose there are n machines and that the smallest, nth machine has size k_n. Suppose the nth worker (in order of decreasing productive ability) has productive ability g_n, and that there are workers with productive ability less than g_n. The wage of the nth worker will be bid down to $\hat{w}$. Any worker with productive ability less than g_n would be unemployed but would be willing to work at wage $\hat{w}$. At the wage of $\hat{w}$, the owner of the smallest machine prefers the worker with the greatest productive ability, g_n. The constant of integration for the wage function is determined by setting $w(g_n) = \hat{w}$ and solving for the constant. The rent for the last machine is the residual value of production, $r(k_n) = f(g_n, k_n) - \hat{w}$. This boundary condition determines the constant of integration for the machine rent function.

4.2. Unemployed machines

The number of machines exceeds the number of workers, and the production obtained from the last machine and worker employed covers the reserve prices.

Again, let g_n be the productive ability of the nth, least able worker and k_n the size of the nth machine. By assumption there exist more machines with size smaller than k_n. The existence of these smaller machines bids the rent on the nth machine down to k_n. The constant of integration for the capital rent function is then determined by setting $r(k_n) = \hat{r}$. The wage rate for the nth worker is $f(g_n, k_n) - \hat{r}$ and the constant of integration is determined by setting $w(g_n)$ equal to this residual.

4.3. Unemployed workers and machines

The general case arises when production falls below $\hat{w} + \hat{r}$ before either machines or workers run out. Both machines and workers would then be unemployed.

Consider a worker of arbitrary productive ability g_0, and suppose $k = k(g_0)$ is the size of the machine he would work with in equilibrium, if he worked. If

$$f(g_0, k_0) < \hat{w} + \hat{r},$$

then neither the worker nor the machine would be employed, since either the worker or the machine owner would receive insufficient compensation. On the other hand, if

$$f(g_0, k_0) > \hat{w} + \hat{r},$$

then output is sufficient to cover the reserve prices of the two factors of production. Furthermore, the factor payments $w(g_0)$ and $r(k_0)$ must equal or exceed the reserve prices. If, say, $r(k_0) < \hat{r}$, then the machine of size k_0 would be withdrawn from production. Then the worker with productive ability g_0 would be willing to work for less than $f(g_0, k_0) - r(k_0)$ rather than not work. This would increase the return to the owner of the machine until $r(k_0) \geq \hat{r}$.

The least-productive worker employed is the one for whom $f(g, k(g)) = \hat{w} + \hat{r}$. Then $w(g) = \hat{w}$ and $r(k) = \hat{r}$. Any worker with a lower productive ability would not work and any machine with a smaller size would not be used. Given the value of g for which $w(g) = \hat{w}$, the whole wage function can be determined from the differential equation (6.4). Similarly, given the value of k at which $r(k) = \hat{r}$, the whole rent function can be determined using (6.2).

Thus, the reserve prices, $\hat{w}$ and $\hat{r}$, determine the least-productive individual and smallest machine employed, the division of output between the last individual and last machine employed, and the constants of integration in the solutions of the differential equations (6.2) and (6.4).

The presence of reserve prices in the determination of the wage and machine rent functions means that the analysis combines elements of both classical and neoclassical income distribution theory. The model is neoclassical in the sense that relative wages and relative machine rents are determined by the differences in production arising from changes in the productive ability of the worker and the size of the machine. Furthermore, the derivatives of the wage and capital rent functions are derived from conditions of equilibrium. In contrast, the absolute level of wages and machine rents are substantially determined by the reserve prices of labor and capital, which in turn are determined exogenously. In this sense the model is classical.

The assumption in the above analysis that the reserve price is the same for all units of a factor can be weakened. For example, the reserve price for labor could be an increasing function of productive ability. Virtually the same preceding analysis applies provided the reserve price for labor increases less rapidly than the wage as productive ability increases. Similarly, it would be possible to assume that the reserve price for machines is an increasing function of the machine size.

5. Examples

5.1. Pareto factor distributions, Cobb-Douglas production function

All the foregoing analyses will now be illustrated for specific functions. The easiest functions to work with are Pareto distributions for the density functions and the Cobb-Douglas for production.

Suppose the density functions for individuals and machines take the following Pareto (exponential) forms:

$$G(g) = cg^{-\gamma}, \quad \text{where} \quad \gamma > 2 \quad \text{and} \quad g \geq 1,$$

and

$$K(k) = hk^{-\delta}, \quad \text{where} \quad \delta > 2 \quad \text{and} \quad k \geq 1.$$

Suppose the production function is given by the Cobb-Douglas form

$$f(g,k) = g^{\alpha}k^{\beta}, \quad \text{where} \quad 0 < \alpha < 1 \quad \text{and} \quad 0 < \beta < 1.$$

The mixed partial derivative $\partial^2 f/\partial g \partial k = \alpha\beta \, g^{\alpha-1} \, k^{\beta-1} > 0$, so that the more-productive individuals will work with larger machines in equilibrium. If k is the size of machine used in equilibrium by the individual with productive ability g, then

$$\int_k^\infty hx^{-\delta} \, dx = \int_g^\infty cx^{-\gamma} dx \quad \text{or} \quad \frac{h}{\delta - 1} \, k^{1-\delta} = \frac{c}{\gamma - 1} \, g^{1-\gamma}$$

or

$$k(g) = \phi^{1/(1-\delta)} g^{(1-\gamma)/(1-\delta)}, \quad \text{where} \quad \phi = c(\delta - 1)/h(\gamma - 1).$$

The partial derivatives of the production function are

$$\frac{\partial f}{\partial g} = \alpha g^{\alpha-1} k^{\beta} \quad \text{and} \quad \frac{\partial f}{\partial k} = \beta g^{\alpha} k^{\beta-1}.$$

Corresponding to (6.2) we thus have $w'(g) = \alpha g^{\alpha-1} k^{\beta}$, where k is given by $k(g)$. Thus,

$$w'(g) = \alpha \phi^{-\beta/(\delta-1)} g^{-1+\theta/(\delta-1)}, \tag{6.7}$$

where $\theta = \alpha(\delta - 1) + \beta(\gamma - 1)$. Integration yields

$$w(g) = \frac{\alpha\phi}{\theta/(\delta-1)} \, g^{\theta/(\delta-1)} + C_1, \tag{6.8}$$

where C_1 is the constant of integration. Similarly,

$$r'(k) = \beta \phi^{-\alpha/(\gamma-1)} k^{-1+\theta/(\gamma-1)} \tag{6.9}$$

and

$$r(k) = \frac{\beta\phi^{-\alpha/(\gamma-1)}}{\theta/(\gamma-1)} \, k^{\theta/(\gamma-1)} + C_2, \tag{6.10}$$

where C_2 is the constant of integration.

The constants of integration can be calculated as follows. First we calculate the productive ability of the worker such that the output obtained is $\hat{w} + \hat{r}$. This is found by setting

$$g^{\alpha}(k(g))^{\beta} = \hat{w} + \hat{r}$$

or

$$\phi^{\beta/(1-\delta)} g^{\alpha+\beta(\gamma-1)/(\delta-1)} = \hat{w} + \hat{r}$$

or

$$g_0 = \phi^{\beta/\theta}(\hat{w} + \hat{r})^{(\delta-1)/\theta}. \tag{6.11}$$

Then

$$k(g_0) = \phi^{-\alpha/\theta}(\hat{w} + \hat{r})^{(\gamma-1)\theta}.$$

Suppose the parameters are such that $g_0 > 1$ and $k(g_0) > 1$. Workers with productive ability less than g_0 and machines with size less than $k(g_0)$ will be unemployed. This is the case discussed in section 4.3.

The constant of integration C_1 is obtained by setting $w(g_0)$ equal to $\hat{w}$:

$$\frac{\alpha\phi^{-\beta/(\delta-1)}}{\theta} \left(\frac{\hat{w} + \hat{r}}{\phi^{\beta/(1-\delta)}} \right) + C_1 = \hat{w},$$

so

$$C_1 = (\beta(\gamma - 1)\hat{w} - \alpha(\delta - 1)\hat{r})/\theta. \qquad (6.12)$$

The constant of integration for $r(k)$ can be calculated in a similar manner and is

$$C_2 = (\alpha(\delta - 1)\hat{r} - \beta(\gamma - 1)\hat{w})/\theta = -C_1. \qquad (6.13)$$

Suppose, instead, that the calculated value of g_0 in (6.11) is less than one while $k(g_0)$ is greater than one. Then all workers will be employed, as discussed in section 4.2. The least-productive worker employed will be the one for whom $g = 1$. The corresponding machine size will be $\alpha^{1/(1-\delta)}$. The rental cost for that machine size will be $\hat{r}$ (because of the presence of unemployed machines) and the wage rate for $g = 1$ would be the difference between the production obtained and $\hat{r}$. The constants of integration would then be determined by these factor payments and not by the expressions in (6.12) and (6.13). The case discussed in section 4.1 can be derived in a similar manner.

Whether or not wages are a convex, concave or linear function of g depends on the exponent of g in (6.7). This exponent in turn can be related to the amounts of inequality in the distributions of productive abilities and machine sizes. In a similar way these amounts of inequality can also be related to the shape of the machine rent function.

The Pareto coefficients $\gamma - 1$ and $\delta - 1$ (from the cumulative form for the Pareto distribution) are measures of the amount of equality in the distributions. A larger Pareto coefficient is regarded as indicating a more equal distribution. Suppose now that the production function has constant returns to scale, so that $\alpha + \beta = 1$ and the exponent of g in (6.7) reduces to $\beta(\gamma - \delta)/(\delta - 1)$. Three cases arise.

(i) Suppose productive abilities are more equally distributed than machine sizes so that $\gamma - 1 > \delta - 1$. Then the exponent of g in (6.7) is positive and wages are a convex function of productive ability. That is, the slope of the wage function goes up as productive ability increases. Also, the exponent of k in (6.9) is negative, so the machine rent is a concave function of machine size. The slope of the rent function decreases as machine size increases.

(ii) Suppose productive abilities are less equally distributed than machine sizes so that $\gamma - 1 < \delta - 1$. Then wages are a concave function of productive abilities and rents are a convex function of machine size.

(iii) Suppose productive abilities are just as equally distributed as machine sizes so that $\gamma - 1 = \delta - 1$. Then wages are a linear function of productive ability and rents are a linear function of machine sizes.

The density function for the distribution of earnings can be derived as described in the previous section and is given by

$$G(g(w))g'(w) = \frac{c\phi^{(1-\gamma)\beta/\theta}}{\alpha} \left[\frac{(w-C_1)\theta}{\alpha(\delta-1)}\right]^{-1-(\gamma-1)(\delta-1)/\theta}. \qquad (6.14)$$

In the general case where $C_1 \neq 0$, earnings will not have the Pareto distribution. Even if $C_1 = 0$, so that earnings follow the Pareto distribution, the exponent will not in general be the same as the exponent in the distribution of productive abilities.

In a previous article Sattinger (1975) demonstrated that a minimum requirement for the distribution of earnings to differ in shape from the distribution of productive abilities is that there be comparative advantage in the performance of different tasks by different individuals. In the example that has been developed above, comparative advantage is ruled out by the multiplicatively separable form of the production function $f(g,k)$. Yet in general the distributions of earnings and productive abilities are different shapes. Hence, the distributions can differ for another reason besides comparative advantage: the distribution of cooperating factors can affect the shape of distribution of earnings.

The inequality in earnings can be investigated in two stages. First, the distribution of g can be compared with that of $w-C_1$ in (6.14), and then this transform of the wage can be compared with the wage itself.

From (6.14) the Pareto coefficient for the distribution of the transform $w-C_1$ is

$$\frac{\gamma-1}{\alpha + \beta(\gamma-1)/(\delta-1)}.$$

This is greater or less than the Pareto coefficient for productive abilities, $\gamma-1$, depending on whether the denominator is less than or greater than one.

For a given level of equality in the distribution of productive abilities, as measured by the Pareto coefficient $\gamma - 1$, the denominator is an increasing function of $1-\delta$, the Pareto coefficient for the distribution of machine sizes. Hence, greater values of the exponents α and β in the production function and more inequality in the distribution of machine sizes (as measured by the Pareto coefficient) result in more inequality in the distribution of the values of the transform $w-C_1$.

Restricting attention to the case where $\alpha + \beta = 1$, i.e. where the production function has constant returns to scale, the denominator will be less or greater than one depending on whether $1-\gamma$ is less or greater than $1-\delta$. Thus, the transform $w-C_1$ will be more (less) equally distributed than the productive abilities if the productive abilities are less (more) equally distributed than machine sizes.

Next, let us compare the equality in the distribution of $w-C_1$ with the equality in the distribution of w. The comparison depends solely on the sign of C_1. If C_1 is positive, wages will be more equally distributed than the transform $w-C_1$. In turn, the sign of C_1 depends on the labor and machine reserve prices.

The effect of a larger reserve price for labor (and a correspondingly lower reserve price for machines) is to add a lump-sum amount to the earnings of all employed individuals, thereby reducing their earnings inequality. The matter is more complicated if the reserve price for labor increases while the reserve price for machines remains the same. Then the wages of each employed individual are increased by the same amount (but not by as much as the increase in the labor reserve price); however, fewer individuals will be employed. The net effect on earnings inequality is ambiguous. An increase in the reserve price of machines is unambiguously to increase labor earnings inequality. Fewer individuals are employed, and an amount, less than the change in the reserve price for machines, is subtracted from each individual's earnings.

In summary, for a given amount of inequality in productive abilities, inequality in earnings will depend positively on

(i)   the exponents of the production function, α and β;

(ii)   the inequality in the distribution of machine sizes;

(iii)   the reserve price for machines, $\bar{r}$;

and will depend negatively on

(iv)   the reserve price for labor, $\hat{w}$, holding the sum $\hat{w} + \hat{r}$ constant.

5.2.   *Lognormal factor distributions, Cobb-Douglas production function*

Now let us consider a slightly more complex case. Suppose the distributions of abilities and machine sizes are lognormal. These distributions are then given by

$$G(g) = \frac{P}{g} \frac{1}{\sqrt{(2\pi)\sigma_1}} \exp\left[\frac{-(\log g - \mu_1)^2}{2\sigma_1^2}\right], \quad g > 0;$$

$$K(k) = \frac{P}{k} \frac{1}{\sqrt{(2\pi)\sigma_2}} \exp\left[\frac{-(\log k - \mu_2)^2}{2\sigma_2^2}\right], \quad k > 0.$$

Under the assumption that one worker is employed at one machine, the correspondence $k(g)$ or $g(k)$ can be found simply by transforming to the standardized normal variates $(\log g - \mu_1)/\sigma_1$ and $(\log k - \mu_2)/\sigma_2$. The cumulative density functions for g and k are equal when these standardized normal variates are equal. Then

$$k(g) = g^{\sigma_2/\sigma_1} \exp \left[\mu_2 - \mu_1 \sigma_2/\sigma_1 \right]$$

and

$$g(k) = k^{\sigma_1/\sigma_2} \exp \left[\mu_1 - \mu_2 \sigma_1/\sigma_2 \right].$$

Suppose that the production function relating productive ability and machine size to output is again Cobb-Douglas and is given by $f(g,k) = g^\alpha k^\beta$, where $\alpha > 0$ and $\beta > 0$. It follows that the derivative of the wage function is given by

$$w'(g) = \alpha g^{\alpha - 1} (k(g))^\beta = \alpha \exp \left[\beta(\mu_2 - \mu_1 \sigma_2/\sigma_1) \right] g^{-1 + \theta/\sigma_1},$$

where now $\theta = \alpha \sigma_1 + \beta \sigma_2$.
    Thus,

$$w(g) = \frac{\alpha \sigma_1 \exp \left[\beta(\mu_2 - \mu_1 \sigma_2/\sigma_1) \right]}{\theta} \, g^{\theta/\sigma_1} + C_1, \tag{6.15}$$

where C_1 is the constant of integration. Similarly,

$$r'(k) = \beta (g(k)^\alpha k^{\beta - 1} = \beta \exp \left[\alpha(\mu_1 - \mu_2 \sigma_1/\sigma_2) \right] k^{-1 + \theta/\sigma_2}$$

and

$$r(k) = \frac{\beta \sigma_2 \exp \left[\alpha(\mu_1 - \mu_2 \sigma_1/\sigma_2) \right]}{\theta} \, k^{\theta/\sigma_2} + C_2. \tag{6.16}$$

Whether or not wages are a convex, linear or concave function of productive ability depends on whether the exponent of g in (6.15) is greater than one, equal to one, or less than one, respectively. The exponent of g is $\theta/\sigma_1 = (\alpha \sigma_1 + \beta \sigma_2)/\sigma_1$. In the case where $f(g,k)$ has constant returns to scale, $\alpha + \beta = 1$ and $\alpha \sigma_1 + \beta \sigma_2$ is a weighted average of the standard deviations of the density functions for g and k. If $\sigma_2 > \sigma_1$, then $\alpha \sigma_1 + \beta \alpha_2 > \sigma_1$, so that $w(g)$ is convex. At the same time, $\alpha \sigma_1 + \beta \sigma_2 < \sigma_2$, so that $r(k)$ will be a concave function. Similarly, still assuming $\alpha + \beta = 1$, if $w(g)$ is concave then $r(k)$ must be convex.
    However, both $w(g)$ and $r(k)$ could be convex if $f(g,k)$ has increasing returns to scale. Similarly, $w(g)$ and $r(k)$ could be concave if $\alpha + \beta < 1$.
    Now let us calculate the constants of integration for $w(g)$ and $r(k)$ in terms of

the reserve prices of labor and capital, $\hat{w}$ and $\hat{r}$. Let us restrict attention to the general case where both workers and machines are unemployed. Setting $f(g,k(g)) = \hat{w} + \hat{r}$ yields

$$g_0 = \left\{ \frac{\hat{w} + \hat{r}}{\exp\left[\beta(\mu_2 - \mu_1 \sigma_2/\sigma_1)\right]} \right\}^{\sigma_1/\theta}, \qquad (6.17)$$

where g_0 is the least-productive worker employed. Setting $w(g_0) = \hat{w}$ yields

$$\frac{\alpha\sigma_1(\hat{w} + \hat{r})}{\theta} + C_1 = \hat{w}$$

or

$$C_1 = \frac{\beta\sigma_2 \hat{w} - \alpha\sigma_1 \hat{r}}{\theta}. \qquad (6.18)$$

Similarly,

$$C_2 = \frac{\alpha\sigma_1 \hat{r} - \beta\sigma_2 \hat{w}}{\theta} = -C_1.$$

Now let us construct explicitly the distribution of earnings. From section 3 this distribution is given by $G(g(w))g'(w)$. Inverting $w(g)$ yields

$$g(w) = (w - C_1)^{\sigma_1/\theta} \left\{ \frac{\theta}{\alpha\sigma_1 \exp\left[\beta(\mu_2 - \mu_1\sigma_2/\sigma_1)\right]} \right\}^{\sigma_1/\theta}.$$

Then

$$G(g(w))g'(w) = P \frac{g'(w)}{g(w)} \frac{1}{\sqrt{(2\pi)}\sigma_1} \exp\left[\frac{-(\log g'(w) - \mu_1)^2}{2\sigma_1^2}\right]$$

$$= \frac{P}{\sqrt{(2\pi)}\,\theta\,(w - C_1)} \exp\left[\frac{-(\log(w - C_1) - \hat{\mu}_1)^2}{2\theta^2}\right]$$

where again $\theta = \alpha\sigma_1 + \beta\sigma_2$ and $\hat{\mu}_1 = \alpha\mu_1 + \beta\mu_2 + \log(\alpha\sigma_1/\theta)$. It follows that the distribution of earnings will also be lognormally distributed, but with parameters that are different from the distribution of productive abilities.

A common measure of inequality in a distribution is the variance of the logarithms of the variable. The inequality in the distribution of productive abilities is therefore given by σ_1^2, while the inequality in the distribution of machine sizes is σ_2^2. In turn, the inequality in the distribution of earnings is given by θ^2, where $\theta = \alpha\sigma_1 + \beta\sigma_2$. It is therefore possible to give a systematic discussion of the determinants of earnings inequality in this case. Following the procedure in the previous case, we can discuss the distribution of $w-C_1$ first and then the effects of C_1 on the distribution of earnings.

The inequality in the distribution of $w-C_1$, as measured by the variance of the logarithms, is an increasing function of α and β, the exponents of g and k in the production function, and σ_1 and σ_2, the standard deviations in the distributions of productive abilities and machine sizes. In particular, the earnings transform $w-C_1$ will be more unequally distributed the more unequal the distributions of productive abilities and machine sizes.

The distribution of $w-C_1$ will be more unequal than the distribution of productive abilities whenever $\alpha\sigma_1 + \beta\sigma_2 > \sigma_1$. If $\alpha + \beta = 1$, then this inequality holds whenever $\sigma_2 > \sigma_1$, i.e. whenever machine sizes are more unequally distributed than productive abilities.

Now consider the effects of the constant of integration C_1 on earnings inequality. If C_1 is positive, earnings will then be more equally distributed than the transform $w-C_1$. For a given distribution of $w-C_1$, the distribution of earnings will be more unequal the lower the value of C_1. From (6.18) it is apparent that many of the parameters which affect the distribution of $w-C_1$ also have a second influence on the distribution of earnings through their effect on C_1.

The effects of increases in α and σ_1 are to reduce C_1 and unambiguously to increase earnings inequality. Decreases in β and α_2 raise C_1 if $\hat{w} > \hat{r}$ and lower C_1 if $\hat{w} < \hat{r}$. In the latter case the effects of increases in β or σ_2 make the distribution more unequal both through their effects on θ and on C_1. If $\hat{w} > \hat{r}$, the increase in C_1 could more than compensate for the increase in θ. If θ is held constant, C_1 and earnings inequality will be increasing functions of α and σ_1 and decreasing functions of β and σ_2.

The reserve prices, $\hat{w}$ and $\hat{r}$, also affect C_1. By inspection, C_1 depends positively on $\hat{w}$ and negatively on $\hat{r}$.

The foregoing analysis neglects changes in the employment of workers. The factors on which g_0 (the productive ability of the least-productive worker employed) depend are given in (6.17). Increases in $\hat{w}$ and $\hat{r}$ raise g_0 in the general case, thereby increasing unemployment. Further inferences depend on whether $(\hat{w} + \hat{r})/\exp[\beta(\mu_2 - \mu_1\sigma_2/\sigma_1)]$ is greater than one.

In summary, for a given value of C_1, earnings inequality (as measured by the variance of the logarithm of earnings) is an increasing function of

(i) the exponents of the factors g and k in the production function;

(ii) the inequality in the distribution of productive abilities, measured by σ_1^2; and

(iii) the inequality in the distribution of machine sizes, measured by σ_2^2. Furthermore, for a given value of θ (the standard deviation of $w - C_1$), earnings inequality is an increasing function of

(iv) α, σ_1, and $\hat{r}$

and an decreasing function of

(v) β, σ_2 and $\hat{w}$.

5.3. Normal factor distributions, CES production function

Suppose that the distributions of individuals and machines are normal, truncated so that only positive values of g and k are included:

$$G(g) = \frac{P}{\sqrt{(2\pi)}\sigma_1} \exp\left[\frac{-(g - \mu_1)^2}{2\sigma_1^2}\right], \quad g > 0,$$

and

$$K(k) = \frac{P}{\sqrt{(2\pi)}\sigma_2} \exp\left[\frac{-(k - \mu_2)^2}{2\sigma_2^2}\right], \quad k > 0.$$

Suppose, further, that the production function takes the constant elasticity of substitution form

$$f(g,k) = (\delta g^{-\rho} + (1 - \delta)k^{-\rho})^{-1/\rho}.$$

Because this production function is not multiplicatively separable, comparative advantage will arise. It can be shown that if ρ is positive, the more productive individuals will have a comparative advantage working with larger machines. If ρ is negative, the more-productive individuals have a comparative advantage working with smaller machines. The borderline case occurs when ρ is zero; this reduces to the Cobb-Douglas case where there is no comparative advantage. Even if ρ is negative, however, the more-productive individuals may be assigned to larger machines in equilibrium. It can be shown by differentiation that as long as $\rho > -1$, $\partial^2 f/\partial g \partial k$ will be positive so that dg/dk must be positive.

Assuming the more-productive individuals work with larger machines, the machine size that will be used by an individual of productive ability g in equilibrium can be found by transforming both k and g to the standardized normal and setting them equal:

$$\frac{g - \mu_1}{\sigma_1} = \frac{k - \mu_2}{\sigma_2} \quad \text{or} \quad k = \mu_2 + \frac{\sigma_2}{\sigma_1}\,(g - \mu_1).$$

When this condition holds, the cumulative density functions will be equal. Substituting $k(g)$ into the partial derivative $\partial f/\partial g$ yields the differential equation for the wage function:

$$w'(g) = \delta \left[\delta + (1 - \delta)\left(\left(\mu_2 - \mu_1\,\frac{\sigma_2}{\sigma_1}\right)\,g^{-1} + \frac{\sigma_2}{\sigma_1}\right)^{-\rho} \right]^{-1-1/\rho}$$

By investigating $w''(g)$, it is possible to establish that the wage function will be a convex (upward-curving) function of productive ability whenever $\mu_2 - \mu_1\sigma_2/\sigma_1$ is negative, i.e. whenever

$$\frac{\sigma_2}{\mu_2} > \frac{\sigma_1}{\mu_1}.$$

The above result states that the wage function will be convex whenever machine sizes are more unequally distributed (as measured by the coefficient of variation) than productive abilities. Similarly, the wage function will be concave whenever machine sizes are less unequally distributed than productive abilities. The borderline case occurs when productive abilities and machine sizes have the same amount of inequality; then wages will be a linear function of productive ability.

As in the previous examples, the shape of the wage function can be related to the amount of earnings inequality. A convex wage function tends to raise the earnings of the more-productive individuals relative to the less-productive individuals, thereby increasing earnings inequality. However, the final result also depends upon the constant of integration.

It does not appear possible to solve the differential equations explicitly to get $w(g)$ and $r(k)$. However, numerical techniques, in which the differential equations are solved via small iterations, can be used to describe the resulting wage and machine rent functions.

6. Perfectly elastic supply of capital

This section investigates the distribution of earnings arising when the supplies of machines of different sizes are perfectly elastic at rental rates proportional to the size of the machine. This situation is consistent with but not necessary for a long-run equilibrium in a perfectly competitive economy. This section should be considered as an alternative to the foregoing analysis rather than an extension. It does not seem reasonable that the distribution of capital among jobs is determined by the distribution of productive abilities, as implied by the underlying hypothesis of this section. The analysis presented here should therefore be regarded as exploratory in nature.

Suppose as before that the distribution of productive abilities is determined exogenously and is given by the density function $G(g)$. Suppose, however, that the distribution of machine sizes is determined endogenously. Assume that each individual selects a machine on the basis of earnings maximization. Suppose that the supply of machines of any size k is perfectly elastic at the rental rate rk, where r is a constant.

The earnings obtained by a worker of productive ability g using a machine of size k is the residual $f(g,k)-rk$. Differentiate this residual with respect to k and set it equal to zero to obtain the optimal machine size k: $\partial f/\partial k - r = 0$. If $f(g,k) = g^\alpha k^\beta$, then the first-order condition becomes $\beta g^\alpha k^{\beta-1} = r$
or

$$k = \left(\frac{\beta g^\alpha}{r} \right)^{1/(1-\beta)} .$$

Let $k(g)$ be the optimal machine size for a worker of productive ability g. The earnings for a worker of productive ability g are then

$$w(g) = f(g,k(g)) - r = \left(\frac{\beta}{r} \right)^{\beta/(1-\beta)} g^{\alpha/(1-\beta)}$$

$$- r \left(\frac{\beta}{r} \right)^{1/(1-\beta)} g^{\alpha/(1-\beta)}$$

$$= (1-\beta) \left(\frac{\beta}{r} \right)^{\beta/(1-\beta)} g^{\alpha/(1-\beta)}. \tag{6.19}$$

In the above Cobb-Douglas case the wage will be proportional to the machine size. Therefore, the distribution of earnings will be the same as the distribution of machine sizes; in particular, the inequality will be the same in each.

As an example, suppose that g is normally distributed:

$$G(g) = \frac{P}{\sqrt{(2\pi)}\sigma_1} \exp \left[\frac{-(g-\mu_1)^2}{2\sigma_1^2} \right] , \quad g > 0,$$

where P is the total number of workers. If $f(g,k)$ is homogeneous of degree one, so that $\alpha + \beta = 1$, then

$$G(g(w))g'(w) = \frac{P}{\sqrt{(2\pi)}\,\tilde{\sigma}_1} \exp\left[\frac{-(w-\tilde{\mu}_1)^2}{2\tilde{\sigma}_1^2}\right] ,$$

where

$$\tilde{\sigma}_1 = \alpha\left(\frac{\beta}{r}\right)^{\beta/\alpha}\sigma_1 \quad \text{and} \quad \tilde{\mu}_1 = \alpha\left(\frac{\beta}{r}\right)^{\beta/\alpha}\mu_1 .$$

It follows that the inequality in the distribution of earnings, as measured by the coefficient of variation (the standard deviation divided by the mean), is the same as the inequality in the distribution of productive abilities: $\tilde{\sigma}_1/\tilde{\mu}_1 = \sigma_1/\mu_1$.

If $\alpha + \beta > 1$, the wage function in (6.19) is convex. This results in the distribution of earnings being skewed to the right relative to the distribution of productive abilities, producing greater earnings inequality. If $\alpha + \beta < 1$, the wage function is concave, the distribution of earnings is skewed to the left relative to the distribution of productive abilities and inequality is less. These results can be obtained more directly from (6.19) by taking logarithms on each side and then variances:

$$\text{var}\,(\log w) = \left(\frac{\alpha}{1-\beta}\right)^2 \text{var}\,(\log g).$$

Using the variance of the logarithms as the measure of inequality, it follows that the inequality in earnings will be greater or less than the inequality in productive abilities depending on whether $\alpha + \beta > 1$ or $\alpha + \beta < 1$.

A further result in the above example is that the inequality in the distribution of earnings would not depend on the interest rate. This result does not hold in general, however, and arises from the use of a simple Cobb-Douglas production function. (It can also be shown to hold whenever $f(g,k)$ is linearly homogeneous.) Unfortunately, the only examples in section 5 that were completely worked out used the Cobb-Douglas production function.

More general results can be obtained by finding how a worker's wages will change as the interest rate changes:

$$\frac{\partial w}{\partial r} = \frac{\partial (f-rk)}{\partial r} = \frac{\partial f}{\partial k}\cdot\frac{\partial k}{\partial r} - k - r\frac{\partial k}{\partial r} = \left(\frac{\partial f}{\partial k} - r\right)\frac{\partial k}{\partial r} - k = -k.$$

The reduction in a worker's wage will be proportional to the amount of capital with which his labor is combined. In the Cobb-Douglas case the capital is proportional to the wage, so that a change in the interest rate changes all wages in the same proportion and the earnings inequality is unaffected. In general, however, the ratio of wages to capital will differ by level of productive ability. The ratio of wages to capital can in turn be related to the ratio of output to capital: $w/k = f/k - r$. This provides a simple empirical test to determine whether reductions in the interest rate (corresponding to capital accumulation in the neoclassical paradigm) will increase earnings inequality if the assumptions of the model are satisfied. If output per unit of capital is greater for the more productive workers, then a reduction in the interest rate will result in an increase in earnings inequality.

Unfortunately, it does not seem possible to find general conditions under which the ratio of output to capital is greater for more productive workers. For example, for a constant elasticity of substitution production function, the optimal level of capital, $k(g)$, cannot be expressed explicitly.

7. Nature of the model

Anyone familiar with the standard human capital treatments of income distribution will have an immediate objection to the models that have been developed in this chapter. The distribution of productive abilities has everywhere been treated as exogenously determined. Since the major source of inequality in earnings comes from inequality in productive abilities, does it not make sense to concentrate attention on explaining that distribution of productive abilities? Will not the individuals' investments in themselves alter the distribution of productive abilities to conform to the distribution demanded?

To answer these questions, let us review the nature of the human capital models. The two basic human capital models, the Mincer and Becker-Chiswick models, determine the distribution of earnings by imposing alternative and inconsistent considerations on the distribution of earnings. The Mincer model operates by imposing the long-run condition that individuals will select among alternative levels of schooling so as to equalize the present value of lifetime earnings. This determines the earnings function and educational differentials, but leaves the determination of the number of individuals at each educational level entirely to the demand side. In contrast, the Becker-Chiswick model operates by imposing the condition that the earnings of labor of different educational levels must correspond to their contributions to production, which in turn are determined by the physical rates of return to schooling. In the Mincer model the distribution of productive abilities (or at least the distribution of schooling) is determined exogenously by the distribution of demands for workers at different educational levels. In the Becker-Chiswick model the distribution of schooling is also determined outside the model, and the model merely relates this exogenously determined distribution to the distribution of earnings. Neither the Mincer nor the Becker-Chiswick model by itself can be used to explain the long-run distribution of earnings.

In contrast, the model developed in this chapter is unabashedly short run. At any one point in time both the distribution of machine sizes and the distribution of productive abilities are determined exogenously (or by previous decisions), and the model describes the resulting wage and capital machine rent functions. The course of earnings inequality over time then depends on what happens to the distribution of machine sizes and productive abilities over time. In describing the course of any long-run phenomenon, the temptation is very great to make everything relevant to the outcome endogenous to the model. In the case of earnings inequality the temptation is to make the distributions of machine sizes and productive abilities endogenous, i.e. explained within a larger model. The problem with this approach is that the assumptions made to determine such distributions within the model would be overly simplistic. Greater realism and predictive power would be gained by taking the distributions as determined exogenously. A complete model of earnings inequality over time would then consist of the short-run model determining the wage function, along with separate explanations of how the distribution of machine sizes and the distribution of productive abilities change over time. This is the point of view taken in the empirical work to follow.

Chapter 7

THE EMPIRICAL APPLICATION OF THE THEORY

1. Introduction

This chapter collects together a number of topics which must be discussed before the empirical work is presented. The major objectives of the chapter are to evaluate the importance of the differences between the assumptions of the formal model and the real world, to present descriptive evidence on the distribution of capital among jobs, and to investigate whether there is a positive assignment of more productive individuals to more capital-intensive jobs. These topics must be addressed because the theory has not been developed directly in terms of observable market phenomena. It is therefore necessary to examine in detail the correspondence between the formal models and the real world they were intended to describe.

2. Transition to an empirical model

Many of the assumptions of the differential rents model of chapter 6 are necessary to produce a model in which the wage and rent functions and the distribution of earnings can be solved explicitly. Without them, the main results of the theory remain valid, but only qualitative results can be stated.

One assumption of the model is that the output obtained from combining labor with a machine is homogeneous. This assumption is necessary because without it the prices of produced goods would become endogenous and it would be difficult to solve for the prices at the same time one solved for the wage and rent functions. A consequence of this assumption is that the distribution of capital among jobs cannot be determined by the demands for goods produced using different machine sizes.

Suppose, instead, that firms produce different types of goods. Suppose the demand for goods produced by more capital-intensive processes increases relative to the demand for goods produced by labor-intensive processes. In response to this greater demand, the prices of those goods produced by capital-intensive processes would tend to go up relative to the prices of labor-intensive goods. Because of the change in relative prices, the profit rate would tend to go up in the capital-intensive sectors relative to the labor-intensive industries. With free entry into industries (and free exit from industries), the capital-intensive sectors would expand relative to the labor-intensive sectors, tending to bring the rates of return back into equality. In the above process the demand for goods, which can be taken as exogenously determined, significantly affects the size of the industries according to capital intensity and thereby affects the distribution of capital among jobs. Furthermore, with heterogeneous goods the rate of return to industries of different capital intensities (corresponding to machines of different sizes) is no longer determined by the relation between the distribution of capital among jobs and the distribution of productive abilities. Essentially, the relative availabilities of labor of different productive abilities affect the prices of the goods produced instead of the rates of return for producing an identical good.

The consequences for the wage function and the distribution of earnings can be simply stated. Assuming the more-productive workers are employed in more capital-intensive sectors, an expansion of the capital-intensive sectors will increase the demand for the more-productive workers, raising their earnings relative to the less-productive workers and increasing earnings inequality. Similarly, a contraction of the labor-intensive sectors will result in a reduction in the demand for the less-productive workers and a lowering of their earnings relative to the more-productive workers. Even with heterogeneous goods, the main outcome of the differential rents theory remains valid: an increase in the inequality in the distribution of capital among jobs (arising from a change in the demand for goods) leads to an increase in earnings inequality. However, more formal or rigorous statements of results are apparently not possible with heterogeneous goods.

A second assumption of the differential rents model is that capital intensity is the only determinant of the productive ability of the workers employed in an industry. Throwing away information is inherent in the process of abstraction. By eliminating all other determinants of the quality of labor in an industry, the differential rents model succeeds in isolating the effect of the distribution of capital among jobs. But one cannot assume, on the basis of the model, that there are no other determinants of the productive ability of the workers of an industry. One must be prepared, therefore, to investigate these other determinants.

Closely related to the above is the model's assumption that an industry (corresponding to a particular machine size) hires only one type of labor. In fact, industries employ labor from a large range of abilities and the distribution of earnings within an industry is approximately as dispersed as the distribution of earnings for the population as a whole. It is rather difficult, therefore, to speak of the productive ability of an industry's labor. Industries differ not only in the average level of productive ability but in the numbers of employees with different levels of productive ability, as reflected in earnings or education. An increase in the demand for the output of one industry therefore affects not only the demand for workers of one level of productive ability but the demands for all levels, in varying proportions. The demand side of the distribution of earnings is therefore more complex than depicted in the simple differential rents model of Chapter 6. These added complications will be discussed in Chapters 11, 12 and 13.

Table 7.1
Manufacturing industry data, 1959.

		Employment (1,000's)	Capital to labor ratio ($1,000 per employee)	Proportion of employees with four years high school	Proportion of employees with four years college
1.	Food	1,651	15.8	0.364	0.034
2.	Tobacco	90	35.6	0.280	0.026
3.	Textiles	913	7.9	0.246	0.022
4.	Apparel	1,141	3.1	0.275	0.017
5.	Lumber and wood	623	9.5	0.226	0.018
6.	Furniture and fixtures	373	5.9	0.314	0.023
7.	Paper	567	22.8	0.405	0.053
8.	Printing and publishing	804	8.9	0.501	0.082
9.	Chemicals	796	30.1	0.564	0.149
10.	Petroleum and coal	209	75.1	0.611	0.135
11.	Rubber and plastics	361	10.2	0.425	0.059
12.	Leather	354	3.4	0.267	0.015
13.	Stone, clay and glass	586	17.7	0.365	0.048
14.	Primary metals	1,167	28.2	0.368	0.046
15.	Fabricated metals	1,106	11.8	0.448	0.064
16.	Machinery, except electrical	1,432	13.7	0.481	0.061
17.	Electrical equipment	1,358	8.5	0.543	0.095
18.	Transportation equipment	1,794	11.5	0.473	0.071
19.	Instruments	337	9.5	0.557	0.105
20.	Miscellaneous manufacturing	372	12.9	0.378	0.043
	All manufacturing	16,034	12.9	0.413	0.053

Data sources: see appendix.

Table 7.2
Nonmanufacturing industry data, 1959.

		Employment (1,000's)	Capital to labor ratio ($1,000 per employee)	Proportion of employees with four years high school	Proportion of employees with four years college
1.	Railroad transportation	917	159.1	0.371	0.019
2.	Nonrail transportation	1,577	27.5	0.375	0.030
3.	Communication	799	48.1	0.734	0.061
4.	Public utilities	594	169.0	0.504	0.062
5.	Trade	9,900	11.2	0.460	0.046
6.	Finance, insurance and real estate	2,471	113.6	0.561	0.140
7.	Services	7,641	7.8	0.569	0.225
	All service-producing industries	23,899	32.6	0.524	0.111
8.	Mining	709	40.6	0.353	0.070
9.	Contract construction	2,761	4.3	0.331	0.031
	Nonfarm nonmanufacturing	27,369	29.9	0.501	0.102
10.	Farm	1,764	18.2	0.044	0.022

Data sources: see appendix.

3. Industry capital to labor ratios

Data on the distribution of capital among jobs are presented in tables 7.1–7.4. The data cover thirty industries, twenty of which are in manufacturing. The Conference Board (1976) has published data, developed by John Kendrick, on real gross capital stocks by major industry for the period 1948–1974. These data have been combined with data on full-time equivalent employees published by the Bureau of Economic Analysis in *The National Income and Product Accounts of the United States, 1929–1974* to produce the employment and capital to labor ratios in tables 7.1–7.4. The data reveal that there are substantial variations in the average amount of capital per worker in different industries. Within manufacturing, some industries, such as textiles, apparel, furniture and fixtures, and leather, employ very little capital per worker. Other industries, such as tobacco, paper, chemicals, petroleum and coal, and primary metals, use relatively large amounts of capital per worker. Of course, within industries, the capital may not be evenly distributed among workers. At a more disaggregated level some of the subindustries will have larger or smaller amounts of capital per

Table 7.3
Manufacturing industry data, 1969.

	Employment (1,000's)	Capital to labor ratio ($1,000 per employee)	Proportion of employees with four years high school	Proportion of employees with four years college	Proportion of employees with earnings less than $6,000
1. Food	1,715	17.1	0.475	0.051	0.468
2. Tobacco	79	35.4	0.404	0.046	0.558
3. Textiles	984	9.1	0.343	0.030	0.713
4. Apparel	1,342	4.2	0.364	0.021	0.827
5. Lumber and wood	588	12.9	0.356	0.030	0.591
6. Furniture and fixtures	472	6.1	0.402	0.030	0.594
7. Paper	705	23.4	0.554	0.069	0.359
8. Printing and publishing	1,012	10.1	0.687	0.111	0.454
9. Chemicals	1,050	33.7	0.697	0.180	0.282
10. Petroleum and coal	186	96.2	0.728	0.182	0.181
11. Rubber and plastics	585	10.6	0.550	0.062	0.449
12. Leather	328	4.9	0.369	0.022	0.762
13. Stone, clay and glass	652	19.0	0.489	0.060	0.385
14. Primary metals	1,344	29.5	0.507	0.053	0.244
15. Fabricated metals	1,420	12.8	0.516	0.053	0.367
16. Machinery, except electrical	2,007	15.3	0.640	0.090	0.283
17. Electrical equipment	2,012	11.9	0.663	0.111	0.432
18. Transportation equipment	2,368	14.6	0.605	0.087	0.219
19. Instruments	475	10.9	0.677	0.123	0.397
20. Miscellaneous manufacturing	429	10.5	0.445	0.052	0.559
All manufacturing	19,753	15.9	0.545	0.071	

Data sources: see appendix.

worker. Even within a firm the capital with which employees work will not be the same.

In nonmanufacturing industries there appears to be a wider variation in the capital to labor ratio. By and large, nonmanufacturing industries use more capital per worker than manufaturing industries ($29.9 thousand versus $12.9 thousand in 1959, and $30.1 thousand versus $15.9 thousand in 1969). The exceptions are contract construction, services and trade, with low amounts of capital per worker. Three sectors, railroad transportation, public utilities, and finance, insurance and real estate, employ extremely large amounts of capital per worker, over $100,000. The data for 1959 are substantially similar to the data for 1969.

The general conclusion from the examination of these tables is that the average amount of capital combined with a unit of labor varies substantially among industries, resulting in an unequal distribution of capital among jobs. The

Table 7.4
Nonmanufacturing industry data, 1969.

	Employment (1,000's)	Capital to labor ratio ($1,000 per employee)	Proportion of employees with four years high school	Proportion of employees with four years college	Proportion of employees with earnings less than $6,000
1. Railroad transportation	637	211.5	0.540	0.027	0.178
2. Nonrail transportation	1,997	29.2	0.546	0.046	0.353
3. Communication	1,001	68.1	0.855	0.072	0.453
4. Public utilities	651	210.0	0.636	0.076	0.296
5. Trade	12,829	11.7	0.568	0.055	0.627
6. Finance, insurance and real estate	3,415	109.8	0.860	0.167	0.520
7. Services	11,193	9.4	0.701	0.274	0.561
All service-producing industries	31,723	32.4	0.651	0.144	
8. Mining	610	47.0	0.512	0.097	0.288
9. Contract construction	3,452	6.3	0.455	0.039	0.377
Nonfarm nonmanufacturing	35,785	30.1	0.630	0.113	
10. Farm	1,240	30.3	0.375	0.039	0.703

Data sources: see appendix.

next task is to develop an objective measure of the extent of inequality or concentration in the distribution of capital among jobs.

4. Capital concentration over time

The data presented in tables 7.1—7.4 can be used to develop a measure of capital concentration, or the inequality in the distribution of capital among jobs. For each sector i, let E_i be the number of full-time equivalent employees (the data presented in the first columns of tables 7.1—7.4) and let C_i be the amount of capital per full-time equivalent employee (the data presented in the second columns).

All the sectors described in tables 7.1—7.4 are used in the calculation of capital concentration with the following exceptions. Farming, real estate and government services are excluded on the grounds that equipment and structures in these cases do not adequately represent the average amount of capital with which a worker's labor is combined. In the case of real estate, the employment and capital quantities were subtracted from the figures for the larger category of finance, insurance and real estate. Real estate by itself has an extremely high capital to labor ratio (over \$400,000 per employee), so that the capital to labor ratio for real estate would have dominated the determination of the capital concentration measure. The figures for services already exclude government employees. As a result of these exclusions, twenty-nine sectors are used in the calculation of capital concentration.

A figure for the mean capital per full-time equivalent employee can be calculated and is given by

$$\text{mean (CW)} = \frac{\sum_{i=1}^{29} C_i E_i}{\sum_{i=1}^{29} E_i} \, .$$

The standard deviation of capital per full-time equivalent employee is then calculated as

$$\text{SD(CW)} = \frac{\sum_{i=1}^{29} (C_i - \text{mean(CW)})^2 E_i}{\sum_{i=1}^{29} E_i} \, .$$

The coefficient of variation of capital per worker, represented by C_ρ in the rest of the tables, is given by the standard deviation divided by the mean, or $C_\rho = \text{SD (CW)}/\text{mean (CW)}$.

The measures of mean (CW), SD (CW) and C_ρ are presented in table 7.5 for 1948–1972. This table reveals that in the postwar US economy, the coefficient of variation of capital per worker has tended to increase over time. However, the increases have not followed a simple time trend. Instead, most of the increase appears to have taken place from 1951 to 1962. Furthermore, the coefficient of variation of capital per worker and mean capital per worker are highly correlated. This indicates that the process of capital accumulation in a developed economy is accompanied by a greater concentration of capital among jobs.[1]

---

[1] An alternative measure of capital concentration, suggested by the analysis of Chapter 6, section 5.2, is the variance of logarithms of the distribution of capital among jobs. Relative to the coefficient of variation presented in table 7.5, the variance of logarithms is more sensitive to changes in labor-intensive jobs and less sensitive to changes in capital-intensive jobs. Over time, the variance of logarithms shows a decline, in contrast to the changes in the coefficient of variation. When used in place of the coefficient of variation in the empirical work in Chapter 8, the estimated coefficients were not significant. For this reason the variance of logarithms of the distribution of capital among jobs has not been investigated further.

Table 7.5
US capital concentration, 1948–1972.

Year	Mean capital per worker (thousands of dollars)	Standard deviation capital per worker	Coefficient of variation capital per worker, C_ρ
1948	14.41	19.98	1.387
1949	15.40	21.65	1.406
1950	15.53	21.79	1.403
1951	15.41	21.52	1.396
1952	15.71	22.28	1.418
1953	15.75	22.82	1.449
1954	16.68	24.89	1.492
1955	16.76	25.24	1.505
1956	16.86	25.41	1.506
1957	17.34	26.40	1.522
1958	18.51	29.02	1.568
1959	18.31	29.32	1.601
1960	18.35	29.68	1.617
1961	18.92	30.80	1.628
1962	18.92	30.81	1.628
1963	19.05	30.96	1.625
1964	19.16	31.13	1.626
1965	18.96	30.89	1.629
1966	18.89	30.72	1.627
1967	19.01	31.12	1.637
1968	18.91	31.36	1.658
1969	19.07	31.77	1.666
1970	19.87	32.64	1.642
1971	20.49	33.84	1.651
1972	20.43	34.44	1.685

Sources: see text.

5. The relation between capital intensity and labor quality

The theoretical conclusion of Chapter 5 and the underlying assumption of Chapter 6 is that the more-productive individuals will be employed at more capital-intensive jobs. The intention of this section is to investigate whether such a correspondence can be observed for the thirty industrial sectors presented in tables 7.1–7.4.

Before looking at the relationships, however, it is important to reiterate the distinction between two very similar theories which are regarded as describing those relationships. The first theory is capital-skill complementarity, put forward by Griliches (1969, 1970) and discussed previously in Chapter 5, section 7. The intention of this theory is to describe what happens to the employment of factors of production as factor prices change. Taking the production function (for a firm or an economy) as given, the assumption of capital-skill complementarity implies that as the interest rate goes down (corresponding to capital accumulation), the capital to labor ratio and the skill to labor ratio both go up. At different interest rates, then, one would observe a positive correspondence between capital intensity and average skill level (holding the production function fixed). In contrast, the theory developed in Chapter 5 asserts that, looking at industries or firms with different productions and different capital to labor ratios but facing the same rate of interest, the more productive workers will be employed at the more capital-intensive processes. For example, the production functions could all be Cobb-Douglas, with the exponent of the capital term varying from industry to industry. At a fixed interest rate, section 6 in Chapter 5 demonstrates that the more capital-intensive firms would employ the more productive workers. It is easy to see why the two theories could be confused, since they both describe the relation between capital intensity and productive ability or skill level of the work force. However, they differ in that the theory of capital-skill complementarity derives the relation by varying the interest rate and holding the production function fixed, whereas the assignment theory of Chapter 5 derives the relation by holding the interest rate fixed and varying the production function.

Since the interest rate must vary to produce the results of the capital-skill complementarity hypothesis, one cannot in general use cross-section data to test for its presence. At any one point in time the interest rate or cost of capital to different industries within a country would be approximately the same, controlling for level of risk. Unfortunately, many of the tests for capital-skill complementarity have used cross-section data. (These studies are summarized by Hamermesh and Grant, 1978, in a review.) The cross-section tests for capital-skill complementarity have apparently picked up the positive assignment of the more productive workers to more capital-intensive jobs and mistaken it for capital-skill complementarity. For example, if one looks closely at Griliches's cross-section test, he does not use the interest rate or cost of capital as the variable which is different across industries. Instead, he uses the gross rate of return, which is more closely associated with the profit rate. A true test of capital-skill complementarity must involve a time-series test, in which capital intensity and skill level change in response to a change in the interest rate and do not arise from differences in technology.

There have been some previous studies of the relation between capital intensity and skill level. Boon (1964) investigates the optimal combinations of physical and human factors of production in such processes as metal-turning, metal-facing, wood-working, producing grains, making field trenches and plowing. He finds that capital intensity or level of mechanization and skill level increase together, supporting the capital-skill complementarity hypothesis. In a cross-section comparison, he also finds a general correspondence between capital-intensity and skill level, although the relation is not strong. Similarly, Donges, Fels, Neu et al. (1973) find that physical capital per employee and human capital per employee are correlated for thirty-one industries in West Germany.

In tables 7.1–7.4, along with the data on employment and capital per worker, are data on the educational levels of employees, expressed in terms of the proportions of employees with four years of high school or more and the proportions of employees with four years of college or more. Within manufacturing, very capital-intensive industries (such as chemicals or petroleum and coal) do employ the more-educated workers, and very labor-intensive industries (textiles, apparel, furniture and fixtures and leather) employ relatively the less-educated workers. There is, however, substantial variation. There is even more variation among the nonmanufacturing industries. The highest proportion of employees with four years of college or more occurs for services which, on average, uses very little capital per worker. However, services are an aggregation of many types of employment, including professional services, with many college graduates, and personal services, with relatively few high school or college graduates.

As a class, nonmanufacturing industries not only employ much more capital per worker, they also have more highly educated employees. The proportion of employees with four years college or more is substantially greater (0.102 versus 0.053 in 1959 and 0.133 versus 0.071 in 1969), as is the proportion with four years high school or more (0.501 versus 0.413 in 1959 and 0.630 versus 0.545 in 1969). Within the category of nonmanufacturing industries, however, there does not appear to be a distinct relation between capital intensity and educational levels of employees.

Table 7.6 presents the results of simple ordinary least squares regressions of proportions of employees with schooling above or below a certain level against capital intensity, using the 1969 data for the thirty industries in tables 7.3 and 7.4. On the average, the greater the capital intensity of the industry, the fewer the employees with eight years of elementary school or less or with four years high school or less, and the greater the proportion of employees with four years college or more. Although the coefficients for the capital to labor ratio all have the correct sign, only in one case is the coefficient significant at conventional levels. Furthermore, the adjusted R^2 statistics are extremely low. It is apparent that capital intensity explains only a small proportion of the variation in educational level between industries.

The relation between capital intensity and productive ability of the workers can be examined further by looking at the earnings of employees by industry.

Table 7.6
Education versus capital intensity, 1969, thiry industries.

Proportion of employees with schooling in described range, 1969

	Eight years elementary school or less	Four years high school or less	Four years college or more
Capital to labor ratio of industry, 1969	−0.207 (2.13)*	−0.038 (1.87)	0.181 (1.59)
Constant	−1.00	−0.098	−3.31
Adjusted R^2	0.109	0.080	0.050

Positive values of t-statistics are given in parentheses under estimated coefficient.
Asterisk denotes significance at 0.05 level.

Data sources: see appendix.

While earnings are not a measure of productive ability, at one point in time earnings are an increasing function of productive ability. The proportion of employees with earnings less than a certain level w would then be equal to the proportion of employees with productive ability less than the productive ability corresponding to w.

Data on the proportions of workers with earnings below $6,000 are presented in the fifth columns of tables 7.3 and 7.4. The correspondence between capital intensity and these proportions tends to be better than the correspondence between capital intensity and educational levels. Some industries with high capital intensities but whose employees had low levels of schooling (rail and nonrail transportation and mining) have low proportions of employees with earnings below $6,000. Also, services, a labor-intensive industry, has a relatively high proportion of employees with earnings below $6,000, which is more in conformity with the conclusions of Chapter 5 than the data on educational levels would indicate.

Ordinary least squares regressions of the relation between earnings and the capital to labor ratio are presented in table 7.7 for 1949 and table 7.8 for 1969. The dependent variables are the logarithm of the capital to labor ratio, taken from tables 7.1−7.4, and a dummy variable for nonmanufacturing industries. The results strongly support the argument that the more productive workers are

Table 7.7
Earnings versus capital intensity, 1949.

	Less than $500	Less than $1,500	Less than $2,500	More than $3,500	More than $4,000	More than $4,500
ln (K/L) logarithm of capital to labor ratio	−0.426* (3.51)	−0.370* (3.75)	−0.212* (3.26)	0.266* (2.38)	0.269* (2.35)	0.260* (2.29)
D_1, dummy variable for nonmanufacturing industry	0.628* (2.53)	0.449* (2.23)	0.229 (1.72)	−0.208 (0.910)	−0.188 (0.803)	−0.179 (0.771)
Constant	−2.14	−0.817	−0.254	−2.25	−2.69	−3.12
Adjusted R^2	0.293	0.308	0.235	0.113	0.109	0.101

Dependent variable: logarithm of proportion of workers in industry with earnings in described range, 30 manufacturing and nonmanufacturing industries.
Positive values of t-statistics are given in parenthesis under estimated coefficients.
Asterisk denotes coefficient significant at 0.05 level.
Data sources: see appendix.

Table 7.8
Earnings versus capital intensity, 1969.

	Less than $1,000	Less than $4,000	Less than $7,000	More than $10,000	More than $12,000	More than $15,000
ln (K/L)	−0.435* (4.16)	−0.401* (4.77)	−0.214* (4.12)	0.262* (2.94)	0.202* (2.34)	0.085 (1.02)
D_1	0.709* (3.15)	0.434* (2.39)	0.169 (1.50)	−0.020 (0.105)	0.051 (0.274)	0.102 (0.564)
Constant	−2.08	−0.441	−0.069	−2.40	−2.81	−3.17
Adjusted R^2	0.372	0.417	0.344	0.231	0.169	0.014

Dependent variable: logarithm of proportion of workers in industry with earnings in described range, 30 manufacturing and nonmanufacturing industries.
Positive values of t-statistics are given in parenthesis under estimated coefficients.
Asterisk denotes significance at 0.05 level.
Data sources: see appendix.

employed at the more capital-intensive jobs, if the implicit relation between earnings and productive abilities is accepted. For both years, the estimated coefficients for the capital to labor ratio are negative and significant for the proportions of workers in the lower tails and are positive and generally significant for the proportions of workers in the upper tails (the exception being the proportion of workers earning more than $15,000 in 1969). On the average, more capital-intensive industries employ fewer low-earnings workers and more high-earnings workers, everything else the same. The results appear to be better for the lower tail than the upper tail. Also, the estimated coefficient for the non-manufacturing industry dummy variable is positive and significant for the proportions of workers in the two lowest ranges, indicating that nonmanufacturing industries tend to have more low-earnings workers than manufacturing industries. The results using earnings are substantially better than those using educational levels, although the regressions still only explain a small amount of the variation in the proportions of employees with earnings in the described ranges. The remaining variation is substantially explained by the addition of other demand determinants; this extension is undertaken in Chapter 12.[2]

It should be noted that there are alternative interpretations to the relation between capital intensity and earnings of employees described above. Many economists, in particular those who work with dual labor markets and internal labor markets, would argue that wages are not determined (or not solely determined) by a worker's contributions to production. Instead, some workers gain access to jobs in the primary labor market. Then their earnings are determined by progress within the internal labor market and not by the market wages of comparable workers. It follows that differences in the earnings of similar workers in different industries would arise. The earnings paid could then be positively related to capital intensity, since one of the features of the secondary labor market is a relatively low amount of capital per worker. The outcome of such phenomena for the distribution of earnings would be substantially the same as developed here, but the derivation would be very different.

A second interpretation can be put forward from the human capital point of view. It is possible that more capital-intensive industries require more on-the-job training. The different distributions of earnings among industries might then reflect the fact that some workers are receiving training (and therefore having their earnings depressed relative to what they could earn without training) and

---

[2] Chapter 12 examines the determinants of the educational levels of employees in an industry in more detail. Other determinants include the ratio of production workers to total employment and the ratio of research and development expenditures to value added. When these variables are included, the explanatory power of the model increases substantially and the coefficient of the capital to labor term is generally significant and has the predicted sign.

some workers are already trained and are receiving some of the benefits of that greater training. This is certainly a hypothesis which warrants further investigation. But the outcome, again, is to lead to substantially the same conclusions regarding the distribution of earnings as the analysis developed here.

6. The measurement of inequality

The study of income distribution has recently generated a great deal of interest in the measurement of inequality. Many conclusions regarding changes in the distribution of income over time or comparisons of different economies are sensitive to the inequality measure used. Among the older measures are the Gini coefficient, based on the Lorenz curve, and the coefficient of variation.[3] The development of the theory of the lognormal distribution by Aitchison and Brown (1957) has led to the use of the variance of logarithms, which is a parameter of that distribution. More recently, Atkinson (1970) has developed a measure of inequality which makes explicit the normative value judgments involved in comparing one distribution with another in terms of the inequality measure. Atkinson's inequality measure involves a parameter, E, which depends on the conditions under which a particular type of income transfer will leave society just as well off as before.

These measures have been compared with respect to how they are affected by different types of redistribution of income (Sawyer, 1976). This discussion is useful for the purpose of examining different tax and transfer schemes, which would redistribute income among a given population with given pretransfer earnings. However, for purposes of studying the distribution of earnings over time or making cross-section comparisons, it is necessary to understand the source of changes in the different inequality measures. How do they change in response to an increase in the number of individuals in a particular earnings bracket? The intention of this section is to reveal the sensitivity of the different inequality measures to marginal changes in the distribution of individuals among the earnings brackets.

The procedure is as follows. First, an initial distribution of earnings is chosen. This is taken to be the earnings in 1969 of males 16 years old and over in the experienced civilian labor force, published in the 1970 US census of population. The data give the number of workers in each of thirteen earnings brackets. Using these thirteen brackets and the mean earnings for each bracket, it is possible to

---

[3]   See recent discussions of the Gini coefficient by Dorfman (1979), Gastwirth (1972), Petersen (1979), and Seiver (1979).

Table 7.9
Elasticities of inequality measures
with respect to change in bracket population.

Earnings range (dollars)	Coefficient of variation	Variance of logarithms	Gini coefficient	Atkinson's $E = 0.5$	Atkinson's $E = 1.5$
0 – 999 or less	0.066	0.366	0.080	0.200	0.239
1,000 – 1,999	0.051	0.095	0.060	0.110	0.067
2,000 – 2,999	0.029	0.005	0.033	0.044	0.008
3,000 – 3,999	0.022	−0.030	0.022	0.017	−0.015
4,000 – 4,999	0.011	−0.052	0.006	−0.010	−0.031
5,000 – 5,999	−0.001	−0.076	−0.011	−0.037	−0.048
6,000 – 6,999	−0.017	−0.087	−0.031	−0.062	−0.058
7,000 – 7,999	−0.034	−0.094	−0.050	−0.085	−0.066
8,000 – 9,999	−0.088	−0.142	−0.108	−0.162	−0.106
10,000 – 11,999	−0.083	−0.067	−0.072	−0.111	−0.057
12,000 – 14,999	−0.067	−0.021	−0.036	−0.063	−0.023
15,000 – 24,999	−0.046	0.025	0.008	−0.006	0.013
25,000 or more	0.156	0.080	0.099	0.165	0.077

calculate the value for each of five different inequality measures, the coefficient of variation, the variance of logarithms, the Gini coefficient, Atkinson's measure with $E = 0.5$ and Atkinson's measure with $E = 1.5$. For each inequality measure it is also possible to calculate the derivative of the measure with respect to an increase in the number of individuals in each bracket. Multiplying each derivative by the number of individuals in the bracket and dividing by the inequality measure yields the elasticity of the inequality measure with respect to a change in the number of individuals in that bracket.

The results of these calculations are presented in table 7.9. As one would expect, the elasticities are positive for the lower and upper tails and negative for the middle part of the earnings distributions. As a check on the calculations, the elasticities add to zero for each measure, reflecting the fact that a proportional increase in all brackets should leave the inequality measure unaffected. Typically the highest elasticities occur in either the highest or the lowest bracket, except for the Gini coefficient. There appears to be a great deal of variation among the measures.

The variance of logarithms is extremely sensitive to the very lowest bracket, i.e. individuals with earnings less than $1,000. It follows that differences in the variance of logarithms across states or over time will be substantially determined by differences in the number of individuals in the very lowest bracket. Remarkably, increases in the number of individuals with earnings between $3,000 and $4,999 reduce the variance of logarithms. The measure appears to be relatively insensitive to changes in the upper tail.

The Gini coefficient is fairly insensitive to changes in the number of individuals in any bracket. The highest elasticity is for the earnings bracket $8,000–$9,999. This result confirms the belief of many economists that the Gini coefficient is relatively insensitive to changes in the distribution of earnings over time.

Atkinson's inequality measures appear to be quite reasonable in the sense that they do not put all the inequality elasticity in one bracket. However, they are fairly sensitive to the lowest bracket.

The coefficient of variation appears to be the least sensitive to changes in the lower bracket. Furthermore, it shifts abruptly from a negative elasticity for the $15,000–$24,999 bracket to a large and positive elasticity for the $25,000 or more bracket.

The above discussion does not provide a basis for choosing among different inequality measures. It is intended only to provide some idea of the source of differences in the values of the inequality measures across observations. In Chapter 8 the variance of logarithms will be used. In Chapter 9 both the coefficient of variation and the Gini coefficient will be used. If some value of E could be agreed upon, it would also be desirable to use Atkinson's inequality measure.

7. Implications of the data for earnings inequality

The general increase in the capital to labor ratio over time is revealed in column four of table 7.10. The increase in the concentration of capital among jobs over

Table 7.10
Time series of capital and education variables.

	(1) Proportion of population with less than five years elementary education	(2) Proportion of population with four years high school or more	(3) Proportion of population with four years college or more	(4) Index of capital units per man-hour (1958=100)	(5) Ratio of manufacturing to total non-agricultural employment
1970	0.053	0.552	0.110	127.6	0.274
1960	0.083	0.411	0.077	100.8	0.310
1950	0.108	0.334	0.060	73.4	0.337
1940	0.135	0.241	0.046	65.5	0.339
1930	0.175	0.191	0.039	68.7	0.325
1920	0.220	0.164	0.033	58.7	0.390
1910	0.238	0.135	0.027	49.0	0.361

Data sources: see appendix.

time is shown in the third column of table 7.5. What are the consequences for earnings inequality of these changes over time?

The aggregate theory of Chapter 4 finally concluded that the effect of capital intensity on earnings inequality is theoretically ambiguous. If the capital-skill complementarity condition holds, then increases in the capital to labor ratio over time should, everything else the same, result in greater earnings inequality. However, this condition need not hold. Without knowing about the relative values of the partial elasticities of complementarity, no definite prediction can be made. The question can only be settled by empirical investigation.

The effect of capital intensity on earnings inequality becomes more complicated within the context of a disaggregated analysis. Then increases in capital intensity can come about in two ways. First, each sector can increase its capital to labor ratio. Whether the demand for the more-skilled workers increases in a sector would then depend on whether that sector's production function exhibited capital-skill complementarity. The second way in which the capital to labor ratio for the economy could increase is if there is a shift in production from labor-intensive to capital-intensive sectors, each sector maintaining its capital to labor ratio. Then the overall capital to labor ratio for the economy would increase, but so would the concentration of capital among jobs. Even if each sector did not exhibit capital-skill complementarity, it is possible for the increase in the economy aggregate capital to labor ratio to be accompanied by an increase in earnings inequality. It would therefore be desirable to separate out economy-wide increases in capital intensity from sectoral shifts to more capital-intensive sectors, in order to determine the mechanism lying beyond any empirical connection between capital intensity and earnings inequality.

The effect of the increasing concentration of capital among jobs over time is theoretically unambiguous. These increases can be expected to result in greater earnings inequality, everything else the same.

Eventually, to give a complete explanation of changes in the distribution of earnings over time, one must explain why the concentration of capital among jobs has gone up. An important element in this answer is revealed in column 5 of table 7.10. Over a long period of time the ratio of manufacturing to total non-agricultural employment has declined.[4] By itself, this shift would result in a greater capital to labor ratio for the economy and an increase in the concentration of capital among jobs, since the nonmanufacturing industries are generally much more capital intensive. They employ larger proportions of workers with

---

[4] The shift towards service industries has been described by Stigler (1956). Some implications of sectoral shifts for earnings inequality were described some time ago by Clark (1940).

four years high school or more and four years college or more, as revealed in tables 7.1–7.4. The shift from manufacturing to nonmanufacturing can therefore definitely be expected to affect the demands for workers at different levels of productive ability and consequently increase the inequality in the distribution of earnings.

Countering the effects of a greater concentration of capital among jobs are the effects of changes in the distribution of education among the labor force. These changes have been described in some detail by Jencks et al. (1972). Of course the average amount of education has been going up steadily over time and the inequality in the distribution of education (measured using years of schooling) has generally been declining. Some relevant information on the distribution of education among the population, taken from the *Digest of Educational Statistics*, is presented in the first three columns of table 7.10.

To what extent can these changes be regarded as exogenously determined? Freeman (1976) has demonstrated that prospective college entrants are sensitive to job prospects. But new entrants into the job market have less of an effect on the overall distribution of education among the work force than those who leave the work force through death or retirement. Furthermore, because new entrants are such a small proportion of the total work force, the distribution of education changes only slowly over time. This is revealed by the education statistics in table 7.10, which change only gradually over time and follow fairly stable trends. In the empirical work to follow, it therefore does not appear necessary to take account of the effect of personal rates of return to education on the distribution of education among the work force.

Appendix: Data sources

Tables 7.1–7.4. Employment figures are taken from *The National Income and Product Accounts of the United States*, 1929–1974, US Department of Commerce, Bureau of Economic Analysis, table 6.8, p. 206. The capital to labor ratios are the ratios of capital stocks to the employment figures in the first columns. The capital stocks by·industry are taken from *The National Wealth of the United States by Major Sector and Industry*, by John W. Kendrick, Kyu Sik Lee and Jean Lomack, The Conference Board, New York, 1976, tables 9 and 10, pp. 78–81. Capital stocks for agriculture are calculated separately by interpolation from data on pp. 76–77. The proportions of employees with four years high school or more and with four years college or more, 1959, are calculated from the *1960 Census of Population, Industrial Characteristics*, US Bureau of Commerce, table 21, pp. 98–101. The corresponding 1969 figures are taken from the *1970 Census of Population, Industrial Characteristics*, US Department of Commerce, table 3, pp. 11–22. Data on the proportion of employees with earnings less than $6,000 are from the same source, table 12, pp. 77–78.

Table 7.5. The sources of data for these figures are the same as those for tables 7.1–7.4. The method of calculation is described in the text.

Table 7.6. The data sources are the same as those for tables 7.3 and 7.4.

Table 7.7. The earnings data are taken from the *1950 United States Census of Population, Industrial Characteristics*, US Department of Commerce, table 17, pp. 75–80. The capital to labor ratios are derived from the same sources as tables 7.1–7.4.

Table 7.8. The sources are the same as those for tables 7.3 and 7.4.

Table 7.10. Educational proportions are from the *1973 Digest of Educational Statistics*, US Department of Health, Education and Welfare, Office of Education, p. 14. The index of capital units per man-hour is taken from *Historical Statistics of the United States, Colonial Times to 1970*, vol. II, US Department of Commerce, Bureau of the Census, p. 948. The ratio of manufacturing to total nonagricultural employment is obtained from the same source, vol. I, p. 137.

Chapter 8

EARNINGS INEQUALITY OVER TIME

1. Introduction

This chapter presents time-series tests of the hypotheses that have been developed in previous chapters and explains what factors have influenced the course of earnings inequality over time. Compared to the apparent reductions in the interwar period, earnings inequality has failed to decline to any significant extent in the postwar period in the United States (Reynolds and Smolensky, 1977, p. 35). The amount of pretransfer poverty (measured without including cash transfers) has been unaffected by recent attention to the issue of poverty (Plotnick and Skidmore, 1975, p. 170). The failure of earnings inequality to decline over time is inconsistent with the expectations of many economists. In the postwar period the general level of education has increased and inequality in the distribution of schooling (at least measured in terms of years of schooling) has generally declined. These changes should have led, according to many economists, to a reduction in earnings inequality. The contrary behavior of earnings inequality constitutes something of a paradox.

In response, the psychologist Arthur Jensen (1969) put forward the argument that earnings and success are primarily determined by genetics, not by education. Similarly, noting the failure of earnings inequality to decline, Thurow (1975) presented a job competition model in which earnings are determined by the job and not by the job holder. Bowles and Gintis (1976, p. 82), in turn, have responded to the paradox with the argument that earnings inequality is created by the capitalist mode of organizing production for the purpose of exerting totalitarian hierarchical control over the activities of workers.

There exists a much more simple explanation of the observed relation: earnings inequality depends on demand variables (capital intensity and the distribution of capital among jobs) as well as supply variables (the distribution of schooling among workers), and the two sets of variables have opposing effects. This is essentially the answer given by Tinbergen (1975a, ch. 6) in describing the course of earnings inequality as a race between technological development and education.

The point to be made here is that one cannot observe the true relation between the distribution of schooling and earnings inequality merely by regressing one on the other. Assuming the relation to be estimated is a reduced form price equation, the relation must include both the supply and the demand variables. Excluding the demand variables results in a substantial mis-specification of the model and leads to biased estimates of the effects of the supply variables.

Two sets of time-series data will be examined in this chapter. The first, covering male income inequality from 1949 to 1969, is taken from an analysis by Chiswick and Mincer (1972) of earnings inequality using the human capital approach. It provides a convenient yardstick with which to compare the results obtained using the theories developed here. The second set of data, compiled by Kuznets (1953), are for the proportions of total earnings received by the upper 1 percent and the upper 5 percent of all income recipients in the period 1918–1948.

2. Male income inequality, 1949–1969

In an attempt to extend the human capital explanation of earnings inequality to time-series analysis, Chiswick and Mincer (1972) used postwar US data to estimate a form for earnings inequality suggested by the Becker-Chiswick model (1966), previously discussed in Chapter 2, section 3. This model implicitly incorporates the efficiency units assumption, so that the derived relation between earnings inequality and the distribution of schooling is consistent with any distribution of schooling. In this Chiswick and Mincer analysis the distributions of schooling, age and weeks worked are assumed to be determined exogenously, and projections of these variables by the US Department of Commerce are used to predict the level of earnings inequality in 1985.

Along with the discussion of their results, the authors of the study published the data on income and schooling inequality. Those data, combined with separately acquired data on the capital variables, are used here to investigate the effects of the capital variables on income inequality and to check on the results of Chiswick and Mincer.

The dependent variable in this data is the variance of the logarithm of income for three groups, males 25 and over, males 25–64, and males 25–34. The variance of the logarithm of income is a standard measure of income inequality and has the feature that it does not depend on the units of measurement. It is closely related to the coefficient of variation, especially for low values.

The major disadvantage with this measure of inequality is that it is for income from all sources, instead of just employment earnings. A major component of income inequality will therefore be the distribution of wealth among individuals. It is conceivable that some of the independent variables will systematically affect the distribution of wealth among individuals or the returns to wealth. In particular, changes in capital intensity could affect factor shares and, via income from capital ownership, the inequality in income distribution. However, if the elasticity of substitution between labor and capital is not too far from one, changes in capital intensity will have a negligible effect on factor shares. The effect of capital intensity on income inequality, via factor shares, could then be ignored. It will be found in the cross-section tests in the following chapter that there is little difference in the results between using income inequality and earnings inequality as the dependent variable.

The corresponding data on the means and standard deviations of schooling also suffer from a shortcoming. These data are calculated separately for each of the three groups. This presumes that the distribution of income for one particular group, say males 25–64, is not affected by the supplies of other workers. In particular, it assumes that the distribution of schooling among females will not affect the distribution of male earnings. This is entirely consistent with the view of the rates of return to schooling for individuals being random variables, as in the Becker-Chiswick analysis, but is inconsistent with these rates of return being affected by supply and demand for workers at different educational levels.

The two major demand variables of interest are the capital to labor ratio, K/L, and the measure of capital concentration, C_ρ. The capital to labor ratio is derived as the ratio of two series, output per man-hour and output per unit of capital, originally developed by Kendrick (1961, 1973). The measure of capital concentration is derived in the previous chapter; its values are given in table 7.7. Simply adding these variables to the list used in the Chiswick and Mincer regressions does not lead to very meaningful results. Twelve parameters are too many to estimate accurately with twenty-one observations. Even the ten parameters estimated by the authors are too many. While the marginal relevance of some of the added supply variables must be granted, their inclusion undoubtedly reduces the accuracy of the estimates of the more fundamental variables. For example, Chiswick and Mincer (1972, p. 46) attribute a substantial amount of income inequality to inequality in weeks worked. But the estimated coefficient for the variance of the logarithm of weeks worked has the wrong sign in all three cases. It is negative, implying that increases in the inequality in the distribution of employment reduce income inequality.

The best estimates of the coefficients can be obtained by reducing the included variables to the basic supply and demand variables, those for schooling and capital. With these four variables included, the typical equation as it will be estimated is

$$V = a_0 + a_1 \ln(\overline{S}) + \ln(S.D.(S)) + a_3 \ln(K/L) + a_4 \ln(C_\rho) + e,$$

where V is the variance of the logarithms of incomes and e is an independently, identically distributed random error term. To use Tinbergen's terminology (1975a, ch. 3), this is a reduced form price equation.

Ordinary least squares regressions of this equation are presented in tables 8.1–8.3. The first column presents the results using the schooling variables alone. (Columns one and two are presented in order to show potential biases from mis-specification.) The coefficient of the logarithm of mean schooling is positive for all three groups, and is significant at conventional levels for the first two. Column two in each table presents the results adding only the term for the capital to labor ratio, $\ln(K/L)$. In all three cases the estimated coefficient is

Table 8.1
Income inequality, males 25 and over, 1949–1969.

	(1)	(2)	(3)	(4)	(5)
$\ln(\overline{S}_1)$, log of mean schooling, males 25 and over	0.917* (3.34)	−1.30 (1.65)	−2.21* (3.18)	−2.96 (1.91)	−2.27* (3.23)
$\ln(S.D.(S_1))$, log of standard deviation of schooling	2.00* (3.57)	0.878 (1.45)	−0.806 (1.13)	−0.851 (0.980)	−1.06 (1.37)
$\ln(K/L)$, log of capital to labor ratio		0.597* (2.94)	−0.004 (0.015)	0.038 (0.126)	−0.047 (0.182)
$\ln(C_\rho)$, log of capital concentration			1.81* (3.20)	1.83* (2.44)	2.09* (3.23)
$\ln(U)$, log of unemployment rate				−0.002 (0.045)	
T, time (year)				−0.039 (0.192)	
$\ln(P)$, log of productivity				0.416 (1.20)	
$\ln(M)$, log of ratio of manufacturing to total nonfarm employment					0.215 (0.897)
Constant	−3.97	2.70	6.19	7.08	6.78
Adjusted R^2	0.350	0.543	0.704	0.685	0.701
Durbin-Watson statistic	1.52	1.80	2.20	2.40	2.23

Dependent variable: variance of logarithms of incomes, males 25 and over, 1949–1969.
Positive values of t-statistics are given in parentheses under estimated coefficients.
Asterisk denotes significance at 0.05 level.
Data sources: see appendix.

Table 8.2
Income inequality, males 25–64, 1949–1969.

	(1)	(2)	(3)	(4)	(5)
ln($\overline{S}_2$)	1.17* (2.77)	−1.68 (1.79)	−2.84* (4.34)	−2.44 (1.98)	−2.77* (4.26)
ln(S.D. (S_2))	2.67* (3.24)	1.35 (1.73)	−1.34 (1.80)	−0.820 (1.01)	−1.03 (1.31)
ln(K/L)		0.741* (3.26)	−0.273 (1.08)	−0.262 (1.04)	−0.222 (0.871)
ln(C_ρ)			2.67* (4.93)	1.85* (3.01)	2.36* (3.93)
ln(U)				0.057 (2.01)	
T				0.032 (0.202)	
ln(P)				0.141 (0.490)	
ln(M)					−0.252 (1.14)
Constant	−5.55	2.90	7.83	6.14	7.14
Adjusted R^2	0.316	0.554	0.812	0.843	0.816
Durbin-Watson statistics	1.08	1.15	1.83	1.87	1.81

Dependent variable: variance of logarithms of incomes, males 25–64, 1949–1969.
Positive values of t-statistics are given in parentheses under estimated coefficients.
Asterisk denotes significance at 0.05 level.
Data sources: see appendix.

positive and significant. This result suggests that increases in the aggregate capital to labor ratio are associated with greater income inequality.

However, following previous discussion, the increases in the capital to labor ratio for the economy can come about in two ways. First, each sector can have increases in the amount of capital per worker. Secondly, the aggregate increase in the capital to labor ratio can come about from shifts in production to the more capital-intensive sectors, which would generally result in greater capital concentration.

Evidence on the source of the positive association between the capital to labor ratio and income inequality is provided by the regressions in column three of each table. When the capital concentration term is added, the coefficient for the logarithm of the capital to labor ratio is no longer significant. The coeffi-

Table 8.3
Income inequality, males 25–34, 1949–1969.

	(1)	(2)	(3)	(4)	(5)
$\ln(\bar{S}_3)$	0.072 (0.274)	−1.59 (2.07)	−1.36 (1.84)	−0.654 (0.522)	−1.63* (2.31)
$\ln(\text{S.D.}\,(S_3))$	1.09 (1.43)	1.07 (1.57)	0.242 (0.297)	−2.03* (2.17)	−1.10 (1.04)
$\ln(K/L)$		0.552* (2.28)	−0.092 (0.205)	−1.60* (2.68)	−0.597 (1.19)
$\ln(C_\rho)$			1.36 (1.67)	1.41 (1.68)	1.80* (2.26)
$\ln(U)$				0.178* (3.01)	
T				0.567* (2.98)	
$\ln(P)$				−1.30* (2.40)	
$\ln(M)$					−0.890 (1.83)
Constant	−0.975	3.03	2.90	6.06	3.95
Adjusted R^2	0.089	0.261	0.332	0.573	0.418
Durbin-Watson statistics	1.64	1.74	1.89	1.82	1.90

Dependent variable: variance of logarithms of incomes, males 25–64, 1949–1969.
Positive values of t-statistics are given in parentheses under estimated coefficients.
Asterisk denotes significance at 0.05 level.
Data sources: see appendix.

cients of the capital concentration terms are positive and are significant for the first two groups. Furthermore, the explanatory power of the model is greatly improved by the addition of the capital concentration term. These results strongly support the argument that intersectoral shifts in employment, and accompanying changes in capital concentration, are responsible for changes in income inequality. Increases in the capital to labor ratios in each industry, holding capital concentration fixed, are apparently not responsible, according to these results.

Comparing columns one and three, the addition of the demand variables alters drastically the estimated impact of increases in mean schooling. In column three of each table the estimated coefficient for the logarithm of the mean level of schooling for each group is negative, and significant for the first two groups.

This indicates that increases in mean schooling reduce income inequality, contrary to the results in column one. Which results should one believe? The large increases in explanatory power obtained by adding the demand variables suggest that the model estimated in column one is mis-specified, so that the estimated coefficients in that column are biased to the extent that they are correlated with the demand variables. It follows that the positive value for the coefficient of the logarithm of the mean schooling in column one is incorrect. The question of the effect of schooling on income and earnings inequality is an extremely important one. A full discussion of these effects will be delayed until after the cross-section results of the next chapter are presented.

The results with both schooling and demand variables included can be compared with those obtained by Chiswick and Mincer. Using nine, nine, and six variables for the three groups, they obtained adjusted R^2 statistics of 0.54, 0.79 and 0.25.[1] Using just four variables, the regressions in column three yield higher adjusted R^2 statistics in all three cases: 0.704, 0.812 and 0.332, respectively.

It is conceivable that the significance of the capital concentration term for the first two groups arises from its correlation with some other, "true" explanatory variable. To investigate this possibility, column four re-estimates the equation with a time variable and the logarithm of the unemployment rate added. Also, the logarithm of a productivity index, as measured by output per unit of input, is added to investigate the possible effects of technological change. The results are presented in column four. For the first two groups, the added coefficients for the added variables are not significant, and the previously estimated coefficients remain more or less unaffected. For the third group, males 25–34, the estimated coefficients are significant, and the coefficients for the standard deviation of schooling and the capital to labor ratio are affected. Probably these results occur because the group males 25–34 represents such a small proportion of total employment, and the labor supply conditions of other groups affect income inequality in this group.

In an attempt to discover if the division of employment between manufacturing and nonfarm nonmanufacturing has any effect on income inequality beyond its effect via capital concentration, the regression equation in column three was re-estimated with a term added for the logarithm of the ratio of manufacturing to total nonfarm employment. The resulting coefficient is not significant for any of the three groups, but the coefficient for the capital concentration term remains positive and significant at conventional levels.

[1] For the second group, males 25–64, Chiswick and Mincer report an adjusted R^2 statistic of 0.87. But the figure obtained by repeating their regression and the figure consistent with their reported multiple R of 0.9365 is 0.79. The 0.87 figure is in fact the unadjusted R^2.

Table 8.4
Income inequality, 1949–1969, linear relation.

	Males 25 and over (1)	Males 25–64 (2)	Males 25–34 (3)
Mean schooling	−0.234* (3.25)	−0.288* (4.21)	−0.137 (1.81)
Standard deviation of schooling	−0.357 (1.46)	−0.500 (1.86)	0.121 (0.572)
K/L	−0.082 (0.276)	−0.273 (0.857)	0.066 (0.164)
C_ρ	1.34* (3.37)	1.73* (4.51)	0.720 (1.79)
Constant	2.51	3.05	0.441
Adjusted R^2	0.706	0.798	0.314
Durbin-Watson statistic	2.21	1.77	1.85

Dependent variable   variance of logarithms of male incomes, various
    age groups.
Asterisk denotes significance at 0.05 level.

To investigate the importance of functional form, the model was also estimated using a linear relation among the variables. The results are presented in
table 8.4 and are substantially the same as when the model is estimated in
loglinear form. For the first two groups, the estimated coefficients for the capital concentration term are positive and significant and for mean schooling they
are negative and significant.

The major conclusions from these time-series tests is that income inequality
depends positively and significantly on the concentration of capital among jobs
and negatively and significantly on the mean level of schooling. The results show
no evidence that economy-wide changes in the capital to labor ratio (i.e. holding
capital concentration fixed) have any systematic effect on income inequality.
The differential rents theory of Chapter 6 is therefore strongly supported.

The shortcomings of this type of time-series analysis are revealed in table 8.5,
which gives the correlation coefficients for the independent variables in table 8.2. It can be seen that the correlations among the schooling and capital
variables are quite high. The multicollinearity among independent variables is of
course as much a problem for the original Chiswick-Mincer study as it is for the
results presented here. One consequence of a high correlation between two
explanatory variables is that there is a correspondingly high correlation between

Table 8.5
Correlation coefficients for variables in table 8.2.

	$\ln(\bar{S}_2)$	$\ln(\text{S.D.}(S_2))$	$\ln(K/L)$	$\ln(C_\rho)$	$\ln(U)$	T	$\ln(P)$	$\ln(M)$
$\ln(\bar{S}_2)$	1.00							
$\ln(\text{S.D.}(S_2))$	−0.943	1.00						
$\ln(K/L)$	0.981	−0.891	1.00					
$\ln(C_\rho)$	0.945	−0.806	0.981	1.00				
$\ln(U)$	−0.059	0.248	0.082	0.218	1.00			
T	0.998	−0.943	0.985	0.950	−0.031	1.00		
$\ln(P)$	0.992	−0.941	0.972	0.936	−0.043	0.995	1.00	
$\ln(M)$	−0.931	0.852	−0.942	−0.938	−0.237	−0.943	−0.930	1.00

the estimated coefficients. Although the expected values of the estimated coefficients are the true values, the *t*-statistics do not necessarily reflect the accuracy of the estimates.

3. Upper income shares

The second set of data is taken from Kuznets's classic study of upper income groups (1953). The data are for the share of total earnings received by the top 1 percent and the top 5 percent of income recipients. That is to say, one finds the 1 (or 5) percent of the population with the highest incomes and finds the share of the total population's earnings going to them. The data cover the period 1917–1948, with two discontinuities arising from changes in underlying measurements.

For the purposes of the investigation undertaken here, the data suffer from two disadvantages. First, the data do not themselves measure earnings or income inequality. However, the share of earnings going to upper income recipients is an important determinant of earnings inequality: the greater the shares, the greater the earnings and income inequality.

The second difficulty with the data is that they are for the top 1 and 5 percent of all income recipients, instead of just earnings recipients. The top 1 percent, for example, includes individuals who receive their incomes from sources other than earnings, in particular, from the ownership of property or capital. It is therefore conceivable that changes in capital intensity could change the proportion of the top 1 or the top 5 percent of income receivers who get their income earnings. However, if fewer upper-income recipients get their income from earnings as capital intensity increases, then one would expect a negative relation between capital intensity and earnings share instead of the positive one predicted by capital-skill complementarity and the theory of Chapter 4. Whether capital intensity affects earnings shares through the proportions of income coming from earnings will be examined by including variables for the proportion of income for each group coming from earnings.

Data on capital concentration are not available for the period under consideration, although the capital to labor ratio is available from the same source as used in the previous section. The results of Chapter 7 suggest that the level of capital concentration is strongly affected by the division of employment between manufacturing and nonfarm nonmanufacturing. This is because as a class nonfarm nonmanufacturing industries have much higher capital to labor ratios. This relation is confirmed by the correlation coefficient between the logarithm of capital concentration and the logarithm of the ratio of manufacturing to total nonfarm employment. From table 8.4 the value of this correlation is -0.938.[2] In the absence of a measurement of capital concentration, therefore, the ratio of manufacturing to total nonfarm employment may be used as a proxy. The greater the value of this variable, the lower the level of capital concentration.

Data on the mean and standard deviation of schooling for the working population are also unavailable. Instead, data on educational attainments for the population as a whole are interpolated from statistics by decades (presented in table 7.10 of Chapter 7). The two variables used are E_1, the proportion of the population with four years of high school or more, and E_2, the proportion of the population with four years of college or more.

The form of the basic model as it will be estimated is

$$\ln(Y_1) = a_0 + a_1 \ln(E_1) + a_2 \ln(E_2) + a_3 T + a_4 \ln(K/L) + a_5 \ln(M) + $$
$$a_6 \ln(Q_1) + e,$$

where

Y_1 = the proportion of total earnings received by the top one per cent of all income recipients;

[2] An ordinary least-squares regression of the measure of capital concentration on the capital to labor ratio and the ratio of manufacturing to total nonfarm employment, covering the period 1948–1970, yields

$$C_\rho = 1.21 + 0.493\ K/L - 0.438\ M,$$
$$\quad\quad\quad (3.89) \quad\quad\quad (0.428)$$

with R^2 equal to 0.926 and the Durbin-Watson statistic equal to 0.491. Using the Cochrane-Orcutt iterative procedure, the R^2 is raised to 0.975 and the coefficient of the capital to labor becomes negative but not significant. Apparently the multicollinearity prevents accurate estimation of the coefficients, even though the explanatory power of the relation is quite high.

E_1 = the proportion of the population with four years high school or more;
E_2 = the proportion of the population with four years college or more;
T = time, in years;
K/L = the capital to labor ratio;
M = the ratio of manufacturing to total nonfarm employment;
Q_1 = the proportion of income coming from compensation for the top one per cent of all income recipients; and
e = the identically, normally distributed random error term.

The time subscripts have been suppressed. The model for the top 5 percent of income recipients is analogous.

Table 8.6
Top 1 percent, 1917–1948.

	(1)	(2)	(3)	(4)	(5)
$\ln(E_1)$, log of proportion of population with four years high school or more	−3.76 (1.23)	−0.260 (0.147)	2.10 (1.69)	0.586 (0.342)	1.22 (0.676)
$\ln(E_2)$, log of proportion of population with four years college or more	−2.73 (0.603)	−5.97* (2.25)	−9.15* (4.98)	−6.42* (2.27)	−7.48* (2.48)
T, time (year)	1.21* (3.24)	0.991* (4.36)	1.08* (7.06)	0.905* (4.36)	1.03* (4.04)
$\ln(K/L)$, log of capital to labor ratio		0.951* (4.72)	0.379 (1.81)	0.091 (0.293)	−0.007 (0.020)
$\ln(M)$, log of ratio of manufacturing to total employment			−0.657* (3.91)	−0.613* (3.61)	−0.684* (3.46)
$\ln(Q_1)$, log of proportion of income from compensation				0.293 (1.26)	0.203 (0.779)
$\ln(P)$, log of productivity					−0.360 (0.852)
$\ln(U)$, log of unemployment rate					−0.001 (0.118)
Constant	15.0	9.77	6.30	6.19	6.42
Rho used in transformation	0.664	0.498	0.323	0.333	0.276
R^2	0.907	0.948	0.966	0.968	0.969
Durbin-Watson statistic	1.47	1.48	1.74	1.83	1.80

Dependent variable: logarithm of share of total earnings received by top 5 percent of all income recipients.
Positive values t-statistics are given in parentheses under estimated coefficients.
Asterisk denotes significance at 0.05 level.

Table 8.7
Top 5 percent, 1917–1948.

	(1)	(2)	(3)	(4)	(5)
$\ln(E_1)$	−4.61 (1.46)	0.427 (0.394)	1.65 (1.54)	0.156 (0.116)	0.994 (0.737)
$\ln(E_2)$	−1.53 (0.329)	−6.61* (4.04)	−8.26* (5.30)	−4.78 (1.92)	−6.61* (2.49)
T	1.25* (3.23)	0.998* (6.77)	1.05* (7.92)	0.723* (3.20)	0.983* (3.37)
$\ln(K/L)$		1.15* (7.78)	0.858* (4.63)	0.360 (1.08)	0.274 (0.777)
$\ln(M)$			−0.354* (2.32)	−0.452* (2.83)	−0.512* (3.06)
$\ln(Q_2)$				0.442 (1.75)	0.251 (0.852)
$\ln(P)$					−0.508 (1.26)
$\ln(U)$					−0.007 (0.643)
Constant	16.9	9.64	7.80	6.01	7.18
Rho used in transformation	0.665	0.273	0.228	0.271	0.154
R^2	0.879	0.954	0.962	0.967	0.968
Durbin-Watson statistic	1.59	1.88	2.04	2.16	1.97

Dependent variable: logarithm of share of total earnings received by top 5 percent of all income recipients.
Positive values of t-statistics are given in parentheses under estimated coefficients.
Asterisk denotes significance at 0.05 level.

Because ordinary least squares estimates of this equation indicate substantial serial correlation of the residuals, the equation has been estimated using the Cochrane-Orcutt iterative technique (Cochrane and Orcutt, 1949). The results are presented in tables 8.6 and 8.7, along with the final values of the rho used in the transformation and the Durbin-Watson statistics. Column one gives the results using only the education and time variables. These variables by themselves explain much of the variance in upper income shares over time. The results in column two show the improvement when the term for the capital to labor ratio alone is introduced. The coefficient for this term is positive and significant for both groups. For the top 5 percent it remains significant when the ratio of manufacturing to total employment is introduced in the third column, although it appears to be reduced. The coefficient for the manufacturing ratio is negative and significant, as expected from the differential rents theory. However, when the term for the proportion of income from compensation is introduced in column four, the coefficient for the capital to labor ratio is no longer significant, although it is still positive. The coefficient for the manufacturing ratio continues to be significant and negative. In column five the possible influence of two other variables is investigated, the unemployment rate and productivity (these are the same series used in the analysis of section 2). Neither of these variables has a coefficient significant at conventional levels and the coefficient of the manufacturing ratio term continues to be negative and significant. These results give strong support to the differential rents theory of Chapter 6.

In all forms of estimation the coefficient for the time term is positive and significant. This comes as something of a surprise. Despite the long-run decrease in upper-income shares over the period in question, the results indicate that there was a strong upward trend, countered by the changes in the other variables. In particular, everywhere but in column one the coefficient for the proportion of the population with four years of college or more is negative and significant. This indicates that the upward trend in this proportion significantly reduced the shares of earnings going to upper income recipients, presumably by reducing the scarcity of individuals with potentially high earnings. Except in the first column, the coefficient for the proportion of the population with four years high school or more is positive, although it is not always significant. The coefficients of the education and time variables may not be reliably estimated because of multicollinearity. This is revealed in table 8.8, which shows substantial correlation among the education and time variables and moderate or little correlation among the capital and other variables.

Table 8.8
Correlation coefficients for variables in tables 8.6 and 8.7.

	$\ln(E_1)$	$\ln(E_2)$	T	$\ln(K/L)$	$\ln(M)$	$\ln(S_1)$	$\ln(S_2)$	$\ln(U)$	$\ln(P)$
$\ln(E_1)$	1.00								
$\ln(E_2)$	0.998	1.00							
T	0.990	0.995	1.00						
$\ln(K/L)$	0.179	0.222	0.269	1.00					
$\ln(M)$	0.239	0.189	0.151	−0.744	1.00				
$\ln(Q_1)$	0.029	0.042	0.080	0.705	−0.530	1.00			
$\ln(Q_2)$	0.343	0.360	0.429	0.787	−0.357	0.666	1.00		
$\ln(U)$	0.060	0.070	0.087	0.092	−0.250	0.161	0.084	1.00	
$\ln(P)$	0.970	0.968	0.962	0.041	0.290	−0.109	0.224	0.070	1.00

4. Conclusions

The time-series estimates of this chapter provide substantial evidence on the validity of the theories developed in Chapters 4, 5 and 6. The results indicate a strong association between capital intensity in the economy and the amount of income inequality. This is indicated by the positive and significant coefficients for the capital to labor term when other demand terms are not included. However, the association between capital intensity and income inequality does not appear to be brought about by economy-wide increases in the capital to labor ratio, as suggested by the aggregate theory of Chapter 4. Instead, increases in the capital to labor ratio and increases in income inequality are both brought about by a deeper, underlying change in the economy, the shift in production and employment from labor-intensive to capital-intensive sectors. When the term for the concentration of capital among jobs is included in the regression equations, the coefficient for the capital to labor term is no longer in general significant. The coefficient of the capital concentration term or its proxy in the Kuznets series, the ratio of manufacturing to total nonfarm nonmanufacturing employment, is almost always positive and significant, even when the time and unemployment variables are included. The results therefore give strong support to the differential rents theory of Chapter 6.

One aspect of the theory of Chapter 4 is strongly supported. This is the negative relation between mean schooling and income inequality. The higher the level of mean schooling, the lower the inequality. The conditions under which this result comes about, developed in Chapter 4, section 6, are independent of the conditions under which greater capital intensity causes greater earnings inequality. It is therefore possible that one set of conditions holds and the other does not. The whole subject of the effect of schooling on earnings inequality will be taken up in Chapter 9. It is sufficient at this point to note that the inclusion of demand variables in the estimated model of earnings inequality removes the bias which invalidates much previous work and indicates a negative and significant coefficient for mean schooling.

The empirical results of this chapter provide an answer to the question of why income inequality has failed to decline significantly in the postwar period, despite substantial increases in mean schooling and reductions in the inequality in the distribution of schooling. The answer is that the positive effects of these changes have been offset by increases in the concentration of capital among jobs. The general process of capital accumulation involves a shift in production and employment to relatively capital-intensive sectors. This process tends to increase the amount of earnings inequality, unless counteracted by other changes in the economy. It is therefore incorrect to state that changes in the distribution of schooling have had no effect or a negligible effect on earnings inequality: these changes have succeeded in preventing the earnings inequality from getting progressively worse.

Appendix: Sources of data

Tables 8.1–8.5. The variances of logarithms of incomes, and the means and standard deviations of schooling for the three groups are published in Chiswick and Mincer (1972, pp. 59–65). The capital per worker time series is the ratio of two time series, output per unit of capital divided by output per man-hour, published in the US Department of Commerce's *Historical Statistics of the United States, Colonial Times to 1970*, part 2, p. 948. The data were originally developed by Kendrick (1961, 1973). The same sources provide a series for output per unit of input, which is used as the measure of productivity. The unemployment rate and the ratio of manufacturing to total nonfarm employment are also taken from *Historical Statistics*, p. 135 and p. 137, respectively.

Tables 8.6–8.8. The data on shares of earnings received by the upper 1 percent and upper 5 percent of all income recipients were developed by Simon Kuznets and published in Kuznets (1953, p. 646, and p. 649, respectively). They are reprinted in *Historical Statistics*, p. 302. The corresponding data on the percentage of income coming from employee compensation is published in Kuznets (1953, p. 668 and p. 671) for the upper 1 percent and upper 5 percent, respectively. The proportion of the population with four years high school or more and four years college or more are interpolated from decade statistics published by the Office of Education, US Department of Health, Education, and Welfare, *Digest of Educational Statistics* (1973, p. 14). The capital to labor ratio, ratio of manufacturing to total nonfarm employment, productivity and unemployment rate are taken from the same sources as tables 8.1–8.5.

Chapter 9

CROSS-SECTION STUDIES

1. Introduction

This chapter uses cross-section data to investigate the relation between earnings inequality and various determinants. Because such data are readily available, many other economists have used similar data (see Ahmad and Miller, 1961; Aigner and Heins, 1967; Burns and Frech III, 1970; Chiswick, 1968, 1974; Conlisk, 1967; Danziger, 1976; Farbman, 1975; Formby and Seaks, 1978; Hirsch, 1978a, 1978b; Sale, 1974; Schultz, 1965; Singh and Sale, 1978; and Tannen, 1976).

Cross-section data have an important advantage over time-series data in the study of earnings inequality. There is generally more widespread variation in the variables among states or regions, so that the problems of serial correlation and multicollinearity are avoided. On the other hand, cross-section data have important disadvantages. Each state or region used for an observation is not a closed economy. Mobility can therefore arise to affect the outcomes. Another difficulty with cross-section data is that there are more differences in unobserved variables, thereby creating a greater potential for biases in estimated coefficients if these variables are correlated with included variables.

Mobility can arise from both movement of workers and movement of industries. With complete mobility, wage differentials and profit rates will be equalized across states or regions. For example, suppose there is an increase in the supply of workers with four years college or more. In a closed economy the wage differential between these workers and workers with four years high school would be reduced. But with complete mobility, in response to any reduction in the wage rate for workers with four years of college, those workers would migrate to areas or regions where the wage rate was not reduced. The supply of workers with four years college would then return to its former level. With wage differentials equalized between observational areas, the distribution of earnings could be described equally well either by the supplies of workers at the common wage differentials or the demands for workers. It would further be impossible to discover the unbiased aggregate effects of either the supply or the demand variables on earnings inequality, since the effects on wage differentials could not be detected. However, mobility between states is undoubtedly not perfect, and the wage differentials that arise will not be equalized across states. It will then be possible to observe the effects of the supply or demand variables on earnings inequality not only through the numbers of individuals at different schooling levels but through the wage differentials that arise. Nevertheless, one should be aware that, using states as observational areas, the effects on wage differentials will be less than if the states were closed economies, with no mobility.

2. Data

2.1. Inequality measures

Most of the data for the cross-section tests of this chapter are taken from the 1960 and 1970 US censuses of the population. The census provides data on the distribution of earnings and income and on the distributions of schooling, employment and age by state and smaller areas. For this study, states are chosen as the observational unit, since they are generally large enough to constitute separate although interdependent economies. Other studies have used standard metropolitan statistical areas as the observational units. Although the 1970 census provides published income concentration statistics (Gini coefficients) for many distributions, the measure of inequality chosen for use in this chapter is the coefficient of variation, the standard deviation divided by the mean. This is the measure suggested by the analysis of Chapter 4. The sensitivity of the results to the measure of inequality will be examined by use of the Gini coefficients as alternative measures. In addition, the results will be reported for both earnings and income inequality (income includes returns from the ownership of property and other sources).

For 1959, the census reports earnings and incomes in nine brackets. For the first eight brackets, all individuals with earnings or income in that bracket were assumed to have earnings or income equal to the midpoint of the bracket. However, the upper bracket is open-ended ($10,000 and above). For this bracket, an average of $14,400 was chosen, based on a study of the distribution of incomes within brackets by Seiver (1979). The same study provides estimates of the true means within brackets for the 1970 census. These figures have been used in place of the simple midpoints of the brackets. The average income for the top bracket ($25,000 and above) is calculated to be $37,500.

The resulting measures of earnings inequality are given in tables 9.1 and 9.2 for males and for males and females combined, along with some of the other data used.

Table 9.1
Selected data for 1959 cross-section estimations.

		Coefficient of variation of male earnings	Coefficient of variation of earnings, males and females	Coefficient of variation of male incomes	Coefficient of variation of incomes, males and females
1.	Alabama	0.822	0.839	0.854	1.012
2.	Arizona	0.702	0.785	0.702	0.854
3.	Arkansas	0.883	0.944	0.928	1.073
4.	California	0.620	0.711	0.630	0.793
5.	Colorado	0.662	0.753	0.666	0.826
6.	Connecticut	0.603	0.700	0.609	0.782
7.	Delaware	0.668	0.772	0.677	0.850
8.	Florida	0.751	0.857	0.774	0.938
9.	Georgia	0.830	0.905	0.844	0.993
10.	Idaho	0.692	0.791	0.677	0.848
11.	Illinois	0.615	0.707	0.635	0.802
12.	Indiana	0.636	0.726	0.647	0.817
13.	Iowa	0.724	0.813	0.726	0.891
14.	Kansas	0.701	0.796	0.708	0.875
15.	Kentucky	0.799	0.853	0.836	0.967
16.	Louisiana	0.778	0.871	0.814	0.983
17.	Maine	0.674	0.761	0.703	0.864
18.	Maryland	0.659	0.750	0.662	0.820
19.	Massachusetts	0.627	0.725	0.640	0.813
20.	Michigan	0.625	0.716	0.633	0.797
21.	Minnesota	0.702	0.791	0.711	0.868
22.	Mississippi	0.963	1.028	0.991	1.131
23.	Missouri	0.707	0.785	0.752	0.910
24.	Montana	0.688	0.782	0.688	0.846
25.	Nebraska	0.737	0.821	0.735	0.886
26.	Nevada	0.624	0.717	0.627	0.766
27.	New Hampshire	0.649	0.740	0.664	0.829
28.	New Jersey	0.598	0.696	0.614	0.785
29.	New Mexico	0.703	0.789	0.704	0.848
30.	New York	0.631	0.713	0.653	0.805
31.	North Carolina	0.842	0.887	0.852	0.969
32.	North Dakota	0.773	0.852	0.766	0.904
33.	Ohio	0.611	0.707	0.630	0.808
34.	Oklahoma	0.748	0.828	0.784	0.944
35.	Oregon	0.629	0.733	0.655	0.836
36.	Pennsylvania	0.636	0.725	0.659	0.822
37.	Rhode Island	0.633	0.724	0.659	0.824
38.	South Carolina	0.856	0.916	0.851	0.873

Table 9.1 continued

		Coefficient of variation of male earnings	Coefficient of variation of earnings, males and females	Coefficient of variation of male incomes	Coefficient of variation of incomes, males and females
39.	South Dakota	0.790	0.875	0.796	0.936
40.	Tennessee	0.837	0.896	0.860	0.991
41.	Texas	0.763	0.847	0.767	0.927
42.	Utah	0.640	0.746	0.609	0.793
43.	Vermont	0.725	0.803	0.726	0.885
44.	Virginia	0.776	0.846	0.782	0.922
45.	Washington	0.619	0.720	0.640	0.813
46.	West Virginia	0.702	0.777	0.758	0.909
47.	Wisconsin	0.644	0.739	0.658	0.833
48.	Wyoming	0.652	0.759	0.645	0.815

		$\overline{S}_m$ mean schooling males (years)	S.D.(S_m) standard deviation of schooling, males (years)	$\overline{S}$ mean schooling males and females (years)	S.D.(S) standard deviation of schooling males and females (years)
1.	Alabama	8.546	4.338	8.603	4.299
2.	Arizona	10.027	4.237	10.171	4.130
3.	Arkansas	8.446	4.171	8.558	4.096
4.	California	10.754	3.881	10.751	3.748
5.	Colorado	10.728	3.796	10.778	3.699
6.	Connecticut	10.249	3.927	10.172	3.863
7.	Delaware	10.249	4.044	10.226	3.885
8.	Florida	9.808	4.130	9.855	4.001
9.	Georgia	8.537	4.498	8.604	4.390
10.	Idaho	10.463	3.444	10.554	3.342
11.	Illinois	10.035	3.759	9.971	3.678
12.	Indiana	10.023	3.531	10.062	3.441
13.	Iowa	10.139	3.373	10.254	3.319
14.	Kansas	10.438	3.546	10.476	3.473
15.	Kentucky	8.423	4.044	8.651	3.985
16.	Louisiana	8.367	4.732	8.337	4.703
17.	Maine	9.934	3.447	10.065	3.352
18.	Maryland	9.861	4.144	9.850	4.000
19.	Massachusetts	10.418	3.851	10.314	3.785
20.	Michigan	9.970	3.645	10.028	3.593
21.	Minnesota	10.066	3.562	10.163	3.510
22.	Mississippi	8.220	4.472	8.367	4.383
23.	Missouri	9.545	3.765	9.567	3.687
24.	Montana	10.227	3.508	10.388	3.468
25.	Nebraska	10.308	3.386	10.387	3.355
26.	Nevada	10.772	3.521	10.893	3.381

Table 9.1 continued

		$\bar{S}_m$ mean schooling males (years)	S.D.(S_m) standard deviation of schooling, males (years)	$\bar{S}$ mean schooling males and females (years)	S.D.(S) standard deviation of schooling males and females (years)
27.	New Hampshire	10.087	3.542	10.125	3.473
28.	New Jersey	10.121	3.941	9.973	3.852
29.	New Mexico	9.992	4.393	10.085	4.359
30.	New York	10.123	4.001	10.025	3.946
31.	North Carolina	8.391	4.372	8.652	4.325
32.	North Dakota	9.489	3.532	9.659	3.578
33.	Ohio	10.068	3.649	10.067	3.574
34.	Oklahoma	9.725	4.068	9.762	3.986
35.	Oregon	10.495	3.522	10.605	3.416
36.	Pennsylvania	9.736	3.754	9.693	3.698
37.	Rhode Island	9.645	3.796	9.527	3.737
38.	South Carolina	8.209	4.560	8.414	4.528
39.	South Dakota	9.835	3.364	9.981	3.396
40.	Tennessee	8.546	4.218	8.772	4.120
41.	Texas	9.413	4.448	9.525	4.339
42.	Utah	11.333	3.446	11.257	3.360
43.	Vermont	10.002	3.477	10.239	3.412
44.	Virginia	9.078	4.501	9.330	4.361
45.	Washington	10.719	3.561	10.760	3.450
46.	West Virginia	8.790	3.925	8.986	3.922
47.	Wisconsin	9.853	3.597	9.910	3.558
48.	Wyoming	10.597	3.517	10.741	3.439

		K/L estimated capital to labor ratio	C_ρ estimated capital concentration	G manufacturing capital per worker ($1000)	M ratio of manufacturing total nonfarm employment
1.	Alabama	17.362	1.685	12.700	0.324
2.	Arizona	11.194	1.688	8.929	0.048
3.	Arkansas	10.715	1.650	7.477	0.074
4.	California	16.678	1.685	7.640	0.291
5.	Colorado	19.111	1.705	7.930	0.187
6.	Connecticut	14.982	1.595	6.568	0.447
7.	Delaware	19.801	1.510	13.199	0.388
8.	Florida	16.581	1.721	10.594	0.235
9.	Georgia	15.977	1.783	7.744	0.321
10.	Idaho	20.732	1.753	11.074	0.183
11.	Illinois	19.376	1.677	8.980	0.371
12.	Indiana	18.652	1.624	12.098	0.413
13.	Iowa	17.701	1.759	9.574	0.254
14.	Kansas	22.062	1.731	10.678	0.212

Table 9.1 continued

		K/L estimated capital to labor ratio	C_ρ estimated capital concentration	G manufacturing capital per worker ($1000)	M ratio of manufacturing to total nonfarm employment
15.	Kentucky	20.597	1.654	10.223	0.272
16.	Louisiana	20.438	1.583	24.260	0.186
17.	Maine	16.109	1.779	8.212	0.389
18.	Maryland	18.659	1.723	11.097	0.305
19.	Massachusetts	14.594	1.673	4.665	0.401
20.	Michigan	16.550	1.581	10.468	0.426
21.	Minnesota	18.212	1.703	7.505	0.363
22.	Mississippi	15.879	1.810	6.865	0.264
23.	Missouri	17.694	1.740	7.031	0.396
24.	Montana	24.879	1.683	20.226	0.134
25.	Nebraska	21.648	1.816	8.941	0.172
26.	Nevada	18.733	1.788	19.440	0.077
27.	New Hampshire	13.485	1.708	5.110	0.452
28.	New Jersey	17.417	1.596	8.915	0.406
29.	New Mexico	21.361	1.666	11.844	0.093
30.	New York	15.878	1.696	5.521	0.329
31.	North Carolina	14.166	1.686	6.515	0.393
32.	North Dakota	20.483	1.832	15.855	0.061
33.	Ohio	18.576	1.609	10.708	0.421
34.	Oklahoma	19.410	1.585	9.619	0.206
35.	Oregon	17.922	1.786	10.296	0.279
36.	Pennsylvania	19.618	1.613	9.388	0.412
37.	Rhode Island	14.436	1.595	5.099	0.453
38.	South Carolina	13.757	1.793	8.300	0.418
39.	South Dakota	16.536	1.787	6.427	0.107
40.	Tennessee	17.317	1.745	8.363	0.318
41.	Texas	20.016	1.634	18.094	0.200
42.	Utah	22.261	1.638	11.750	0.199
43.	Vermont	16.659	1.752	5.743	0.308
44.	Virginia	18.558	1.707	7.872	0.279
45.	Washington	17.506	1.707	10.375	0.293
46.	West Virginia	26.477	1.428	19.926	0.264
47.	Wisconsin	16.711	1.652	7.584	0.402
48.	Wyoming	27.121	1.578	24.902	0.126

Table 9.2
Selected data for 1969 cross-section estimations.

		Coefficient of variation of male earnings	Coefficient of variation of earnings, males and females	Coefficient of variation of male incomes	Coefficient of variation of incomes males and females
1.	Alabama	0.892	0.998	0.939	1.090
2.	Arizona	0.879	0.997	0.880	1.035
3.	Arkansas	0.958	1.051	0.998	1.130
4.	California	0.847	0.955	0.856	1.002
5.	Colorado	0.901	1.025	0.887	1.047
6.	Connecticut	0.842	1.002	0.832	1.014
7.	Delaware	0.835	0.969	0.845	1.021
8.	Florida	0.941	1.056	0.960	1.123
9.	Georgia	0.925	1.020	0.948	1.084
10.	Idaho	0.908	1.067	0.870	1.036
11.	Illinois	0.801	0.932	0.812	0.979
12.	Indiana	0.778	0.912	0.779	0.956
13.	Iowa	0.874	1.020	0.862	1.047
14.	Kansas	0.917	1.039	0.905	1.069
15.	Kentucky	0.895	0.987	0.941	1.076
16.	Louisiana	0.898	1.013	0.948	1.106
17.	Maine	0.849	0.972	0.848	1.004
18.	Maryland	0.832	0.942	0.836	0.988
19.	Massachusetts	0.840	0.971	0.842	1.013
20.	Michigan	0.774	0.913	0.780	0.958
21.	Minnesota	0.876	1.021	0.861	1.040
22.	Mississippi	0.993	1.082	1.041	1.172
23.	Missouri	0.865	0.979	0.891	1.050
24.	Montana	0.889	1.033	0.872	1.043
25.	Nebraska	0.917	1.049	0.896	1.069
26.	Nevada	0.787	0.898	0.791	0.926
27.	New Hampshire	0.817	0.949	0.815	0.982
28.	New Jersey	0.808	0.939	0.817	0.993
29.	New Mexico	0.900	1.013	0.911	1.056
30.	New York	0.835	0.937	0.860	1.010
31.	North Carolina	0.942	1.012	0.963	1.070
32.	North Dakota	0.980	1.102	0.949	1.108
33.	Ohio	0.770	0.912	0.784	0.973
34.	Oklahoma	0.917	1.031	0.939	1.094
35.	Oregon	0.865	1.013	0.848	1.029
36.	Pennsylvania	0.800	0.925	0.826	0.998
37.	Rhode Island	0.863	0.976	0.872	1.026
38.	South Carolina	0.904	0.982	0.932	1.045
39.	South Dakota	1.005	1.127	0.974	1.131
40.	Tennessee	0.924	1.011	0.965	1.094
41.	Texas	0.920	1.037	0.927	1.086
42.	Utah	0.867	1.019	0.830	1.017
43.	Vermont	0.879	1.007	0.873	1.034
44.	Virginia	0.897	0.989	0.919	1.052

Table 9.2 continued

		Coefficient of variation of male earnings	Coefficient of variation of earnings, males and females	Coefficient of variation of male incomes	Coefficient of variation of incomes, males and females
45.	Washington	0.823	0.955	0.817	0.985
46.	West Virginia	0.792	0.909	0.864	1.027
47.	Wisconsin	0.824	0.965	0.822	1.005
48.	Wyoming	0.867	1.024	0.843	1.026

		$\overline{S}_m$ mean schooling males (years)	S.D.(S_m) standard deviation of schooling, males (years)	$\overline{S}$ mean schooling males and females (years)	S.D.(S) standard deviation of schooling males and females (years)
1.	Alabama	9.964	4.032	9.999	3.910
2.	Arizona	11.381	3.725	11.371	3.584
3.	Arkansas	9.774	4.002	9.883	3.834
4.	California	11.793	3.547	11.681	3.433
5.	Colorado	11.853	3.426	11.807	3.288
6.	Connecticut	11.405	3.654	11.274	3.536
7.	Delaware	11.364	3.604	11.295	3.404
8.	Florida	10.912	3.759	10.883	3.594
9.	Georgia	10.120	4.133	10.102	3.971
10.	Idaho	11.420	3.218	11.428	3.035
11.	Illinois	11.171	3.495	11.052	3.394
12.	Indiana	11.041	3.275	11.018	3.152
13.	Iowa	11.220	3.132	11.279	3.023
14.	Kansas	11.517	3.277	11.488	3.167
15.	Kentucky	9.817	3.927	9.964	3.784
16.	Louisiana	9.966	4.283	9.961	4.204
17.	Maine	10.983	3.201	11.050	3.081
18.	Maryland	11.270	3.864	11.151	3.670
19.	Massachusetts	11.520	3.560	11.390	3.447
20.	Michigan	11.100	3.374	11.096	3.272
21.	Minnesota	11.299	3.362	11.331	3.212
22.	Mississippi	9.786	4.228	9.882	4.053
23.	Missouri	10.814	3.550	10.764	3.426
24.	Montana	11.292	3.338	11.396	3.222
25.	Nebraska	11.323	3.226	11.342	3.115
26.	Nevada	11.763	3.041	11.743	2.916
27.	New Hampshire	11.354	3.245	11.311	3.133
28.	New Jersey	11.205	3.672	10.994	3.557
29.	New Mexico	11.125	4.008	11.112	3.900
30.	New York	11.231	3.691	11.074	3.618
31.	North Carolina	9.913	3.971	10.038	3.829
32.	North Dakota	10.726	3.500	10.839	3.464

Table 9.2 continued

		$\overline{S}_m$ mean·schooling males (years)	S.D.(S_m) standard devia- tion of schooling, males (years)	$\overline{S}$ mean schooling males and females (years)	S.D.(S) standard devia- tion of schooling males and females (years)
33.	Ohio	11.121	3.337	11.071	3.227
34.	Oklahoma	10.959	3.736	10.916	3.589
35.	Oregon	11.535	3.334	11.556	3.159
36.	Pennsylvania	10.910	3.435	10.799	3.356
37.	Rhode Island	10.896	3.541	10.721	3.475
38.	South Carolina	9.867	4.084	9.922	3.973
39.	South Dakota	10.860	3.304	11.007	3.235
40.	Tennessee	10.000	3.991	10.100	3.812
41.	Texas	10.686	4.052	10.677	3.890
42.	Utah	12.237	3.132	12.108	2.975
43.	Vermont	11.258	3.319	11.378	3.167
44.	Virginia	10.609	4.131	10.680	3.912
45.	Washington	11.781	3.239	11.747	3.121
46.	West Virginia	9.998	3.741	10.112	3.678
47.	Wisconsin	11.064	3.367	11.085	3.261
48.	Wyoming	11.538	3.281	11.610	3.147

		K/L estimated capital to labor ratio	C_ρ estimated capital concentration	G manufacturing capital per worker ($1000)	M ratio of manufacturing to total nonfarm employment
1.	Alabama	18.789	1.798	17.399	0.302
2.	Arizona	23.092	1.879	12.306	0.155
3.	Arkansas	23.970	1.942	12.107	0.276
4.	California	23.988	1.902	13.886	0.214
5.	Colorado	25.203	1.899	14.319	0.149
6.	Connecticut	19.802	1.852	11.538	0.337
7.	Delaware	24.570	1.766	17.429	0.300
8.	Florida	24.959	1.939	14.303	0.142
9.	Georgia	24.048	1.924	11.870	0.296
10.	Idaho	26.685	1.883	16.564	0.174
11.	Illinois	25.851	1.863	14.156	0.299
12.	Indiana	23.629	1.826	19.087	0.363
13.	Iowa	23.171	1.926	14.596	0.239
14.	Kansas	26.940	1.879	14.327	0.188
15.	Kentucky	26.070	1.851	16.488	0.265
16.	Louisiana	28.823	1.781	45.857	0.154
17.	Maine	22.389	1.942	14.897	0.349
18.	Maryland	25.069	1.668	16.005	0.174
19.	Massachusetts	20.748	1.943	9.617	0.289
20.	Michigan	21.723	1.831	15.279	0.359

Table 9.2 continued

		K/L estimated capital to labor ratio	C_ρ estimated capital concentration	G manufacturing capital per worker ($1000)	M ratio of manufacturing to total nonfarm employment
21.	Minnesota	24.493	1.918	10.774	0.221
22.	Mississippi	22.481	1.975	12.354	0.274
23.	Missouri	25.646	1.915	10.598	0.250
24.	Montana	28.967	1.841	31.434	0.114
25.	Nebraska	26.706	1.915	12.944	0.150
26.	Nevada	23.657	1.938	28.671	0.049
27.	New Hampshire	18.420	1.927	9.613	0.358
28.	New Jersey	25.416	1.842	14.070	0.314
29.	New Mexico	25.286	1.830	12.179	0.078
30.	New York	23.536	1.928	11.043	0.328
31.	North Carolina	20.918	1.997	11.144	0.368
32.	North Dakota	26.083	1.941	16.819	0.058
33.	Ohio	18.783	1.674	15.924	0.367
34.	Oklahoma	26.721	1.804	12.324	0.182
35.	Oregon	24.443	1.936	16.967	0.230
36.	Pennsylvania	24.264	1.847	14.201	0.340
37.	Rhode Island	19.479	1.906	9.407	0.357
38.	South Carolina	19.610	1.985	13.830	0.371
39.	South Dakota	22.938	1.961	9.139	0.095
40.	Tennessee	23.641	1.929	13.407	0.309
41.	Texas	25.864	1.836	24.088	0.187
42.	Utah	26.141	1.845	17.572	0.163
43.	Vermont	20.802	1.948	10.631	0.240
44.	Virginia	24.695	1.910	12.785	0.245
45.	Washington	31.097	1.848	18.378	0.219
46.	West Virginia	30.580	1.634	27.138	0.232
47.	Wisconsin	21.884	1.882	12.386	0.325
48.	Wyoming	33.273	1.660	35.695	0.073

2.2. Schooling variables

As with the time-series study of income inequality, the distribution of schooling
will be used to describe the distribution of productive abilities. The two major
variables are the mean and standard deviation of schooling for each state. These
variables are calculated from census tables on the distribution of schooling
among income recipients.

Typically, in cross-section studies the distribution of earnings for a group is
related to the distribution of schooling for that group. This approach presumes
that the return to schooling, or wage differentials, are unaffected by the distribution of schooling in the labor force. For example, the distribution of earnings

among males is related to the distribution of schooling among males. In a general supply and demand context, this procedure is clearly incorrect. The distribution of schooling among females should affect the returns to schooling for males and therefore the earnings inequality among males. Following this line of reasoning, two other schooling variables have been added in the estimation of male earnings and income inequality. These are the ratio of male to female mean schooling and the ratio of male to female standard deviation of schooling. These ratios were chosen instead of simply the mean and standard deviation of the distribution of schooling among females to reduce the amount of multicollinearity among the variables.

Some of the schooling data is provided in tables 9.1 and 9.2.

2.3. Capital measures

The capital data used in the time-series studies are unavailable for the cross-section analysis. Although the *Annual Survey of Manufactures* has published data on manufacturing capital per worker (or more accurately total assets per worker), there is no data on the overall capital to labor ratio for each state. Similarly, the absence of the capital to labor ratios for most industries by state makes it impossible to calculate explicitly the capital concentration variable used in the time-series studies.

These shortcomings are overcome as follows. For each state, the census provides the distribution of employment among the twenty-nine industries used to construct the capital concentration variable in Chapter 8. For each state, an estimate of the capital to labor ratio and capital concentration were obtained by assuming that the capital to labor ratios in each of the twenty-nine sectors in a state were proportional to the national averages for that year. Specifically, let C_i be the national capital to labor ratio for sector i, and let E_{ij} be the number of employees in sector i in state j. Then for state j, the estimated capital to labor ratio is

$$\left(\frac{K}{L} \right)_j = \frac{\sum\limits_{i=1}^{29} C_i E_{ij}}{\sum\limits_{i=1}^{29} E_{ij}} \, .$$

The estimated capital concentration for state j is then

$$(C_\rho)_j = \frac{\left[\sum_{i=1}^{29} (C_i - (K/L)_j)^2 \, E_{ij} / \sum_{i=1}^{29} E_{ij} \right]^{1/2}}{(K/L)_j}$$

Two other demand variables are investigated in this chapter. One is the capital to labor ratio for manufacturing, published by the *Annual Survey of Manufactures*. The theoretical implications of this variable are ambiguous, as will be discussed in following sections, but it provides an accurate measure of the capital to labor ratio for at least one important sector of each state economy. The second variable is simply the ratio of manufacturing to total nonfarm nonmanufacturing employment. The time-series estimates revealed that this variable is a close proxy for the capital concentration term when the latter is calculated directly. The variable is included here to indicate whether it provides additional information on the demands for workers. (Aigner and Heins, 1967, used a similar variable in their cross-section study.)

All of the demand variables for each state are listed in tables 9.1 and 9.2.

The basic model, estimated in loglinear form, is

$$\ln(E_m) = a_0 + a_1 \ln(\overline{S}_m) + a_2 \ln(\text{S.D.}(S_m)) + a_3 \ln(K/L) + a_4 \ln(C_\rho) + e,$$

where

E_m	= the coefficient of variation of earnings for males in a state,
$\overline{S}_m$	= the mean schooling for males in a state,
$\text{S.D.}(S_m)$	= the standard deviation of schooling for males,
K/L	= the estimated capital to labor ratio,
C_ρ	= the estimated capital concentration, and
e	= an independent, identically distributed normal random variable.

The subscripts for state have been suppressed. The additional variables that will be investigated are:

$\overline{S}_m/\overline{S}_f$	= the ratio of the male to the female mean schooling,
$\text{S.D.}(S_m)/\text{S.D.}(S_f)$	= the ratio of the female to male standard deviation of schooling,
G	= the manufacturing capital to labor ratio, and
M	= the ratio of manufacturing to total nonfarm employment.

The equation to be estimated is a reduced-form price equation which includes both supply and demand variables. In addition to the supply variables included here, other economists have used the distribution of age and weeks worked.

Table 9.3
Male earnings and income inequality, 1959.

	Earnings					Income				
	(1)	(2)	(3)	(4)	(5)	(6)	(7)	(8)	(9)	(10)
$\ln(\bar{S}_m)$, logarithm of mean schooling, males with income	−1.22* (7.11)	−0.759* (3.52)	−1.11* (7.72)	−0.767* (3.99)	−1.16* (5.69)	−1.35* (8.96)	−1.03* (5.16)	−1.27* (9.49)	−1.03* (5.56)	−1.43* (7.44)
$\ln(S.D.(S_m))$, logarithm of standard deviation of schooling	−0.095 (0.647)	0.132 (0.856)	0.082 (0.643)	0.217 (1.60)	0.054 (0.416)	−1.20 (0.925)	0.039 (0.274)	0.018 (0.155)	0.107 (0.815)	−0.054 (0.437)
$\ln(\bar{S}_m/\bar{S}_f)$, logarithm of ratio of male to female mean schooling		−1.49* (3.89)		−1.06* (2.93)	−0.461 (1.25)		−1.12* (3.17)		−0.777* (2.24)	−0.191 (0.550)
$\ln(S.D.(S_m)/S.D.(S_f))$, logarithm of ratio of male to female standard deviation of schooling		−0.204 (0.595)		−0.249 (0.830)	0.248 (0.815)		−0.085 (0.268)		−0.123 (0.423)	0.397 (1.38)
$\ln(K/L)$, logarithm of estimated capital to labor ratio			0.079 (1.62)	0.038 (0.800)	0.139* (2.17)			0.057 (1.28)	0.028 (0.605)	0.143* (2.37)
$\ln(C\rho)$, logarithm of estimated capital concentration			0.847* (4.82)	0.679* (3.90)	0.483* (2.87)			0.668* (4.10)	0.541* (3.22)	0.331* (2.08)
$\ln(G)$, logarithm of manufacturing capital to labor ratio					−0.073* (2.16)					−0.083* (2.61)
$\ln(M)$, logarithm of ratio of manufacturing to total nonfarm employment					−0.066* (3.56)					−0.068* (3.85)
Constant	2.55	1.18	1.39	0.630	1.60	2.91	1.93	2.01	1.50	2.47
Adjusted R^2	0.652	0.731	0.764	0.796	0.838	0.747	0.786	0.810	0.822	0.865

Dependent variables: logarithm of coeffient of variation of male earnings (columns 1–5) or incomes (columns 6–10), 48 states.
Positive values of t-statistics are presented in parentheses under estimated coefficients.
Asterisk denotes significance at 0.05 level.

Table 9.4
Earnings and income inequality, males and females combined, 1959.

	Earnings			Incomes		
	(1)	(2)	(3)	(4)	(5)	(6)
$\ln(\bar{S})$, logarithm of mean schooling, males and females	−0.870* (4.62)	−0.790* (4.99)	−0.938* (6.61)	−0.998* (6.24)	−0.958* (6.27)	−1.09* (7.64)
$\ln(S.D.(S))$, logarithm of standard deviation of schooling, males and females	−0.037 (0.241)	0.117 (0.902)	0.028 (0.243)	−0.127 (0.986)	−0.039 (0.310)	−0.105 (0.910)
$\ln(K/L)$		0.083 (1.82)	0.114 (1.97)		0.057 (1.29)	0.112 (1.93)
$\ln(C_\rho)$		0.773* (4.72)	0.539* (3.43)		0.430* (2.72)	0.208 (1.32)
$\ln(G)$			−0.041 (1.35)			−0.055 (1.80)
$\ln(M)$			−0.060* (3.92)			−0.054* (3.48)
Constant	1.80	0.769	1.27	2.31	1.72	2.11
Adjusted R^2	0.500	0.656	0.743	0.610	0.654	0.720

Dependent variable: logarithm of coefficient of variation of earnings (columns 1−3) or incomes (colums 4−6), males and females combined, 48 states.

While such variables are potentially significant, they are not immediately relevant to the issues examined in this chapter and are therefore excluded. To the extent that they are correlated with the included variables, there may be some specification bias in the estimates of the included coefficients.

3. Results

The results of ordinary least squares regressions for 1959 are presented in table 9.3 for males and table 9.4 for males and females combined. The corresponding results for 1969 are presented in table 9.6 for males and table 9.8 for males and females combined. For purposes of examining the validity of the theoretical work of Chapters 4, 5, and 6, the results for males alone should be used. The implications of the theoretical work for males and females combined are less clear because of the possibility of market segregation and discrimination.

Table 9.5
Correlation coefficients for tables 9.3 and 9.4.

	$\ln(\bar{S}_m)$	$\ln(S.D.(S_m))$	$\ln(\bar{S}_m/\bar{S}_f)$	$\ln\left(\dfrac{S.D.(S_m)}{S.D.(S_f)}\right)$	$\ln(K/L)$	$\ln(C_p)$	$\ln(G)$	$\ln(M)$
$\ln(\bar{S}_m)$	1.00							
$\ln(S.D.(S_m))$	−0.712	1.00						
$\ln(\bar{S}_m/\bar{S}_f)$	0.474	−0.121	1.00					
$\ln(S.D.(S_m)/S.D.(S_f))$	0.384	−0.014	0.158	1.00				
$\ln(K/L)$	0.254	−0.268	−0.061	0.004	1.00			
$\ln(C_p)$	−0.014	−0.158	−0.300	−0.006	−0.247	1.00		
$\ln(G)$	0.027	0.013	−0.175	0.083	0.697	−0.301	1.00	
$\ln(M)$	−0.082	0.032	0.340	0.095	−0.103	−0.214	−0.422	1.00

Table 9.6
Male earnings and income inequality, 1969.

	Earnings					Incomes				
	(1)	(2)	(3)	(4)	(5)	(6)	(7)	(8)	(9)	(10)
$\ln(\bar{S}_m)$	−0.278 (1.21)	0.489 (1.66)	−0.213 (1.14)	0.391 (1.53)	−0.200 (0.728)	−0.506* (2.71)	0.104 (0.423)	−0.460* (3.05)	−0.005 (0.022)	−0.500* (2.22)
$\ln(\text{S.D.}(S_m))$	0.154 (1.06)	0.449* (3.00)	0.208 (1.77)	0.434* (3.43)	0.241 (1.98)	0.253* (2.13)	0.487* (3.91)	0.296* (3.12)	0.465* (4.43)	0.302* (3.03)
$\ln(\bar{S}_m/\bar{S}_f)$		−2.28* (3.99)		−1.76* (3.47)	0.848 (1.61)		−1.79* (3.76)		−1.31* (3.10)	0.555 (1.28)
$\ln\dfrac{\text{S.D.}(S_m)}{\text{S.D.}(S_f)}$		−0.065 (0.202)		−0.053 (0.200)	−0.254 (1.03)		−0.093 (0.352)		−0.083 (0.381)	−0.172 (0.853)
$\ln(K/L)$			0.182* (3.12)	0.109 (1.97)	0.094 (1.64)			0.163* (3.47)	0.111* (2.40)	0.103* (2.20)
$\ln(C_\rho)$			0.819* (4.98)	0.694* (4.62)	0.463* (3.01)			0.668* (5.04)	0.578* (4.63)	0.369* (2.93)
$\ln(G)$					−0.063* (2.64)					−0.058* (2.92)
$\ln(M)$					−0.059* (3.50)					−0.049* (3.54)
Constant	0.333	−1.87	0.985	−2.41	−0.495	0.760	−0.990	−0.342	−1.42	0.803
Adjusted R^2	0.155	0.375	0.456	0.569	0.672	0.497	0.612	0.684	0.734	0.189

Dependent variables: logarithm of coefficient of variation of male earnings (columns 1–5) or incomes (columns 6–10), 48 states.

Table 9.7
Male earnings and income Gini coefficients, 1969.

	Earnings					Income				
	(1)	(2)	(3)	(4)	(5)	(6)	(7)	(8)	(9)	(10)
$\ln(\bar{S}_m)$	0.135 (0.653)	0.866* (3.47)	0.180 (1.04)	0.779* (3.49)	0.160 (0.719)	-0.070 (0.424)	0.516* (2.54)	-0.046 (0.341)	0.407* (2.26)	-0.107 (0.623)
$\ln(\text{S.D.}(S_m))$	0.300* (2.29)	0.584* (4.61)	0.343* (3.15)	0.569* (5.14)	0.369* (3.74)	0.440* (4.23)	0.666* (6.47)	0.470* (5.55)	0.640* (7.16)	0.471* (6.19)
$\ln(\bar{S}_m/\bar{S}_f)$		-2.25* (4.64)		-1.82* (4.10)	-0.824 (1.93)		-1.76* (4.47)		-1.34* (3.74)	-0.555 (1.68)
$\ln \dfrac{\text{S.D.}(S_m)}{\text{S.D.}(S_f)}$		0.064 (0.239)		0.074 (0.319)	-0.398 (2.00)		-0.017 (0.075)		-0.009 (0.050)	-0.256 (1.67)
$\ln(K/L)$			0.172* (3.17)	0.093 (1.92)	0.066 (1.41)			0.159* (3.78)	0.103* (2.63)	0.094* (2.61)
$\ln(C_\rho)$			0.683* (4.47)	0.549* (4.18)	0.335* (2.68)			0.536* (4.52)	0.440* (4.15)	0.229* (2.38)
$\ln(G)$					-0.058* (2.96)					-0.058* (3.88)
$\ln(M)$					-0.062* (4.59)					-0.051* (4.83)
Constant	-1.58	-3.70	-2.72	-4.11	-2.12	-1.27	-2.96	-2.21	-3.27	-1.61
Adjusted R^2	0.114	0.422	0.394	0.575	0.722	0.499	0.658	0.672	0.752	0.851

Dependent variables: logarithm of Gini coefficients for male earnings (columns 1–5) or incomes (columns 6–10), 48 states.

Table 9.8
Earnings and income inequality, males and females combined, 1969.

	Earnings			Income		
	(1)	(2)	(3)	(4)	(5)	(6)
$\ln(\bar{S})$	0.003 (0.012)	0.007 (0.035)	−0.292 (1.38)	−0.275 (1.49)	−0.289 (1.75)	−0.523* (3.19)
$\ln(S.D.(S))$	0.080 (0.571)	0.103 (0.838)	0.008 (0.071)	0.159 (1.48)	0.170 (1.79)	0.092 (1.03)
$\ln(K/L)$		0.153* (2.71)	0.097 (1.55)		0.132* (3.04)	0.108* (2.22)
$\ln(C_\rho)$		0.585* (3.72)	0.357* (2.13)		0.419* (3.46)	0.219 (1.69)
$\ln(G)$			−0.047 (1.78)			−0.046* (2.24)
$\ln(M)$			−0.056* (3.54)			−0.040* (3.23)
Constant	−0.112	−1.00	0.190	0.501	−0.162	0.759
Adjusted R^2	−0.024	0.220	0.378	0.309	0.471	0.570

Dependent variables: logarithm of coefficient of variation of earnings (columns 1–3) or incomes (columns 4–6) for males and females combined, 48 states.

In addition to results using the coefficient of variation as the measure of inequality, table 9.7 presents the results using Gini coefficients. Also, as a means of investigating the importance of functional form, all regressions have been run using both the loglinear and linear forms. The results are substantially the same. Table 9.9 presents the results for male earnings and income inequality using the linear relation.

The possibility of heteroscedasticity with respect to state size has also been investigated. The absolute values of the residuals from the regressions for male earnings and income inequality (table 9.3, columns 3 and 8, table 9.6, columns 3 and 8) and for male and female earnings and income inequality (table 9.4, columns 2 and 5, table 9.8, columns 2 and 5) have been regressed against total male and female employment. The estimated coefficients are never significant at conventional levels, and the *t*-statistics are less than one except for male and female earnings inequality. Similar results hold when the logarithm of total male and female employment is used as the measure of state size. These results indicate that there is no substantial heteroscedasticity of residuals with respect to state size.

Table 9.9
Male earnings and income inequality, linear form.

	Earnings		Income		Earnings Gini	Income Gini
	1959 (1)	1969 (2)	1959 (3)	1969 (4)	1969 (5)	1969 (6)
$\bar{S}_m$	0.083* (7.54)	−0.017 (1.11)	−0.097* (9.14)	−0.037* (3.00)	0.0076 (1.13)	−0.0009 (.170)
S.D.(S_m)	.025 (1.07)	.051 (1.80)	.012 (.518)	.075* (3.25)	.040* (3.23)	.056* (5.77)
K/L	.0034 (1.73)	.0067* (3.16)	.0025 (1.33)	.0060* (3.48)	.0029* (3.13)	.0026* (3.64)
C_ρ	.394* (5.13)	.408* (5.09)	.317* (4.25)	.339* (5.21)	.160* (4.51)	.126* (4.61)
Constant	.691	−.051	1.04	.239	−.183	−.075
Adjusted R^2	.774	.463	.809	.694	.395	.680

Dependent variables: Coefficient of variation of earnings (columns 1 and 2) or of incomes (columns 3 and 4), and Gini coefficient for earnings (column 5) and for incomes (column 6).

Table 9.10
Correlation coefficients for tables 9.6 and 9.7.

	$\ln(\bar{S}_m)$	$\ln(\text{S.D.}(S_m))$	$\ln(\bar{S}_m/\bar{S}_f)$	$\ln\left(\dfrac{\text{S.D.}(S_m)}{\text{S.D.}(S_f)}\right)$	$\ln(K/L)$	$\ln(C_\rho)$	$\ln(G)$	$\ln(M)$
$\ln(\bar{S}_m)$	1.00							
$\ln(\text{S.D.}(S_m))$	−0.758	1.00						
$\ln(\bar{S}_m/\bar{S}_f)$	.543	−0.149	1.00					
$\ln\dfrac{\text{S.D.}(S_m)}{\text{S.D.}(S_f)}$	.259	−.107	−0.068	1.00				
$\ln(K/L)$	.143	−.068	−.116	0.153	1.00			
$\ln(C_\rho)$	−.089	−.014	−.169	−.015	−0.368	1.00		
$\ln(G)$	.011	−.032	−.157	.065	.588	−0.557	1.00	
$\ln(M)$	−.289	.199	.216	−.055	−.525	.084	−0.415	1.00

Table 9.5 presents the correlation coefficients for the variables in the 1959 regressions and table 9.10 presents the corresponding results for 1969. These tables indicate that correlation between the capital and schooling variables is not substantial, although there remains a moderate amount of correlation among the

schooling variables. In addition, there is substantial correlation between the estimated capital to labor ratio and the manufacturing capital to labor ratio. The consequence of such correlation, again, is to reduce the precision of the estimates of the corresponding coefficients in the regressions.

The results for the coefficient of the capital concentration term are very stable. The estimated coefficient is positive and significant in all regressions for earnings inequality and is positive and significant in almost all cases for income inequality (the exceptions arise when the other demand variables are included). The results therefore give strong support to the differential rents theory of Chapter 6.[1]

The coefficient for the estimated capital to labor ratio is positive in all cases but is only significant in some of the 1969 regressions. The results therefore give mild support to the hypothesis of Chapter 4, i.e. that increases in the capital to labor ratio result in greater earnings inequality, everything else the same.[2]

The coefficient for the manufacturing capital to labor ratio term is always negative. For the 1959 regressions, the coefficient is never significant, while for the 1969 regressions the coefficients are almost always significant. The differences may arise because the 1969 figures are more accurate. The 1959 figures are actually taken from 1962 and include only total assets owned by firms. The 1969 figures are for 1969 and include an adjustment for rented assets. The implications for the theory of the negative sign for the manufacturing capital to labor ratio are unclear. A greater manufacturing capital to labor ratio could indicate a greater capital to labor ratio for the state as a whole or it could indicate a smaller level of capital concentration. Alternatively, it could result in reduced earnings inequality within the manufacturing sector. A more disaggregated approach is necessary to discover the way in which the manufacturing capital to labor ratio affects earnings inequality.

In an attempt to investigate whether the sign of the manufacturing capital to labor term arises from multicollinearity, some of the results were re-estimated under the assumption that the economy can be disaggregated into two sectors, manufacturing and nonmanufacturing. The three variables used to describe the

[1]   In response to an earlier presentation of the differential rents theory of Chapter 6, Hirsch and Hoftyzer (1979) tested for the significance of the capital to labor ratio and capital concentration in the context of a cross-section human capital model using observations from Standard Statistical Metropolitan Areas. They found that the estimated coefficients for capital concentration were significant at conventional levels, but the coefficients for the capital to labor ratio were not significant.

[2]   The aggregate model of Chapter 4 assumes a closed economy in which the interest rate declines as capital intensity increases. To the extent that rates of return to capital are equalized across states, the cross-section study may not validly test the aggregate theory.

demand side are then the manufacturing capital to labor ratio, the nonmanufacturing capital to labor ratio and the ratio of manufacturing to total nonfarm employment. The second variable, the nonmanufacturing capital to labor ratio, is not observed directly but is calculated under the assumption that each individual subsector has the national capital to labor ratio for that subsector. Variations in this variable therefore arise from variations in the distribution of employment among the subsectors. The use of these three variables allows one to draw inferences about the effects of an economy-wide increase in capital intensity. If both the manufacturing and nonmanufacturing sectors have the same proportionate increase in capital to labor ratios, the effects on earnings or income inequality would then be indicated by the sum of the coefficients of the two terms. Similarly, the coefficient for the manufacturing employment ratio indicates the effects of a shift in employment from manufacturing to nonmanufacturing, holding the capital to labor ratios in each sector constant.

The results of ordinary least squares regressions using these three demand variables are presented in table 9.11. As in previous estimations, the coefficients for the manufacturing employment and manufacturing capital to labor ratio terms are negative and significant in all cases. This confirms the previous esti-

Table 9.11
Male earnings and income inequality, alternative capital variables.

	Earnings		Income	
	1959	1969	1959	1969
$\ln(\overline{S_m})$	−1.28* (9.31)	−0.577* (3.31)	−1.40* (11.40)	−0.752* (5.38)
$\ln(\text{S.D.}(S_m))$	−.046 (.371)	.095 (.885)	−.074 (.667)	.204* (2.38)
$\ln(G)$, logaritm of manufacturing capital to labor ratio	−.086* (2.57)	−.099* (4.43)	−.080* (2.68)	−.084* (4.66)
logarithm of nonmanufacturing capital to labor ratio	.113 (1.63)	.070 (1.15)	.101 (1.63)	.075 (1.54)
$\ln(M)$, logarithm of ratio of manufacturing to total nonfarm employment	−.098* (5.06)	−.089* (6.03)	−.084* (4.88)	−.073* (6.17)
Constant	2.34	1.03	2.72	1.28
Adjusted R^2	0.778	0.546	0.833	0.739

Dependent variables: Logarithm of coefficient of variation of male earnings or income, 48 states.

mates. The coefficient for the nonmanufacturing capital to labor ratio is always positive but is not significant, perhaps because the variable is less accurately measured. In three out of four cases the coefficient for the nonmanufacturing capital to labor ratio is larger in absolute size than the coefficient for the manufacturing capital to labor ratio, indicating that a proportionate increase in both capital to labor ratios would result in a slight increase in earnings or income inequality. However, the nonmanufacturing capital to labor ratio is not measured accurately enough to draw any final conclusions.

The explanatory power of the model using the three demand variables is fairly close to the explanatory power using the capital concentration term. It appears that the two capital to labor ratios and the manufacturing employment ratio capture most of the information in the capital concentration term and provide a more interpretable and simplified system.

The estimated coefficients for the ratio of manufacturing to nonfarm employment is negative and significant in all cases. The influence of this variable is surprisingly strong and indicates that the estimated capital to labor ratio and capital concentration do not entirely describe the demands for workers. The sign of the term is consistent with the theories developed in Chapters 4, 5, and 6. A lower ratio of manufacturing to total nonfarm employment results in a greater capital to labor ratio and, in general, greater concentration of capital. However, it is also possible that the term influences the distribution of earnings for reasons not strictly predicted by the theory. In particular, the distribution of earnings is much more unequal for nonmanufacturing than it is for manufacturing. A larger proportion of manufacturing employment would therefore be predicted to result in less earnings inequality, as observed.

The estimated coefficients for the schooling or supply variables are substantially less stable than the capital or demand variables. The coefficient of mean schooling is always negative and significant in the 1959 estimates, but is occasionally positive and significant in the 1969 estimates. Also, the coefficient for the standard deviation of schooling is generally positive and significant for the 1969 estimates, but for the 1959 estimates the coefficient is never significant and is often negative. Of course, the simplest explanation for this instability is multicollinearity among the schooling variables, but this answer does not tell us very much. A more complete answer requires a disaggregation of the schooling variables. (Instability in cross-section studies of earnings inequality has previously been observed by Formby and Seaks, 1978.) One possible explanation is that migration ‿ualized wage differentials more completely in 1969 than in 1959, so that the effects of average schooling on rates of return were not detected.

As expected from a supply and demand point of view, the distribution of schooling among females affects the distribution of earnings for males. The coefficient for the ratio of the male to female mean schooling is generally negative and significant, except when the demand terms G and M are included. The term for the ratio of the standard deviation of schooling is generally negative but not significant. According to these results, an increase in the mean schooling of females raises male earnings and income inequality, everything else the same. The mechanism by which females in the labor force affect the earnings of men is not clear from these results and would require further investigation.

The results are substantially the same whether the Gini coefficient or the coefficient of variation is used as the measure of inequality. This suggests that the results that have been obtained here do not depend strongly on the way in which inequality is measured.

4. Alternative schooling variables

For purposes of understanding the way in which the distribution of schooling affects the distribution of earnings, the mean and standard deviation are too abstract. This section presents the results using alternative schooling variables in the hope of shedding some light on the instability of the schooling coefficients between 1959 and 1969 and revealing the way in which different schooling groups affect the distribution of earnings.

Consider three classes of workers: those with less than four years of high school, those with four years of college or more, and those inbetween. Suppose there is an increase in the number of workers in the lower bracket, those with less than four years of high school. What are the effects on the distribution of earnings? There are two effects. First, for given wage rates (or educational differentials), there will be more workers receiving the wage rates for less-educated workers, so that earnings inequality will increase. The second effect is that the wage rates for less-educated workers will be bid down because of the increased supply, and this will also raise the amount of earnings inequality. Both effects work in the same direction.

Suppose now there is an increase in the number of workers in the upper bracket, those with four years of college or more. Again, there are two effects. For given wage rates, there are now more workers receiving the earnings for more-educated workers, tending to raise the earnings inequality. However, the greater supply of more-educated workers bids down their wage rates, which reduces earnings inequality. The two effects operate in opposite directions, so that the net effect on the distribution of earnings inequality is small and ambiguous.

The above analysis is of course undertaken from a simple supply and demand

Table 9.12
Male earnings and income inequality, alternative schooling variables, 1959.

	Earnings		Income	
	(1)	(2)	(3)	(4)
Logarithm of proportion of males with less than four years high school	0.491* (4.51)	0.449* (4.33)	0.509* (4.93)	0.472* (4.74)
Logarithm of proportion of males with four years college or more	.084 (.790)	.029 (.279)	.047 (.462)	−.001 (.013)
$\ln(K/L)$	.011 (.176)	−.039 (.482)	−.007 (.122)	−.052 (.663)
$\ln(C_\rho)$	.696* (3.20)	.588* (2.59)	.532* (2.58)	.440 (2.01)
$\ln(G)$		.021 (.476)		.019 (.457)
$\ln(M)$		−.046 (1.99)		−.040 (1.80)
Constant	−.166	−.211	−.060	−.098
Adjusted R^2	.605	.654	667	.700

Dependent variables: logarithm of coefficient of variation of male earnings (columns 1 and 2) or income (columns 3 and 4), 48 states.

Table 9.13
Male earnings and income inequality, alternative schooling variables, 1969.

		Coefficient of variation			Gini coefficient			
		Earnings	Income		Earnings		Income	
	(1)	(2)	(3)	(4)	(5)	(6)	(7)	(8)
Logarithm of proportion of males with less than four years high school	0.187* (2.65)	0.266* (4.24)	0.325* (5.06)	0.392* (6.64)	0.168* (2.52)	0.257* (4.67)	0.335* (5.50)	0.411* (7.84)
Logarithm of proportion of males with four years college or more	.025 (.485)	.032 (.694)	.036 (762)	.043 (1.00)	.090 (1.84)	.103* (2.59)	.119* (2.66)	.129* (3.39)
$\ln(K/L)$	.207 (3.25)	.122 (1.91)	.205* (3.55)	.130* (2.17)	.201* (3.35)	.099 (1.76)	.211* (3.85)	.125* (2.34)
$\ln(C_\rho)$	.836* (4.77)	.598* (3.47)	.705* (4.42)	.513* (3.16)	.700* (4.22)	.480* (3.17)	.580* (3.83)	.387* (2.68)
$\ln(G)$		−.049 (1.82)		−.039 (1.52)		−.042 (1.77)		−.037 (1.65)
$\ln(M)$		−.074* (4.64)		−.063* (4.15)		−.079* (5.65)		−.068* (5.09)
Constant	−1.11	−.592	−.878	−.440	−1.62	−1.07	−1.38	−.907
Adjusted R^2	0.392	0.585	0.550	0.669	0.297	0.587	0.475	0.664

Dependent variables: logarithm of coefficient of variation of male earnings (columns 1 and 2) or incomes (columns 3 and 4) and logarithm of Gini Coefficients for male earnings (columns 5 and 6) or income (columns 7 and 8).

point of view. That is to say, the rate of return to schooling and the wage rates for workers with different levels of education are determined endogenously, within the system. In contrast, the Becker-Chiswick human capital model assumes that the rates of return to schooling are determined exogenously and are unaffected by either the supply or demand variables. It follows that in such a model an increase in the number of workers in either the upper or the lower tail of the distribution of schooling will lead to an increase in earnings inequality of about the same magnitude.

The empirical evidence on this question is presented in tables 9.12 and 9.13. Instead of using the mean and standard deviation of the distribution of schooling, the two variables are the proportion of males with less than four years of high school and the proportion of males with four years college or more. The results for the demand variables are substantially the same as in previous estimations. As expected from the simple supply and demand analysis, the coefficient for the proportion of males with four years high school or less is positive and significant in all cases. In contrast, the coefficient for the proportion of males with four years college or more is positive but insignificant when the coefficient of variation is used as the measure of inequality.

This result is consistent with the estimates of the Kuznets time-series data in Chapter 8. From those regressions the increase in the proportion of the population with four years college or more actually reduced the share of total earnings going to the upper 1 and 5 percent of all income recipients.

When the Gini coefficient is used as the measure of inequality in the cross-section estimates, the coefficient for the proportion of males with four years college is positive and significant (in three out of four cases), although the value is much less than the coefficient for the proportion of males with less than four years high school. The difference in results using the Gini coefficient is not surprising. The Gini coefficient is known to weigh the extreme upper and lower tails of the earnings distribution less heavily than the coefficient of variation. It is therefore possible that reductions in the wages for upper-income individuals do not strongly affect the Gini coefficient.

If the distribution of schooling for each state followed the same functional form, then the distribution for each state could be adequately described by the mean and standard deviation. However, if the distributions take different shapes, then the relation between the mean and standard deviation of schooling and earnings inequality is not fixed. The relation would depend on the particular numbers of workers at the lower and upper tails of the distribution of schooling. The results of this section could therefore account for the instability in the coefficients for the schooling terms between 1959 and 1969. In this regard, it should be noted that the estimated coefficients for the proportion of males with

Table 9.14
Educational differentials

| | 1959 | | | | Estimated rate of return | | 1969 | | | |
| | Slope of log income/-log schooling relation, males | | Slope of log income/-log schooling relation, females | | | | Slope of log income/-log schooling relation, males | | Slope of log income/-log schooling relation, females | |
	(1)	(2)	(3)	(4)	(5)	(6)	(7)	(8)	(9)	(10)
$\ln(\bar{S})$	-0.106* (4.32)	-0.100* (4.33)	-0.072* (4.15)	-0.075* (4.26)	-0.133* (4.68)	-0.129* (4.63)	-0.105* (3.80)	-0.110* (3.95)	-0.112* (4.00)	-0.133* (5.33)
$\ln(\text{S.D.}(S))$	.023 (1.16)	.038 (1.98)	.050* (3.59)	.050* (3.44)	.011 (.499)	.002 (.077)	.014 (.869)	.013 (.846)	.024 (1.48)	.017 (1.48)
$\ln(K/L)$		.010 (1.55)		.005 (.969)		.012 (1.45)		.013 (1.79)		.021* (3.18)
$\ln(C_\rho)$		.070* (2.92)		-.008 (.436)		.060* (2.09)		.026 (1.27)		-.023 (1.28)
Constant	.298	.199	.178	.176	.424	.332	.318	.272	.330	.336
Adjusted R^2	.589	.645	.735	.732	.485	.518	.549	.565	.625	.717

less than four years of high school are greater for 1959 than they are for 1969. The possible relevance of this difference is not clear.

5. Further effects of schooling

This section presents further evidence on the effect of schooling on earnings inequality, prior to a complete discussion in the following section. Earnings or income inequality can be disaggregated into two contributing elements: earnings or income differences between schooling levels and the distribution of earnings or income within schooling levels. This section examines the effects of the schooling and capital variables on each of these elements.

Table 9.14 presents the effects of the schooling and capital variables on educational differentials. One measure of educational differentials is obtained by regressing, for each state, the logarithm of mean income for each schooling level on the logarithm of the years of schooling, using the eight different schooling brackets as observations. The slope of the estimated relation, for each state, is then taken as the measure of the educational differential. Separate measures have been obtained for males and females. These measures are, of course, extremely crude. The relationship between schooling and earnings, the subject of substantial research, is quite complex and the simple measures used here are subject to biases because of the exclusion of innate ability variables. An alternative measure is available from Chiswick's cross-section study (1974, pp. 180–182). This measure was obtained in a similar fashion, using more detailed data.

All of the measures of educational differentials yield substantially similar results. The coefficient for the mean level of schooling is negative and significant in all cases. The coefficient for the standard deviation of schooling is generally positive but not significant. It follows that educational differentials, or the returns to schooling, are endogenously determined. They are systematically and strongly affected by the average level of schooling. As predicted by simple supply and demand considerations, the greater the amount of schooling, the smaller the returns to schooling.

The capital terms do not substantially improve the accuracy of the regressions, as measured by the adjusted R^2 statistics. The coefficient of the estimated capital to labor term is always positive but is not in general significant. This lends mild support to the hypothesis of Chapter 4 that greater capital intensity results in greater wage differentials. The coefficient for the capital concentration term is positive for males and negative for females. The other demand variables did not greatly increase the explanatory power of the model. Apparently, the

Table 9.15
Male income inequality by schooling level.

	1959				1969			
	Four years college of more		Four years high school		Four years college		Four years high school	
	(1)	(2)	(3)	(4)	(5)	(6)	(7)	(8)
$\ln(\overline{S})$	−0.400*	−0.462*	−0.655*	−0.737*	−0.305*	−0.325*	−0.345*	−0.637*
	(3.42)	(3.89)	(6.45)	(8.36)	(3.37)	(3.27)	(2.30)	(5.91)
$\ln(K/L)$	−.034	.028	.054	.113*	.111*	.116*	.228*	.095
	(.664)	(.389)	(1.21)	(2.10)	(2.73)	(2.26)	(3.39)	(1.70)
$\ln(C_\rho)$	.596*	.428*	.797*	.557*	.500*	.455*	.888*	.547*
	(3.32)	(2.23)	(5.10)	(3.90)	(4.43)	(3.39)	(4.75)	(3.76)
$\ln(G)$		−.053		−.059*		−.013		−.066*
		(1.38)		(2.06)		(.610)		(2.90)
$\ln(M)$		−.042*		−.066*		−.005		−.105*
		(2.17)		(4.63)		(.400)		(7.52)
Constant	.062	.177	.356	.537	−.230	−.143	−.777	.579
Adjusted R^2	.339	.377	.568	.704	.378	.355	.365	.717

Dependent variable: logarithm of coefficient of variation of male incomes for described schooling levels, 48 states.

capital variables do not affect earnings inequality through the educational differentials but through the number of workers at each educational level or the dispersion of earnings at each level.

The next step is to investigate the effects of the supply and demand variables on the income inequality within schooling levels. The results of this investigation are presented in table 9.15. The dependent variable for the regressions is the logarithm of the coefficient of variation of income for all males with the particular level of schooling, e.g. all males with four years of college.

The coefficient for the mean schooling term is negative and significant in all cases. This result indicates that an increase in the mean level of schooling not only reduces educational differentials but also differentials arising from unobserved differences among workers. It follows that the negative conclusions drawn by Christopher Jencks and others discussed in Chapter 4, section 10, are unjustified. Even if the earnings inequality for workers with a single level of schooling is the same as the earnings inequality for all workers, it does not follow that a change in the distribution of schooling will have no effect on the distribution of earnings. This is because the distribution of earnings within schooling levels is itself affected by the distribution of schooling. Furthermore, the proportion of earnings inequality attributable to schooling (as opposed to genetic inheritance, socio-economic background and luck) does not place an upper limit on the effect of changes in the distribution of schooling on earnings inequality.

The coefficient for the capital concentration term is always positive and almost always significant. The coefficient for the capital to labor ratio is generally positive and is sometimes significant in the 1969 regressions. Everything else the same, increases in these capital variables therefore tend to raise income inequality for given levels of schooling, apparently by raising wage differentials for unobserved variations in worker abilities.

The estimated coefficients for the manufacturing capital to labor ratio and the ratio of manufacturing to total nonfarm employment are all negative and are occasionally significant. In particular, the manufacturing employment term has a strong effect on the income inequality for males with four years high school.

It should be noted that the results for the lower level of schooling are substantially better, in terms of the adjusted R^2. The reasons for this are not immediately clear.

6. The effect of the average level of education on inequality

This chapter has so far presented considerable evidence on the effect of education on the distribution of earnings. Before drawing conclusions, it is useful to consider the predictions of the human capital approach.

Following the Becker-Chiswick model (Chiswick, 1974, p. 41, and Mincer, 1974, p. 27), suppose individual i's earnings function is given by $\ln E_{s,i} = \ln E_0 + r_i s_i + U$, where $E_{s,i}$ is individual i's earnings with s years of schooling, E_0 is the earnings with the minimum years of schooling, r_i is the average adjusted rate of return for individual i, s_i is the years of schooling and U is the residual. The variance of the logarithms of earnings, var $(\ln E)$, is then given by the variance of the rate of return times the years of schooling, var $(r_i s_i)$. At this point both Chiswick and Mincer assume that individual rates of return to schooling are uncorrelated with individual years of schooling, following Becker's analysis (1975, p. 94). However, this assumption has been taken to imply a much stronger, and demonstrably false, result, namely that the rate of return is exogenously determined and does not depend on the average level of schooling. It is possible that the rate of return for an individual is independent of the individual's years of schooling, and yet the average rate of return for the whole economy is completely determined by the average level of schooling.

This result can be demonstrated formally as follows. Suppose x and y are independently distributed random variables and suppose a and b are two arbitrary parameters. Because x and y are independently distributed, the expected value $E((x - \mu_x)(y - \mu_y)) = 0$, where μ_x and μ_y are the mean values of x and y. Then $E((ax - a\mu_x)(by - b\mu_y)) = ab\,E((x - \mu_x)(y - \mu_y)) = 0$, so that ax and *by* are also independently distributed for any values of the parameters a and b. These two parameters could be related linearly and ax and by would still be independent. In particular, the mean of ax could be completely determined by the mean of by and the random variables ax and by would still be independent. In the context of the human capital model, the average rate of return to schooling can be completely determined by the average level of schooling, and individual rates of return and years of schooling can be independent and uncorrelated.

Under the assumption that the rate of return and years of schooling for individuals are independently distributed random variables,

$$\text{var}(\ln E) = \text{var}(r_i s_i) = \bar{r}^2 \text{var}(S_i) + \bar{S}^2 \text{var}(r_i) + \text{var}(r_i)\,\text{var}(s_i) \tag{9.1}$$

This relation holds whether or not the average rate of return, $\bar{r}$, depends on the average level of schooling, $\bar{s}$, or other variables, i.e. it is a tautology. To draw conclusions about the effects of the average level of schooling on earnings inequality, it is necessary to assume that the mean and variance of the individual rates of return do not depend on the schooling variables, i.e., that they are exogenously determined. This is in fact the assumption that is made. Then the partial derivative of earnings inequality (as measured by the variance of logarithms of earnings) with respect to the average level of schooling is $2\bar{s}\,\text{var}(r_i)$. This yields the standard prediction of the human capital model, namely that an increase in the average level of schooling raises earnings inequality, everything else the same.

The empirical results derived by Chiswick do not support this prediction (1974, pp. 71–73). Even holding the rate of return and the variance of schooling constant, Chiswick observes a negative relation between the average level of schooling and income inequality in four out of seven cases. The point is that this approach is the incorrect procedure for estimating the effects of the average level of schooling on income inequality, since it neglects the effects of the average level of schooling on the average rate of return.

Other authors have also disputed the human capital prediction (Tinbergen, 1972; Marin and Psacharopoulos, 1976; Winegarden, 1979). Marin and Psacharopoulos argue that the rate of return to schooling for an individual and the individual's schooling level are not independent, as required for the specific human capital conclusion. Although Marin and Psacharopoulos conclude that an increase in the schooling level can reduce earnings inequality, they do not reject the underlying human capital model.

Let us now examine the evidence on the determinants of the rate of return. Chiswick (1974, p. 56) himself provides evidence that the rate of return is endogenously determined. He reports a correlation between his calculated rates of return and the average schooling levels of -0.66. However, Chiswick dismisses the negative correlation as arising from mobility.

The evidence from section 5 strongly supports the argument that the rate of return is determined endogenously. It depends strongly and negatively on the average level of schooling, as one would expect from a simple supply and demand point of view. Furthermore, the results of that section indicate that income inequality by schooling level depends negatively on the average level of schooling and positively on capital concentration. These results suggest that the variance of the rates of return to schooling also is endogenously determined. The consequence of these results is that the effect of an increase in the average level of schooling on earnings inequality is not given by $2\bar{s}$ var (r_i), as suggested by (9.1). One must also add in the effects of the change in $\bar{s}$ on the mean rate of return $\bar{r}$ and on the variance of the rates of return.

With the rate of return and the variance of returns endogenously determined, the expression for earnings inequality given in (9.1) loses its usefulness. One cannot explain the distribution of earnings in terms of $\bar{r}$ and var (r_i) if these latter terms are not explained. Chiswick's methodology consists in getting separate estimates of the rate of return, assumed to be determined exogenously, and using the estimated rates of return to explain income and earnings inequality. The foregoing remarks suggest that little explanation is given by this procedure.

The evidence from Chapters 8 and 9 strongly supports the conclusion that an increase in the average level of schooling reduces earnings and income inequality, everything else the same. The time-series estimates for 1949—1969 yield a negative and significant coefficient for the average level of schooling. The 1959 cross-section results similarly yield a negative and significant coefficient for the average level of schooling. For 1969, using the coefficient of variation as the measure of inequality, the coefficient for the average level of schooling is negative when the terms involving female schooling are excluded but are not significant for earnings inequality. In other cases, the 1969 regressions yield positive coefficients. The possible sources of this instability have previously been discussed. Subject to some qualification regarding the source of changes in the average level of schooling, the general conclusion is that an increase in the average schooling reduces earnings and income inequality.

Finally, it should be noted that the average level of schooling is not a very meaningful descriptive statistic. It certainly is not a direct policy variable. A more relevant way of describing the distribution of schooling is in terms of the proportion of the labor force with less than four years of high school and the proportion with four years college or more, or similar statistics. The effects of these variables on earnings and income inequality are unambiguous and stable between the 1959 and 1969 estimates. An increase in the proportion of the labor force with less than four years high school substantially raises earnings and income inequality. An increase in the proportion of the population with four years college or more has a negligible influence on earnings inequality, although it does appear to raise income inequality.

7. Poverty

The 1970 census published data on poverty rates by state, and these data make it possible to investigate the influence of the schooling and capital variables on the lower tail of the distribution of income. By and large, the analysis of poverty has been undertaken from the point of view of the individual. That is, the characteristics of households or individuals that tend to be in poverty (age, race, sex, marital state, number of children, education) have been identified. But identifying who ends up being poor and who ends up out of poverty does not explain the total amount of poverty. Instead of explaining poverty in terms of the characteristics of the population, it is possible to explain the amount of poverty in terms of the economy in which a population is placed. This section investigates the extent to which variations in the poverty rate between states can be explained by differences in the economies of those states.

The theoretical foundation of this chapter has partly been established in Chapter 4, section 9. That section indicated that it was possible for increases in capital intensity to worsen absolutely the economic condition of lower income individuals. Similarly, under a separate set of conditions, increases in the average level of productive ability would raise the absolute economic condition of individuals with lower levels of productive abilities. These results did not necessarily hold, however, and depended on the nature of the production function and in particular on the partial elasticities of complementarity. The implications of the differential rents theory, in contrast, are unambiguous and easy to state. An increase in the concentration of capital among jobs reduces the capital with which the labor of less-productive individuals is combined, thereby reducing their relative and perhaps absolute incomes. Similarly, an increase in the standard deviation of schooling (holding the functional form of the distribution of schooling fixed) means that less education is received by individuals at the lower tail of the distribution of schooling. This can be expected to reduce their incomes and increase the incidence of poverty.

The poverty rates used in this investigation are the proportion of households with pretransfer income below the poverty line, each household being compared to a poverty line specific to its conditions (e.g. number of children). Three poverty rates are observed; one for the entire population of households, one for those with heads between 25 and 64, and one for those with heads between 25 and 64 with one to three years of high school. The explanatory variables are the same as those used in the investigation of earnings and income inequality. Demographic variables, such as race and age distribution and number of households with single heads, are specifically excluded, following the simple argument that these variables only determine which households in the population end up in poverty and do not determine the total amount of poverty. Undoubtedly, this simple argument is not valid and a more complete explanation of poverty must inevitably incorporate the excluded demographic characteristics of the population.

The results, using the mean and standard deviation of schooling, are presented in table 9.16. These results strongly support the implications of Chapter 4, section 9. The coefficient for the mean level of schooling is negative and significant in all cases. The coefficient for the standard deviation of schooling is positive and occasionally significant. The demand variables, the capital to labor ratio and capital concentration, have positive and generally significant coefficients when the other demand variables are excluded. Increases in these demand

Table 9.16
Poverty rates, 1968.

	Poverty rate		Poverty rate age 25 to 64		Poverty rate, age 25 to 64, one to three years high school	
	(1)	(2)	(3)	(4)	(5)	(6)
$\ln(\bar{S})$	−4.50* (4.06)	−5.64* (5.09)	−4.17* (3.51)	−5.42* (4.66)	−2.26* (2.16)	−3.40* (3.31)
$\ln(S.D.(S))$	1.03 (1.62)	0.711 (1.19)	1.50* (2.19)	1.16 (1.85)	1.43* (2.37)	1.11 (2.00)
$\ln(K/L)$	.988* (3.40)	0.509 (1.55)	1.06* (3.40)	0.473 (1.37)	0.955* (3.47)	0.469 (1.54)
$\ln(C_\rho)$	1.67* (2.06)	1.09 (1.25)	1.91* (2.19)	1.35 (1.46)	1.40 (1.82)	.829 (1.02)
$\ln(G)$		−.055 (.395)		−.029 (.202)		−.051 (.397)
$\ln(M)$		−.273* (3.26)		−.311* (3.55)		−.274* (3.53)
Constant	7.69	12.43	5.75	10.97	2.12	6.85
Adjusted R^2	0.654	0.715	0.654	0.728	0.551	0.643

Dependent variables: logarithms of poverty rates, various age groups, 48 states.

variables raise the level of poverty, everything else the same. The coefficient for the ratio of manufacturing to total nonfarm employment is negative and significant, indicating that states with more manufacturing have less poverty, everything else the same. The coefficient of the manufacturing capital to labor ratio is negative but not significant.

Table 9.17
Poverty rates, alternative schooling measures, 1969.

	Poverty rate		Poverty rate, age 25 to 64		Poverty rate, age 25 to 64, one to three years high school	
	(1)	(2)	(3)	(4)	(5)	(6)
Logarithm of proportion with less than four years high school	1.57* (4.31)	1.93* (5.41)	1.77* (4.43)	2.20* (5.77)	1.23* (3.63)	1.59* (4.93)
Logarithm of proportion with four years college or more	−0.305 (.940)	−0.227 (.731)	−0.185 (.521)	−0.079 (.239)	−0.072 (.237)	−0.0003 (.001)
$\ln(K/L)$	1.12* (3.19)	.549 (1.38)	1.23* (3.18)	.519 (1.22)	1.08* (3.29)	.507 (1.41)
$\ln(C_\rho)$	1.68 (1.71)	1.37 (1.28)	1.94 (1.81)	1.66 (1.45)	1.40 (1.53)	1.01 (1.04)
$\ln(G)$		.006 (.039)		.034 (.192)		−.014 (.095)
$\ln(M)$		−.299* (2.97)		−.353* (3.27)		−.311* (3.40)
Constant	−1.58	.439	−1.84	.556	−1.04	1.05
Adjusted R^2	0.507	0.581	0.487	0.584	0.380	0.500

The results using the alternative schooling variables are presented in table 9.17. As one would expect, the proportion of income recipients with less than four years high school has a strong and positive influence on the poverty rates, while the proportion with four years college or more has virtually no effect. The demand variables are substantially the same, although the coefficient for the capital concentration term is no longer positive.

The explanatory power obtained is quite high, particularly when the mean and standard deviation of schooling are used. These results suggest that the approach to the explanation of poverty taken in this section is valid and deserves further development.

8. Conclusions

This chapter has presented substantial cross-section evidence on the validity of the theories developed in Chapters 4, 5, and 6. The evidence strongly supports the differential rents theory of Chapter 6, while the aggregate theory of Chapter 4 is only partially supported. The estimated coefficient for the capital concentration term is almost always positive in the regressions for income and earnings inequality. The estimated coefficient for the capital to labor ratio is generally positive, as predicted by the inequality multiplier analysis of Chapter 4 under the assumption that capital-skill complementarity holds. But it is not always significant in the inequality regressions when the capital concentration term is included.

Unlike what one would conclude from the Becker-Chiswick human capital model, the estimated coefficient for the mean level of schooling is negative and significant in most cases, instead of positive. Occasionally the coefficient is positive or not significant in the 1969 regressions. The standard deviation of schooling, which is supposed to be a major determinant of earnings and income inequality, does not strongly affect inequality in the 1959 regressions, although the coefficient for the term is often positive and significant in the 1969 regressions. There appears to be substantial instability in the results for the education variables between 1959 and 1969. The reasons for this instability may lie in the different effects of changes in the upper and lower tails of the schooling distribution on earnings inequality. As one would predict from a simple supply and demand analysis, increases in the lower tail have strong effects on earnings inequality, while the price and quantity effects of changes in the upper tail tend to cancel out. As a result, the estimated coefficients for the mean and standard deviation of schooling depend on the source of variation in these variables among states. It is quite reasonable to suppose that the source of variation changed between 1959 and 1969.

The rate of return to schooling, as measured by the slope of the log income-log schooling relation, appears to be endogenously determined. The rate of return to schooling depends negatively and significantly on the mean level of schooling within a state. This is the result one would expect from a simple supply and demand analysis, but it differs substantially from the treatment of the rate of return in the human capital analysis. Furthermore, income inequality within schooling levels depends positively and significantly on both the capital to labor ratio and capital concentration. It depends negatively on the mean level of schooling. This breakdown of inequality into between schooling level differences and within schooling level differences reveals the mechanisms by which the variables affect inequality.

Following the analysis of Chapter 4, section 9, the effects of the supply and demand variables on poverty rates have also been investigated. Poverty depends negatively on the mean schooling level, as one would expect, and positively on the capital to labor ratio and capital concentration.

Additional demand variables, the manufacturing capital to labor ratio and the ratio of manufacturing employment to total nonfarm employment, were included in many of the regressions. The estimated coefficients for these terms were consistently negative and generally significant, particularly in the case of the manufacturing employment ratio. These variables will be discussed further in later chapters.

Appendix: Data sources

Tables 9.1, 9.3–9.5, 9.11, and 9.12. The coefficient of variation of incomes for males and for males and females combined and the mean and standard deviation of schooling for males and for males and females combined are derived from tables 138, Income in 1959 of Persons 25 Years Old and Over, by Years of School Completed, Color, and Sex, *1960 US Census of Population*, Detailed Characteristics, vol. 1, parts 2–52. For each sex, the table provides an eight-by-nine matrix of the distribution of male or female income recipients by schooling level and income level. The marginal distributions from this matrix are used to calculate the distributions of schooling and income. For most brackets the level of schooling and incomes used in the calculations are the bracket means. For the upper, open-ended brackets, the means used are 17 years of schooling (for the bracket four or more years of college) and $14,400 (for $10,000 and over). The same source is used for the alternative schooling variables in table 9.11. The coefficient of variation of earnings for males and for males and females combined are derived from table 124, Earnings in 1959 of Persons in the Experienced Civilian Labor Force, by Occupation, Color and Sex, *1960 US Census of Population, Detailed Characteristics*, vol. 1, parts 2–52.

The estimated capital per worker and capital concentration are derived from the statistics for the employed in table 126, Detailed Industry of the Experienced Civilian Labor Force and of the Employed, by Sex, *1960 US Census of Population, Detailed Characteristics*, vol. 1, parts 2–52. Both variables are calculated using the national capital to labor ratios for each industry given in tables 7.1 and 7.2. The same employment data are used to calculate the ratio of manufacturing to total nonfarm employment and the estimated nonmanufacturing capital to labor ratio used in Table 9.11.

Capital per worker in manufacturing is given by the gross book value of depreciable assets, table 2, *Annual Survey of Manufactures, Special Geographic Supplement to 1962–1964 Data on Book Value of Fixed Assets and Rental Payments for Building and Equipment* (M65(AS)–6), US Bureau of the Census, 1972. The data are for 1962.

Tables 9.2, 9.6–9.11 and 9.13. The coefficient of variation of incomes for males and for males and females combined and the mean and standard deviation of schooling are derived from table 197, Income in 1969 of Persons 18 Years Old and Over by Years of School Completed, Age, Race and Sex, *1970 US Census of Population, Detailed Characteristics*, vol. 1, parts 2–52. The method of derivation is the same as for 1959. The mean incomes used for each income bracket in calculating the distribution of income are taken from Seiver (1979). The mean used for the upper schooling bracket (five years college or more) is 18 years. The income Gini coefficients used in table 9.7 are given by the index of income concentration provided in the same table. The same source yields the alternative schooling variables in table 9.13.

The coefficient of variation of earnings and the earnings Gini coefficient are derived from table 195, Earnings in 1969 of Persons by Weeks Worked in 1969, Race and Sex, *1970 US Census of Population, Detailed Characteristics*, vol. 1, parts 2–52. The data are for males and females, 14 years old and over, who worked in 1969.

The estimated capital per worker, capital concentration, ratio of manufacturing to total nonfarm employment and capital per worker for nonmanufacturing are derived in the same manner as for 1959, using employment data for the experienced civilian labor force, 16 years old and over, taken from table 138, Detailed Industry of the Experienced Civilian Labor Force and Employed Persons, by Sex, *1970 US Census of Population, Detailed Characteristics*, vol. 1, parts 2–52.

The manufacturing capital per worker is the sum of the gross book value of depreciable assets for machinery and equipment and for buildings and structures, plus ten times the rental payments for these categories. The data on gross book values of depreciable assets are given in columns 1 and 2, table 3, ch. 7, p. 168, *Annual Survey of Manufactures, 1968–1969*, US Bureau of the Census, 1973. Rental payments are for 1968 and are given in ch. 7, table 4, p. 172 from the same source.

Table 9.14. The slopes of the log income versus log schooling relations for each state and each sex are derived from ordinary least squares regressions. Using eight schooling brackets, the dependent variable is the logarithm of the mean income for each schooling bracket and the independent variable is the logarithm of the mean years of schooling for that bracket. For 1959 the data are taken from table 138 (cited above) and for 1969 from table 197 (cited above). The estimated rate of return is provided by Chiswick (1974, pp. 180–182).

Table 9.15. For each schooling level the coefficient of variation of income is calculated from table 138 (cited above) for 1959 and from table 197 (cited above) for 1969.

Tables 9.16 and 9.17. The poverty rates are given in table 211, Poverty Status in 1969 of Families by Years of Schooling Completed, Age, Sex, and Race of Head, *1970 US Census of Population, Detailed Characteristics*, vol. 2, parts 2–52.

Chapter 10

WAGE DIFFERENTIALS

This chapter briefly investigates whether the results that have been obtained for earnings inequality are consistent with changes in wage differentials that have taken place over time. The data are for readily available series covering intervals in the period 1926–1970. The wage differentials are for building trades, drivers and helpers, manufacturing skilled and semiskilled versus unskilled, and occupational wage differentials. These series appear to be the standard data sets used in the analysis of wage differentials.

The same independent variables are used in all estimations. Detailed information on the distribution of schooling among the population are not available, so data by decades has been interpolated to provide the proportion of the population with five years or less elementary school, E_1, and the proportion with four years college or more, E_2. These data are from the same source used in the examination of the Kuznets' data on upper-income shares in Chapter 8.

The data needed to calculate the capital concentration term used in the previous two chapters is not available. However, the results of Chapter 9, section 3 (table 9.10) suggests that substantially the same information is contained in the capital to labor ratios for the manufacturing and the nonfarm nonmanufacturing sectors and the ratio of manufacturing to total nonfarm employment. To obtain the capital to labor ratios, figures on the capital stocks in the manufacturing and nonfarm nonmanufacturing sectors, taken from a Bureau of Economic Analysis study, have been combined with employment data in *The National Income and Product Accounts of the United States, 1925–1970*. These employment data also provide the ratio of manufacturing to total nonfarm nonmanufacturing employment. Finally, time and an index of overall productivity (output per unit of input), as a measure of technological change, are also included in the estimated relations. The relation will be estimated in the following loglinear form.

$$\ln W = a_0 + a_1 T + a_2 \ln E_1 + a_3 \ln E_2 + a_4 \ln M + a_5 \ln G_1$$
$$+ a_6 \ln G_2 + a_7 \ln P + e, \quad (10.1)$$

where

W = the wage differential,
T = the time period (year),
E_1 = the proportion of the population with five years or less of elementary school,
E_2 = the proportion of the population with four years college or more,
M = the ratio of manufacturing to total nonfarm employment,
G_1 = the manufacturing capital to labor ratio,
G_2 = the nonfarm nonmanufacturing capital to labor ratio,
P = the measure of productivity, and
e = an identically distributed random error term.

The three demand variables M, G_1 and G_2 are related to the previously used demand variables, capital concentration and the aggregate capital to labor ratio, as follows. Since the nonfarm nonmanufacturing sector is substantially more capital intensive than the manufacturing sector, capital concentration will depend positively on the capital to labor ratio in the nonfarm nonmanufacturing sector and will depend negatively on the manufacturing capital to labor ratio. The aggregate capital to labor ratio of course depends positively on the capital to labor ratios of the two sectors and negatively on the ratio of manufacturing to total nonfarm employment. From the effects of the demand variables via the capital concentration term, one would expect the coefficients of G_2 to be positive and the coefficients of M and G_1 to be negative. These are in fact the signs obtained when these variables were used in the cross-section analysis of Chapter 9, section 3. Furthermore, the estimated coefficients of M and G_1 were consistently negative when these variables were included elsewhere in the regressions of Chapter 9. Alternatively, the theory developed in Chapter 4 could apply separately to the manufacturing and nonfarm nonmanufacturing sectors, with different effects of capital intensity on the demands for workers of different productive abilities.

Using time-series data from 1948 to 1970, the ordinary least squares estimates of the loglinear relation between capital concentration and the above demand variables is

$$\ln(C_\rho) = -0.449 + 0.0489 \ln(M) + 0.118 \ln(G_1) + 0.401 \ln(G_2),$$
$$(0.239) \qquad (0.960) \qquad (3.21)$$

$$R^2 = 0.963; \quad \text{Durbin-Watson statistic} = 0.422.$$

Employing the Cochrane-Orcutt iterative technique, the final value of rho used in the transformation of data is 0.917. The R^2 is raised to 0.975 and the Durbin-Watson statistic is raised to 0.868, so there is substantial remaining serial correlation of the residuals. None of the estimated coefficients is significant using this technique. While capital concentration is therefore definitely and strongly related to the demand variables used here, the specific values of the coefficients of the relation do not appear to be accurately estimated using the time-series data.

The correlation coefficients for the independent variables are presented in table 10.1. These coefficients reveal that there is substantial multicollinearity among the time, productivity and education variables. The consequence of the multicollinearity is that the estimated coefficients in any ordinary least squares regressions will not be reliable and the t-statistics will not describe the accuracy of the estimates. There is also multicollinearity among the demand variables, although not as much. The two capital to labor ratios are positively correlated (0.809) and they are both negatively correlated with the ratio of manufacturing to total nonfarm employment.

A second problem with the data is that the variables are serially correlated. That is to say, they change gradually over time, so that the value at one time period is close to the value in the next time period. Neither multicollinearity nor serial correlation make the estimated coefficients biased. Both are severe econometric problems, however, because they reduce the accuracy of the estimates and cast doubt on the validity of the results.

By itself, no single regression can be taken as conclusive evidence regarding the effects of the demand variables. The intention of this chapter is instead to demonstrate the consistency of the results among different wage differentials and between wage differentials and earnings inequality.

Table 10.1
Correlation coefficients for variables in tables 10.2–10.5, 1920–1970.

	T	$\ln(E_1)$	$\ln(E_2)$	$\ln(M)$	$\ln(G_1)$	$\ln(G_2)$	$\ln(P)$
T	1.00						
$\ln(E_1)$	−0.993	1.00					
$\ln(E_2)$	0.994	−0.997	1.00				
$\ln(M)$	−0.456	0.502	−0.520	1.00			
$\ln(G_1)$	0.209	−0.249	0.279	−0.934	1.00		
$\ln(G_2)$	−0.213	0.144	−0.130	−0.669	0.809	1.00	
P	0.995	−0.985	0.988	−0.419	0.166	−0.244	1.00

Under the assumption that the error terms are generated by a first-order autoregressive process, the data are transformed using the Cochrane-Orcutt iterative technique (Cochrane and Orcutt, 1949). The results using this procedure are substantially the same as the results obtained with ordinary least squares applied to the untransformed data.

The first set of wage differentials is for union hourly wage rates in the building trades. The dependent variable is the logarithm of the ratio of the hourly wage rate for journeymen to the hourly wage rate for helpers and laborers, covering the period 1925—1970. The results are presented in table 10.2. The estimated coefficient for the manufacturing capital to labor ratio is negative

Table 10.2
Building trades, 1925—1970.

	(1)	(2)	(3)
T, time	−0.025* (5.04)	−0.012* (3.89)	−0.009* (3.69)
$\ln(E_1)$, logarithm of proportion of population with five years or less elementary school	−0.768* (4.45)	−0.561* (4.55)	−0.587* (5.29)
$\ln(E_2)$, logarithm of proportion of population with four years college or more	−0.285 (1.29)	−0.533* (3.49)	−0.576* (4.10)
$\ln(M)$, logarithm of ratio of manufacturing to total nonfarm employment		−0.183 (1.75)	−0.150 (1.51)
$\ln(G_1)$, logarithm of manufacturing capital to labor ratio		−0.174* (3.68)	−0.175* (3.97)
$\ln(G_2)$, logarithm of nonfarm, nonmanufacturing capital to labor ratio		0.262* (6.43)	0.265* (7.74)
$\ln(P)$, logarithm of productivity			−0.102 (1.68)
Constant	3.13	2.31	2.63
Rho used in transformation	0.803	0.593	0.427
R^2	0.994	0.997	0.997
Durbin-Watson statistic	1.96	2.43	2.18

Dependent variable: logarithm of ratio of hourly wage rate for journeymen to hourly wage rate for helpers and laborers.
Positive values of t-statistics are given in parentheses under estimated coefficients.
Asterisk denotes significance at 0.05 level.
Date sources: See appendix.

Table 10.3
Drivers and helpers, 1937–1970.

	(1)	(2)	(3)
T	−0.010* (3.83)	−0.009* (6.70)	−0.008* (5.18)
$\ln(E_1)$	−0.264* (3.91)	−0.159* (4.54)	−0.154* (3.81)
$\ln(E_2)$	−0.043 (0.299)	−0.098 (0.143)	−0.004 (0.052)
$\ln(M)$		−0.260* (6.83)	−0.262* (6.67)
$\ln(G_1)$		−0.084* (6.01)	−0.086* (5.32)
$\ln(G_2)$		0.016 (1.62)	0.018 (1.49)
$\ln(P)$			−0.012 (0.253)
Constant	2.43	0.379	0.377
Rho used in transformation	0.368	−0.478	−0.482
R^2	0.978	0.988	0.988
Durbin-Watson statistic	2.22	2.07	2.06

Dependent variable: logarithm of ratio of union wage rates for drivers to union wage rates for helpers.

and significant and the coefficient for the nonfarm nonmanufacturing capital to labor ratio is positive and significant. The coefficient for the ratio of manufacturing to total employment is negative but not significant. The test statistic for the hypothesis that the coefficients for the demand variables are all zero is 10.26, which far exceeds the critical value of the F distribution at the 0.05 level of significance.[1] The hypothesis that the coefficients for the demand variables M, G_1 and G_2 are zero should therefore be rejected.

The second set of data is for union wage rates for local trucking. The measure of the wage differential is the ratio of the wage rate for drivers to the wage rate for helpers. The results are presented in table 10.3. The coefficients for M and

---

[1] The consequence of using a separate estimate of rho for the regression with the demand variables excluded is to reduce the residual sum of squares in that regression, thereby reducing the test statistic for the hypothesis that the coefficients of the demand variables are zero. The use of different estimates of rho therefore does not bias the test towards rejection of the hypothesis.

G_1 are negative and significant and the coefficient for G_2 is positive and not significant. The Durbin-Watson statistic from the ordinary least squares regressions is in excess of two, suggesting negative serial correlation (this is reflected in the fact that the value of rho used to transform the data is negative). This negative serial correlation could arise if the wage rate for one of the occupations is affected by current market conditions and the other wage rate adjusts after a lag. The test statistic for the hypothesis that the coefficients of the demand variables are zero is 7.50, leading one to reject the hypothesis at the 0.05 level of significance.

The third data set uses average hourly earnings for male production workers in 25 manufacturing industries, 1925–1948. The wage differential is the ratio of the average hourly earnings for skilled and semiskilled males to the average hourly earnings for unskilled males. The results are presented in table 10.4. The coefficients for M and G_1 are negative and significant and the coefficient for G_2 is positive and significant. The test statistic for the hypothesis that the coeffi-

Table 10.4
Manufacturing skilled and semiskilled versus unskilled, 1925–1948.

	(1)	(2)	(3)
T	−0.009 (0.142)	−0.080* (2.18)	−0.077 (2.05)
$\ln(E_1)$	−0.454 (0.237)	−2.01 (1.72)	−1.91 (1.58)
$\ln(E_2)$	−0.280 (0.395)	1.55* (3.01)	1.51* (2.87)
$\ln(M)$		−0.599* (3.77)	−0.591* (3.62)
$\ln(G_1)$		−0.378* (5.00)	−0.373* (4.80)
$\ln(G_2)$		0.394* (4.78)	0.401* (4.56)
$\ln(P)$			0.026 (0.287)
Constant	2.09	3.89	3.59
Rho used in transformation	0.532	0.121	0.103
R^2	0.752	0.913	0.914
Durbin-Watson statistic	1.54	1.68	1.69

Dependent variable: logarithm of ratio of average hourly earnings for skilled and semiskilled male production workers to average hourly earnings for unskilled male production workers.

Table 10.5
Occupational wage differentials, 1947–1968.

	Craftsmen, foremen and kindred versus laborers			Operatives and kindred versus laborers		
	(1)	(2)	(3)	(4)	(5)	(6)
T	0.015 (0.794)	0.024 (1.23)	0.034 (0.531)	−0.009 (0.452)	0.024 (1.55)	0.034 (1.97)
$\ln(E_1)$	0.461 (0.441)	−0.334 (0.482)	−0.318 (0.466)	1.08 (0.915)	0.554 (0.980)	0.557 (0.01)
$\ln(E_2)$	0.353 (0.227)	−1.39 (1.38)	−1.78 (1.62)	1.75 (0.994)	−0.131 (0.159)	−0.554 (0.631)
$\ln(M)$		−1.26* (4.74)	−1.18* (4.23)		−1.40* (6.54)	−1.31* (5.94)
$\ln(G_1)$		−1.04* (4.91)	−0.878* (3.17)		−1.16* (6.73)	−0.990* (4.50)
$\ln(G_2)$		1.37* (2.08)	0.521 (0.462)		0.795 (1.49)	−0.090 (0.010)
$\ln(P)$			0.662 (0.904)			0.699 (1.18)
Constant	−1.46	1.22	1.62	−5.26	−2.33	−1.86
Rho used in transformation	−0.072	−0.570	−0.608	−0.044	−0.726	−0.757
R^2	0.730	0.906	0.912	0.559	0.904	0.913
Durbin-Watson statistic	1.99	2.16	2.28	2.01	2.64	2.94

Dependent variable: Logarithm of ratio of median incomes of craftsmen, foremen and kindred to median incomes of laborers (columns 1, 2, 3) or ratio of median incomes of operatives and kindred to median incomes of laborers (columns 4, 5, 6).

cients for the demand variables are zero is 9.31, leading to rejection of the hypothesis.

The fourth set of data is for occupational wage differentials using median incomes for males 14 years old and over, 1947–1968. Two wage differentials are constructed. The first is the ratio of the median incomes of craftsmen, foremen and kindred workers to the median incomes of laborers. The second is the ratio of median incomes of operatives and kindred to median incomes of laborers. The results are presented in table 10.5. The estimated coefficients for M and G_1 are negative and significant for both wage differentials. The coefficient for G_2 is positive when the productivity variable is excluded (and significant for the first wage differential). However, the estimated coefficient is negative but not significant for the second wage differential when the productivity variable is included. The test statistics for the hypothesis that the coefficients of the demand variables are zero are 8.17 and 15.59 for the first and second wage differentials, respectively. The hypothesis should therefore be rejected. The Durbin-Watson statistics for the ordinary least squares regressions again exceed two, suggesting negative serial correlation.

Except for occupational wage differences, the time trend is negative and is often significant. The measure of productivity or technological change shows no consistent effect on wage differentials. However, it should be remembered that this variable is highly correlated with the time and education variables.

Despite the fact that the wage differentials used in this chapter are taken from different sources and cover different intervals, the results are remarkably consistent. The wage differentials depend negatively on the ratio of manufacturing to total nonfarm employment and the manufacturing capital to labor ratio and depend positively on the nonfarm nonmanufacturing capital to labor ratio. These results are furthermore in substantial conformity to the results using the same variables to explain earnings inequality. The coefficients for M and G_1 have the same sign as those obtained throughout Chapter 9. This chapter therefore reconfirms several empirical regularities that have been observed in previous chapters. It also demonstrates that the results that have been obtained with earnings inequality are consistent with changes in wage differentials over time. Finally, the chapter demonstrates that data on manufacturing and nonmanufacturing sectors can be used to analyze the effects of demand on the distribution of earnings.

Appendix: Data sources

The proportions of the population with five years or less elementary school and with four years college or more, E_1 and E_2, are interpolated from decade statistics published in the *1973 Digest of Educational Statistics*, US Department of Health, Education and Welfare, Office of Education, p. 14. The capital stocks used in calculating the manufacturing and nonmanufacturing capital to labor ratios, G_1 and G_2, are provided in *Fixed Nonresidential Business Capital in the United States, 1925–73*, Bureau of Economic Analysis, US Department of Commerce, published by the National Technical Information Service, January 1974, p. 7 (for manufacturing) and p. 11 (for nonfarm nonmanufacturing). Net stocks were used as the measure of capital.

The corresponding employment data used to calculate the capital to labor ratios are taken from *Historical Statistics of the United States, Colonial Times to 1970*, US Department of Commerce, Bureau of the Census, part 1, p. 137. The same data provide the ratio of manufacturing to total nonfarm employment.

The productivity series is real gross private domestic product per unit of total factor input, published in *Historical Statistics*, part 2, p. 948.

The same source provides the wage series for the building trades (part 1, p. 171) and for manufacturing skilled and semiskilled versus unskilled (part 1, p. 172). The wage series for local trucking are published in the *1975 Handbook of Labor Statistics*, US Department of Labor, p. 226. The occupational wage differentials are published in *Current Population Reports, Consumer Income, Income Growth Rates 1939–1968*, series P60, no. 69, p. 82.

Chapter 11

DISAGGREGATED ANALYSIS

1. Introduction

The empirical work that has been undertaken in the last four chapters leaves several questions unanswered. The most important question concerns the effect of capital intensity on earnings inequality. Chapter 4 presented an aggregate theory relating earnings inequality to capital intensity, among other variables. However, the effect of capital intensity is theoretically ambiguous — it depends on the particular production function. The major condition derived is that if the capital-skill complementarity condition holds, then increases in the capital to labor ratio raise earnings inequality, everything else the same.

The empirical evidence on the effect of capital intensity is not consistent. Often the coefficient of the capital to labor term is positive and significant, but usually the term is not significant and the value depends on the presence or absence of other variables. The problem with the previous estimations is that it has been necessary to estimate the effect of economy-wide increases in capital intensity at the same time that the effects of sectoral shifts are estimated. The effects of the two changes are then not clearly distinguishable. What is needed is a means of examining the effects of changes in capital intensity in such a manner that sectoral shifts do not affect the results. The disaggregated analysis presented in the next section satisfies this requirement.

In addition to the effects of capital intensity, there are a number of other phenomena which deserve further clarification. Both Chapters 9 and 10 found that the effect of a reduction in the proportion of employment in manufacturing raises the level of earnings inequality. Similarly, an increase in the manufacturing capital to labor ratio results in a reduction in earnings inequality, according to the results of the previous chapters. These results are consistent with the theory already developed, but are not predicted by them. An explanation of these results is therefore desirable.

2. Data

The disaggregated analysis of the effects of capital intensity on earnings inequality is based on the observation of changes in the distribution of earnings within an industry over time. For 1949 and 1969, the distributions of earnings by industry are available from the US censuses of population.

There are several reasons why the distribution of earnings within an industry would change over time. The major reason of course is changes in factor prices. For example, the wage rates corresponding to various grades of labor may have changed over the twenty-year span. However, in an economy with substantial labor mobility, the changes in factor availability or factor prices will be substantially the same for all industries. In a cross-section analysis (where each industry provides one observation), the effects of the changes in factor prices could not be observed. Differences in the mean earnings in 1969 relative to the mean earnings in 1949 for industries would therefore be attributable to the production conditions in those industries. In response to the changes in factor prices and other variables, some industries will have larger proportional increases in their capital to labor ratios than other industries. It is then possible to examine whether industries which have had greater than average increases in capital to labor ratios have also had greater than average increases in the grade of labor employed.

The industries chosen for this analysis are the thirty industries (twenty manufacturing and ten nonmanufacturing) described in Chapter 7, tables 7.1–7.4. These industries account for all domestic civilian employment. The average quality of the work force in an industry is not observed directly, of course. Instead, the mean earnings is taken as a measure of labor quality. In an economy with more or less perfectly competitive labor markets, the level of earnings will correspond to the quality or productivity of the labor. Of course, many economists would argue that differences in mean earnings between industries do not reflect differences in labor quality but instead arise from market segmentation and imperfections. These points of view will by analyzed later in this chapter.

Mean earnings for an industry in 1969 are assumed to depend on mean earnings for the industry in 1949 and on the change in the capital to labor ratio. This relation is estimated using the following loglinear form:

$$\ln Y_{69} = a_0 + a_1 \ln Y_{49} + a_2 \ln (K_{69}/_{49}) + e,$$

where

$Y_{69} =$ mean earnings for the industry in 1969,
$Y_{49} =$ mean earnings for the industry in 1949,
$K_{69}/K_{49} =$ ratio of 1969 to 1949 industry capital to labor ratio, and
$e =$ an independent, identically distributed normal random variable.

A stricter test for the effects of capital intensity would be to relate changes in mean earnings to changes in the capital to labor ratio. The dependent variable would then be $\ln (Y_{69}/Y_{49})$. However, when this is done using the loglinear form, the explanatory power of the model is extremely low and no coefficients are significant at conventional levels.

3. Results

The results of ordinary least squares regressions are presented in table 11.1. The first two columns present the results using all thirty industries. The coefficient for the capital term is positive and significant. These results indicate that on the average those industries which have had larger proportional increases in capital to labor ratios have had larger proportional increases in mean earnings. That is, for a given level of mean earnings in 1949, mean earnings in 1969 are greater in the industries which have had greater increases in the capital to labor ratio. This result gives strong indirect support for the hypothesis of capital-skill complementarity. A reasonable inference from the results is that an economy-wide increase in capital intensity should result in an increase in the demand for more-productive workers relative to less-productive workers, everything else the same.

The last two columns of table 11.1 present the results using only the twenty manufacturing industries. Again, the coefficient of the capital term is positive, but it is smaller and is not significant. Apparently, capital-skill complementarity also holds for manufacturing taken alone, but it is much weaker and the effect is less certain.

Table 11.1
Changes in mean earnings by industry, 1949–1969.

	30 industries		20 manufacturing industries	
Logarithm of mean earnings for industry in 1949	0.729* (8.37)	0.761* (9.89)	0.978* (9.80)	0.948* (9.31)
Logarithm of ratio of 1969 to 1949 industry capital to labor ratio		0.200* (3.09)		0.129 (1.18)
Constant	1.26	1.15	0.979	0.971
Adjusted R^2	0.704	0.774	0.833	0.837

Dependent variable: logarithm of mean earnings for industry, 1969.
Positive values of t-statistics are reported in parentheses under estimated coefficients.
Asterisk indicates coefficient is significant at 0.05 level.

Another inference that can be drawn from these results is that mean earnings within industries show strong temporal continuity. That is, the primary determinant of mean earnings in 1969 is the level of mean earnings in 1949.

4. Upper and lower tails

The use of mean earnings to investigate the effects of changes in capital intensity is not completely revealing. The problem is that few workers in an industry receive the mean level of earnings; it is merely a statistical abstraction. It is necessary to recognize that not all workers in an industry receive the same level of earnings. This represents an important step beyond the previous work in this monograph. The theoretical models of Chapters 4 and 5 assume that each industry (or more precisely each machine or unit of capital) uses only one grade of labor. An increase in the productive ability of the labor demanded by an industry then unambiguously raised inequality. When any one particular industry requires a whole range of services from a hierarchy of labor, the analysis becomes more complicated. A change, for example, in the capital to labor ratio for an industry may result not only in a change in the mean productive ability of labor demanded but also in the dispersion of productive abilities demanded.

The first step in studying the distribution of earnings within industries is to examine the source of changes in those distributions over time. The major question concerns how changes in the capital to labor ratio affects the entire distribution of earnings within an industry.

Rather than work with such abstractions as the mean, coefficient of variation or other measures of inequality, it is more revealing to work separately with the upper and lower tails of the distributions. The data on the upper and lower tails of the distribution of earnings are presented in table 11.2 for 1949 and table 11.3 for 1969. For 1949, the lower tail is described by the proportions of workers with less than $500, less than $1,500 and less than $2,500. The upper tail is described by the proportions of workers with more than $3,500, more than $4,000 and more than $4,500. The corresponding earnings levels in 1969 ($1,000, $4,000 and $7,000 for the lower tail and $10,000, $12,000 and $15,000 for the upper tail) were chosen so that the proportions of the working population in the corresponding range would be roughly the same.

The procedure taken here is to relate the 1969 proportion of workers in an industry in a given range (say, less than $4,000) to the 1949 proportion of workers in the corresponding range (less than $1,500) and the change in the capital to labor ratio. The results of ordinary least squares regressions are presented in table 11.4 for all thirty industries and table 11.5 for the twenty manu-

Table 11.2
Distribution of earnings by industry, 1949.

	Proportion of workers with earnings in described range					
	Less than $500	Less than $1,500	Less than $2,500	More than $3,500	More than $4,000	More than $4,500
Food and kindred	0.061	0.225	0.504	0.215	0.136	0.082
Tobacco	0,097	0.384	0.795	0.068	0.045	0.032
Textiles	0.052	0.265	0.697	0.096	0.063	0.041
Apparel	0.080	0.418	0.775	0.093	0.066	0.046
Lumber and wood	0.118	0.465	0.725	0.110	0.068	0.041
Furniture and fixtures	0.058	0.259	0.608	0.142	0.087	0.052
Paper	0.038	0.163	0.465	0.222	0.139	0.088
Printing and publishing	0.122	0.241	0.456	0.354	0.285	0.212
Chemicals	0.031	0.127	0.363	0.315	0.211	0.143
Petroleum and coal	0.011	0.054	0.168	0.579	0.418	0.254
Rubber and plastics	0.025	0.117	0.382	0.267	0.161	0.094
Leather	0.061	0.329	0.723	0.085	0.051	0.034
Stone, clay and glass	0.037	0.178	0.492	0.203	0.125	0.075
Primary metals	0.021	0.097	0.352	0.243	0.145	0.089
Fabricated metals	0.032	0.140	0.422	0.242	0.153	0.097
Machinery except electrical	0.022	0.106	0.337	0.298	0.186	0.116
Electrical equipment	0.044	0.169	0.444	0.250	0.165	0.103
Transportation equipment	0.020	0.091	0.270	0.324	0.193	0.116
Instruments	0.030	0.138	0.430	0.264	0.177	0.120
Miscellaneous manufacturing	0.069	0.273	0.598	0.171	0.115	0.073
Agriculture	0.294	0.711	0.906	0.033	0.022	0.014
Mining	0.037	0.161	0.453	0.247	0.157	0.100
Contract construction	0.066	0.261	0.525	0.243	0.170	0.110
Rail transport	0.019	0.089	0.286	0.349	0.214	0.124
Nonrail transport	0.042	0.176	0.415	0.265	0.161	0.091
Communications	0.038	0.150	0.504	0.225	0.166	0.110
Utilities	0.025	0.113	0.354	0.302	0.187	0.111
Trade	0.112	0.352	0.634	0.171	0.117	0.080
Finance	0.052	0.216	0.558	0.239	0.182	0.137
Services	0.135	0.371	0.620	0.169	0.104	0.068
Manufacturing	0.0502	0.2058	0.4865	0.2275	0.1476	0.0943
Nonfarm nonmanufacturing	0.0944	0.2862	0.5297	0.1838	0.1205	0.0785
All industries	0.0921	0.2904	0.5575	0.2027	0.1324	0.0857

Data sources: see appendix.

facturing industries. In table 11.4, for purposes of comparison, the top three rows present the results excluding the capital term. The estimated coefficient for the capital term is negative and significant in the lower tail and positive and significant (except in the highest range) in the upper tail. On the average, then,

Table 11.3
Distribution of earnings by industry, 1969.

	Proportion of workers with earnings in described range					
	Less than $1,000	Less than $4,000	Less than $7,000	More than $10,000	More than $12,000	More than $15,000
Food and kindred	0.059	0.279	0.565	0.177	0.087	0.041
Tobacco	0.060	0.296	0.719	0.099	0.058	0.029
Textiles	0.046	0.361	0.805	0.070	0.042	0.026
Apparel	0.070	0.583	0.872	0.064	0.044	0.030
Lumber and wood	0.064	0.370	0.685	0.128	0.072	0.038
Furniture and fixtures	0.050	0.312	0.699	0.121	0.071	0.040
Paper	0.030	0.170	0.468	0.221	0.112	0.052
Printing and publishing	0.093	0.286	0.529	0.260	0.153	0.076
Chemicals	0.024	0.130	0.382	0.318	0.189	0.103
Petroleum and coal	0.015	0.086	0.255	0.395	0.224	0.113
Rubber and plastics	0.045	0.235	0.545	0.210	0.111	0.047
Leather	0.060	0.460	0.837	0.063	0.041	0.027
Stone, clay and glass	0.030	0.175	0.504	0.206	0.105	0.050
Primary metals	0.019	0.111	0.357	0.267	0.125	0.048
Fabricated metals	0.031	0.174	0.480	0.231	0.128	0.060
Machinery, except electrical	0.024	0.131	0.382	0.304	0.172	0.083
Electrical equipment	0.032	0.203	0.532	0.244	0.149	0.076
Transportation equipment	0.017	0.099	0.314	0.333	0.196	0.090
Instruments	0.032	0.194	0.493	0.281	0.175	0.091
Miscellaneous manufacturing	0.087	0.352	0.646	0.156	0.089	0.045
Agriculture	0.181	0.533	0.761	0.133	0.087	0.056
Mining	0.024	0.141	0.386	0.266	0.150	0.072
Contract construction	0.043	0.210	0.468	0.294	0.176	0.082
Rail transport	0.014	0.077	0.303	0.275	0.132	0.036
Nonrail transport	0.044	0.204	0.444	0.267	0.141	0.066
Communications	0.045	0.222	0.556	0.257	0.157	0.069
Utilities	0.025	0.140	0.397	0.289	0.145	0.054
Trade	0.145	0.462	0.696	0.151	0.094	0.055
Finance	0.053	0.258	0.551	0.303	0.181	0.099
Services	0.122	0.398	0.643	0.177	0.114	0.066
All manufacturing	0.0428	0.2336	0.5203	0.2257	0.1282	0.0627
Nonfarm nonmanufacturing	0.1071	0.3667	0.6173	0.1941	0.1207	0.0669
All industries	0.0928	0.3375	0.5968	0.2002	0.1214	0.0654
All manufacturing, workers employed 50–52 weeks	0.0261	0.2078	0.5255	0.2864	0.1643	0.0808
Nonfarm nonmanufacturing, workers employed 50–52 weeks	0.0725	0.2984	0.5946	0.2610	0.1648	0.0927

Table 11.4
Changes in distribution of earnings by industry, 1949–1969, thirty industries.

	Less than $1,000	Less than $4,000	Less than $7,000	More than $10,000	More than $12,000	More than $15,000
$\ln(F)$, logarithm of proportion of workers in 1949 with earnings in corresponding range	0.851* (13.3)	0.859* (12.4)	0.815* (14.6)	0.718* (8.02)	0.636* (7.32)	0.490* (5.06)
Constant	−0.560	−0.093	−0.058	−0.458	−0.875	−1.66
Adjusted R^2	0.859	0.841	0,879	0.686	0.644	0.459
$\ln(F)$	0.849* (14.3)	0.849* (13.5)	0.799* (15.3)	0,728* (9.10)	0.645* (8.32)	0.501* (5.35)
$\ln(K_{69}/K_{49})$, logarithm of ratio of 1969 to 1949 capital to labor ratio	−0.358* (2.33)	−0.349* (2.61)	−0.169* (2.43)	0.486* (2.86)	0.484* (2.88)	0.352 (1.75)
Constant	−0.432	0.022	−0.007	−0.625	−1.04	−1.76
Adjusted R^2	0.878	0.868	0.897	0.750	0.718	0.496

Dependent variables: logarithms of proportions of workers with earnings in described range, 1969.

Table 11.5
Changes in distribution of earnings by industry, 1949–1969, twenty manufacturing industries.

	Less than $1,000	Less than $4,000	Less than $7,000	More than $10,000	More than $12,000	More than $15,000
$\ln(F)$	0.707* (9.68)	0.823* (9.68)	0.803* (12.77)	0.934* (10.78)	0.820* (9.73)	0.709* (9.36)
$\ln(K_{69}/K_{49})$	−0.696* (2.77)	−0.364 (1.39)	−0.119 (0.898)	0.203 (0.780)	0.325 (1.24)	0.429 (1.84)
Constant	−0.816	−0.010	−0.001	−0.251	−0.675	−1.30
Adjusted R^2	0.870	0.853	0.910	0,871	0,851	0.848

Dependent variables: logarithms of proportions of workers with earnings in described range, 1969.

those industries which have had larger proportional increases in the capital to labor ratio have had greater reductions in the number of workers in the lower tail and greater increases in the number of workers in the upper tail. These results are consistent with and support the hypothesis of capital-skill complementarity. The results are somewhat different when the twenty manufacturing industries are considered separately. The only significant effect of the capital term for this group of industries is in the very lowest range of the lower tail. Manufacturing industries with greater increases in capital intensity have on the average had significantly greater reductions in the extreme lower tail of the distribution of earnings. The coefficients for the other ranges are the same sign as for all thirty industries, and the magnitudes of the coefficients are comparable, but the coefficients are not significant at conventional levels.

5. Productivity, growth and other variables

The next step is to investigate the effects of other variables on the distribution of earnings within an industry. The aggregate analysis of the previous three chapters reveals no significant or consistent effect of productivity on earnings inequality, although the possibility of such an effect was established in Chapter 4. Generally, the measures of productivity have been too highly correlated with other explanatory variables to reveal anything. Kendrick (1973), in his study of postwar US productivity trends, has published productivity series for each of the thirty industries used in the analysis of this chapter. Productivity is measured by output per unit of input. As a measure of the change in productivity, the ratio of the 1966 to the 1949 productivity level is used. Additionally, the ratio of outputs in the same period is used as a measure of the growth of the industry. Finally, a dummy variable for nonmanufacturing industries is added to investigate systematic differences between manufacturing and nonmanufacturing industries.

Table 11.6

Change in distribution of earnings by industry, 1949–1969, thirty industries.

	Less than $1,000	Less than $4,000	Less than $7,000	More than $10,000	More than $12,000	More than $15,000
$\ln(F)$	0.869*	0.919*	0.846*	0.661*	0.551*	0.384*
	(12.5)	(11.99)	(14.5)	(6.98)	(6.36)	(3.69)
$\ln(K_{69}/K_{49})$	−0.436*	−0.301	−0.102	0.388	0.410*	0.340
	(2.46)	(1.93)	(1.29)	(1.99)	(2.25)	(1.57)
$\ln(P_{66}/P_{49})$, logarithm of ratio of 1966 to 1949 productivity	−0.055	−0.014	0.013	−0.139	−0.249*	−0.440
	(0.221)	(0.063)	(0.122)	(0.519)	(2.25)	(1.49)
$\ln(Q_{66}/Q_{49})$, logarithm of ratio of 1966 to 1949 output	0.198	0.224	0.073	0.240	0.352	0.463*
	(1.40)	(1.75)	(1.17)	(1.44)	(0.995)	(2.50)
D_1, dummy variable for nonmanufacturing industry	0.148	−0.013	−0.068	0.193	0.206	0.180
	(1.49)	(0.145)	(1.57)	(1.77)	(2.01)	(1.48)
Constant	−0.519	−0.044	−0.038	−0.877	−1.42	−2.25
Adjusted R^2	0.882	0.869	0.903	0.762	0.760	0.575

Dependent variable: logarithms of proportions of workers in described range, 1969.

The results are presented in table 11.6. The coefficients for the change in the capital to labor ratio retain their previously estimated signs. The magnitudes are approximately the same as their former levels, although the coefficients are often no longer statistically significant.

The results indicate that on the average changes in productivity are unrelated to the proportion of workers in the lower tail. However, increases in productivity definitely appear to be negatively related to the number of workers in the upper tail (although the estimated coefficient is only significant for the more than $12,000 range). The particular reason why productivity affects the upper tail of the distribution of earnings in this manner requires further investigation.

Growth appears to have a peculiar pattern of effects. Greater growth of output on the average is related to increases in both the upper and lower tail. Only in the case of the extreme upper tail, however, is the estimated coefficient significant. Growth could be related to the changes in the distribution of earnings within an industry in several ways. If demand for an industry's output goes up, profits in the industry will go up. Wage rates will be increased in order to draw more labor resources into the industry. Alternatively, increased industry profits could be shared among the employees. Either of these arguments could explain the relation between growth and the upper tail but give no explanation of the lower tail. The lower tail may be explained by labor supply shifts. Suppose that there has been a large increase in the supply of workers willing to take jobs at lower wages (in particular secondary wage earners). This increase in supply will lead to the expansion of those industries which can use such labor. Then growth would be associated with increases in the number of workers in the lower tail.

The estimated coefficients for the dummy variable for nonmanufacturing industries indicate that on the average, nonmanufacturing industries have had greater increases in the number of workers in the upper tail and in the extreme lower tail. None of the estimated coefficients is significant at conventional levels, however.

One important variable which could not be included for all thirty industries is for the division of employment between production and nonproduction workers (for nonmanufacturing industries, the distinction is between nonsupervisory and supervisory workers). Let N_{69} be the proportion of workers in 1969 that are production workers, and let N_{49} be the corresponding proportion in 1949. The ratio N_{69}/N_{49} then describes the change in the division of employment between production and nonproduction workers. The results for the twenty manufacturing industries and five nonmanufacturing industries using this term are presented in table 11.7. The excluded industries are agriculture, rail and nonrail transportation, trade and services.

Table 11.7
Changes in distribution of earnings by industry, 1949–1969, twenty-five industries.

	Less than $1,000	Less than $4,000	Less than $7,000	More than $10,000	More than $12,000	More than $15,000
$\ln(F)$	0.752*	0.798*	0.759*	0.822*	0.658*	0.549*
	(7.79)	(7.82)	(9.66)	(8.21)	(8.09)	(6.58)
$\ln(K_{69}/K_{49})$	−0.534*	−0.268	−0.071	−0.059	−0.005	−0.034
	(2.35)	(1.38)	(0.709)	(0.336)	(0.036)	(0.219)
$\ln(P_{66}/P_{49})$	0.140	0.338	0.175	−0.714*	−0.785*	−0.605*
	(0.370)	(1.04)	(1.05)	(2.42)	(3.07)	(2.30)
$\ln(Q_{66}/Q_{49})$	0.098	0.062	0.034	0.283	0.415*	0.357*
	(0.535)	(0.379)	(0.421)	(1.84)	(3.17)	(2.68)
D_1	0.084	−0.084	−0.121*	0.240*	0.256*	0.221*
	(0.696)	(0.820)	(2.30)	(2.43)	(2.98)	(2.46)
$\ln(N_{69}/N_{49})$, logarithm of	1.22	1.72	1.03	−1.92*	−2.29*	−2.36*
ratio of 1969 to 1949	(1.09)	(1.74)	(2.01)	(2.18)	(2.99)	(2.98)
production worker proportion						
Constant	−0.756	−0.139	−0.065	−0.414	−1.08	−1.78
Adjusted R^2	0.840	0.857	0.902	0.891	0.908	0.877

Dependent variables: logarithms of proportions of workers with earnings in described range, 1969.

The results for the previously discussed variables are substantially the same as for the thirty industries in table 11.6, with the following exceptions. The estimated coefficient for the productivity term is now negative and significant for all three measures of the upper tail. The effect of growth is now positive and significant for the two higher measures of the upper tail (more than $12,000 and more than $15,000), and is negligible for the lower tail. For the twenty-five industries under consideration, the coefficient for the nonmanufacturing dummy variable indicates that the five nonmanufacturing industries have had significantly greater increases in the proportions of workers in the upper tail and a reduction in the lower tail (as measured by the proportion of workers with earnings less than $7,000). For the extreme lower tail there is apparently no significant difference between the five nonmanufacturing industries and the twenty manufacturing industries. With the production worker term added, the estimated coefficients for the capital term for the upper tail are no longer significant and are negative. This does not mean that the capital to labor ratio has no relation to the proportion of workers in the upper tail. It is possible that the capital to labor ratio affects the division of employment between production and nonproduction workers, and the latter in turn affects the upper tail.

The effects of the production worker term are fairly strong. On the average the estimated coefficients for the term are negative and significant for the upper tail and positive for the lower tail. On the average those industries which have had greater increases in the proportion of nonproduction workers have had significantly greater increases in the proportion of workers in the upper tail and have had decreases in the proportion of workers in the lower tail. Since nonproduction workers are generally white-collar, higher-paid workers, this is exactly the result one would expect. However, the determinants of the division of employment between production and nonproduction workers require further analysis, which will be provided in the following chapters.

Table 11.8 presents the results using the twenty manufacturing industries. In these regressions the dummy variable for nonmanufacturing industries is of course dropped. A dummy variable for durable goods industries is added. The results for the capital, productivity, growth and production worker terms are substantially the same as for the twenty-five industry and thirty industry regressions. This is not surprising, since the manufacturing industry data are a large subset of the previously used data. The estimated coefficient for the durable goods dummy variable is positive and significant for the upper tail and negative for the lower tail. Durable goods industries have on the average had greater increases in the proportions of workers in the upper tail, and have had reductions in the proportions in the lower tail.

The addition of the production worker term in tables 11.7 and 11.8 appears

Table 11.8
Changes in distribution of earnings by industry, 1949–1969, twenty manufacturing industries.

	Less than $1,000	Less than $4,000	Less than $7,000	More than $10,000	More than $12,000	More than $15,000
$\ln(F)$	0.668* (7.18)	0.760* (7.03)	0.754* (9.81)	0.797* (8.43)	0.643* (9.74)	0.521* (9.64)
$\ln(K_{69}/K_{49})$	−0.573 (2.00)	−0.175 (0.636)	−0.028 (0.207)	−0.077 (0.336)	−0.017 (0.100)	−0.099 (0.719)
$\ln(P_{66}/P_{49})$	0.325 (0.754)	0.298 (0.717)	0.178 (0.892)	−0.538 (1.58)	−0.616* (2.45)	−0.282 (1.38)
$\ln(Q_{66}/Q_{49})$	0.003 (0.014)	0.079 (0.371)	0.031 (0.316)	0.209 (1.18)	0.367* (2.84)	0.302* (2.88)
$\ln(N_{69}/N_{49})$	1.16 (1.08)	1.85 (1.72)	0.944 (1.78)	−1.96* (2.23)	−2.18* (3.37)	−2.19* (4.16)
D_2, dummy variable for durable goods industry	−0.092 (0.903)	−0.143 (1.46)	−0.072 (1.52)	0.172* (2.10)	0.169* (2.81)	0.144* (2.94)
Constant	−0.983	−0.141	−0.053	−0.564	−1.23	−2.06
Adjusted R^2	0.856	0.862	0.919	0.916	0.948	0.956

Dependent variables: logarithms of proportions of workers with earnings in described range, 1969.

Table 11.9
Correlation coefficients for thirty industries.

	$\ln(K_{69}/K_{49})$	$\ln(P_{66}/P_{49})$	$\ln(Q_{66}/Q_{49})$	D_1
$\ln(K_{69}/K_{49})$	1.00			
$\ln(P_{66}/P_{49})$	0.282	1.00		
$\ln(Q_{66}/Q_{49})$	−0.097	0.298	1.00	
D_1	0.439	0.047	−0.228	1.00

Table 11.10
Correlation coefficients for twenty manufacturing industries.

	$\ln(K_{69}/K_{49})$	$\ln(P_{66}/P_{49})$	$\ln(Q_{66}/Q_{49})$	$\ln(N_{69}/N_{49})$	D_2
$\ln(K_{69}/K_{49})$	1.00				
$\ln(P_{66}/P_{49})$	0.133	1.00			
$\ln(Q_{66}/Q_{49})$	0.265	0.651	1.00		
$\ln(N_{69}/N_{49})$	−0.436	−0.449	−0.473	1.00	
D_2	0.148	−0.057	0.275	0.023	1.00

to have substantially increased the explanatory power of the regressions for the upper tail. Apparently, the upper tail of the distribution of earnings within an industry is strongly affected by changes in the division of employment between production and nonproduction workers, as one would expect.

The correlation coefficients for the dependent variables are presented in table 11.9 for all thirty industries and in table 11.10 for the twenty manufacturing industries. For all thirty industries, increases in productivity are correlated with increases in capital intensity and growth of output. Nonmanufacturing industries have apparently had greater increases in capital intensity and smaller growth in output. For the twenty manufacturing industries, changes in productivity are highly correlated with growth in output. Also, the production worker term is negatively correlated with the capital, productivity and growth terms. More nonproductive workers go along with increases in capital intensity, productivity and growth. The causal relations among these variables remain to be sorted out (see Kendrick, 1973, ch. 6 for a discussion of these relations).

6. Effects of sectoral shifts

Comparing table 11.6 with table 11.4, an important inference is that the major determinant of an industry's proportion of workers in 1969 in a given range is the corresponding proportion in 1949. The other variables, while occasionally significantly modifying these proportions, do not add large amounts to the explanatory power of the regression models, as measured by the adjusted R^2. It follows that, as observed for the mean earnings by industry, there is substantial temporal continuity in the distribution of earnings by industry. This does not necessarily mean that the distribution of earnings within an industry is stable over time. It is possible that the distributions of earnings within industries change substantially over time, but that the changes are the same for each industry. It is also apparent from tables 11.2 and 11.3 that there is a great deal of variation among industries in the distribution of earnings. It would seem to follow from these two observations that the distribution of earnings should be strongly affected by shifts in output and employment among different sectors and should be only slightly modified by economy-wide changes in capital intensity or productivity.

The large variation in the distributions of earnings among industries relative to the variation between different time periods suggests that it is possible to describe the demands for workers of different productive abilities in two stages. The first stage is to explain the distribution of earnings within each industry. At any one point in time, with the prices of different labor services the same across industries, the distribution of earnings within an industry can be taken as reflecting the distribution of demands for workers of different productive abilities. Higher earnings would represent higher productive abilities, although the correspondence between the two would not be explicitly known. Secondly, one could explain the division of output and employment among the various industries.

There are two major difficulties with the description of demand in this manner. The first is with the interpretation of the distribution of earnings within an industry. There are important objections to regarding the distribution as reflecting the distribution of demands for workers of different productive abilities. The second difficulty is that it is not clear how a shift in employment from one sector to another will affect the distribution of earnings.

To make the discussion concrete, consider the distribution of earnings within manufacturing as compared to the distribution in nonmanufacturing. The mean level of earnings is lower in nonmanufacturing, but the dispersion of earnings is much greater. In particular, there are many more workers in the lower tail of distribution in nonmanufacturing, arising from the services and trade areas. At the upper tail, the proportions are close, but in the extreme upper tail, nonmanufacturing has a higher proportion than manufacturing. Given these differences, what would be the consequences of a shift in output and employment from manufacturing to nonmanufacturing (assuming all industries within each category change in the same proportion)? If the distribution of earnings were rigidly determined within the two sectors, the shift from manufacturing to nonmanufacturing would increase the level of earnings inequality. In contrast, suppose that the distribution of earnings within each sector reflected the distribution of demands for workers of different levels of productive ability. Then the increase in nonmanufacturing jobs would raise the demands for the less-productive, low-income workers. For a given distribution of workers according to productive ability, the increased demand for the less-productive workers will tend to raise their earnings levels, and the effect of the shift via the lower tail would be to reduce earnings inequality. At the same time, the increase in nonmanufacturing jobs would raise the demand for workers with earnings currently in the extreme upper tail, thereby raising their earnings further.

The above discussion should make it apparent that the consequences of a shift in employment from one sector to another are not immediately obvious. The empirical work indicates that a shift from manufacturing to nonmanufacturing results in an increase in earnings inequality, everything else the same. In the cross-section studies of Chapter 9, the estimated coefficient for the ratio of manufacturing to total nonfarm employment is consistently negative and significant. The ratio also significantly affected the shares of earnings received by the top 1 and top 5 percent of all income recipients. The variable was also significant in the wage differential regressions, although not in the income inequality regressions of Chapter 8. Let us now consider several points of view regarding the interpretation of the distribution of earnings within an industry and the consequences of sectoral shifts.

The human capital model developed by Mincer gives a clear-cut answer to the above questions. In the Mincer model, as discussed in Chapter 2, individuals choose among schooling levels so as to maximize the present value of life-time incomes. The consequence is that the supply curves for workers at any level of schooling will be horizontal, i.e. they will be perfectly elastic. It follows that the number of individuals at any schooling level is completely determined by the location of the demand curve. If schooling were the only determinant of productive ability, or if the supplies of workers at any level of productive ability were perfectly elastic, then the distribution of earnings for the economy would be the simple sum of the distributions of earnings within each industry. The consequence of a shift in employment from manufacturing to nonmanufacturing would be to change the weights of the linear combination of the two sectoral distributions of earnings. In other words, in the long run the supply of workers would change in exactly the same way as the distribution of demands. The study of the distribution of earnings would be exceedingly simple, because the changes in demand would cause no changes in the relative earnings of workers with different levels of productive ability.

An opposing point of view (which nevertheless yields the same conclusion as the Mincer model) is that the wage and employment structures within firms and industries are rigidly determined and are by and large unaffected by labor market conditions. This point of view is most closely associated with the work of Doeringer and Piore (1971). However, there is an important distinction between the rigidity of the distribution of earnings and the rigidity of the rules governing the pricing and allocation of labor in internal labor markets. The possible connection between the two deserves further attention. The argument for rigidly determined distributions of earnings within industries has been put more forcefully by Bowles and Gintis (1976) in their radical critique of the US educational system. Their argument is that the distribution of earnings is determined by the control requirements of the capitalist way of organizing production. Inequality is created with a hierarchical organization for the purpose of exerting control over workers' labor activity by the owners of the means of production. The consequences are that workers have little discretion in their work activities, the relationships between workers at different levels are primarily authoritarian, differences in earnings are created and tied to production-irrelevant criteria (e.g. race, sex and social background), and the distribution of earnings within an industry is unrelated to labor market conditions or the employment-relevant characteristics of employees (such as skills, experience and abilities). Furthermore, the authoritarian hierarchy and the corresponding division of labor (job fragmentation) are not required for any technological reasons and are not necessarily more efficient. Instead, the hierarchical division of labor is merely an element in the capitalist way of organizing production. By inference, it is this way of organizing production which is responsible for inequality.

The problem with this theory is that it has not been elaborated to the extent where it is operational. It does not explain why there are differences in the distribution of earnings by industry, and it does not explain variations in earnings inequality over time. Finally, the testable hypotheses of the theory have not been specified in sufficient detail. The type of evidence that has been cited in support of the theory arises from the observation that workers' earnings do not depend solely on their observable work-relevant characteristics but also on the industry in which they are placed (see, for example, Bluestone, Murphy and Stevenson, 1973). Such evidence strongly supports the argument that there are noncompeting groups and labor market segmentation (see the discussion by Cain, 1976). Some of the difficulties with this type of evidence are that many of the work-relevant characteristics of employees are unobservable (such as training), and that there are alternative explanations of why earnings differ among industries for what appears to be the same type of worker.

Thurow (1975) has put forward a third interpretation of the distribution of earnings within industries, closely related to Doeringer and Piore's theory of internal labor markets and on-the-job training. According to Thurow, most of the skills required for the performance of a job are learned on the job. The qualifications of the worker upon entry into a firm are irrelevant, although they may affect the length of time needed to learn the job. The wage paid is then related to the job itself and is not related to the characteristics of the employee. A change in the distribution of worker characteristics (the supply side) would have no effect on the distribution of earnings, which would be determined solely by the distribution of jobs. Again, the distribution of earnings would be rigidly determined within industries. A difficulty with this point of view is that it is hard to reconcile the rigid association between wages and jobs with any sort of optimizing behavior on the part of firms.

Osberg (1975, ch. 5), in his doctoral thesis, has presented a fourth interpretation of the distribution of earnings within an industry based on the rate of learning. Workers in an industry undergo learning by doing, with the result that their earnings go up over time. The rate at which the learning takes place affects the age-earnings relation and consequently the distribution of earnings within the industry. Osberg has estimated the rates of learning for a number of industries. Unfortunately, the sample appears to be too small to investigate whether there are any systematic differences among industries. More generally, the distribution of earnings within an industry will clearly depend on the amount of training given in that industry and the way in which the costs and benefits of training will be shared. In this regard the human capital discussion of training has concentrated on the conditions under which workers would be willing to undergo training. Although the marginal condition for optimizing behavior by the employer have been specified (e.g. the increased revenues from training one more employee must equal the increased costs), the determinants of the absolute amount of training have not been specified.

The point of view taken in this monograph is that the distribution of earnings within an industry reflects the distribution of numbers of workers of different productive abilities demanded by firms in that industry. This distribution of demands is determined by the production requirements of the firms in the industry in combination with the relation between wages and productive ability. (The necessary production theory will be developed in the next chapter.) The distribution of earnings within an industry is therefore not rigidly determined. The empirical work of this chapter generally supports this point of view. Changes in the distribution of earnings within industries are associated with changes in the capital to labor ratio, productivity, growth and the division of employment between production and nonproduction workers.

The mechanism by which a shift in employment and output from manufacturing to nonfarm nonmanufacturing results in greater earnings inequality is, according to the differential rents theory, as follows. Compared to manufacturing, nonfarm nonmanufacturing has a much more unequal distribution of capital among jobs. There are jobs in some industries, such as utilities, communication, railroads and transportation, that have large amounts of capital per worker. Other industries, such as trade and services, have low amounts of capital per worker. The effect of the shift in production and employment towards nonmanufacturing is to increase the amount of capital concentration. As a result, some of the less-productive workers previously employed in manufacturing find that their labor is combined with less capital, and some of the more-productive workers find that their labor is combined with more capital. The wages of the more-productive workers are pushed up by the shift and the wages of the less-productive workers are pushed down. Earnings inequality therefore increases, as observed.

In terms of supply and demand, the increase in employment raises the demands both for very low skilled and very highly skilled workers, as reflected in the distribution of earnings in nonfarm nonmanufacturing. However, the corresponding reduction in manufacturing reduces the demands for workers in the middle ranges of productive abilities. Taking both of the changes together, the effect is to raise earnings inequality, according to the differential rents model.

There are several important qualifications to the interpretation of the distribution of earnings in an industry as reflecting the distribution of demands for workers. The predictions of the differential rents model are based on an economy in which the labor force is fixed, except for changes at the extensive margin, the least-productive workers employed. There is no intensive margin in the model as it now stands. That is to say, the supplies of workers with productive abilities above those of the least-productive employed workers are fixed and are unaffected by changes in wage rates or job opportunities. In examining the effects of shifts among industrial sectors, it is therefore necessary to take account of changes in employment as well as changes in capital concentration. Because of unemployment, mobility or changes in labor force participation rates, a shift towards nonfarm nonmanufacturing could result in greater numbers of low-earnings workers being employed or entering the labor force. As a result, earnings inequality would go up, for reasons unrelated to capital concentration. These employment effects could account for the significance of the coefficients for the manufacturing ratio in the cross-section regressions even when the capital concentration term is included.

The size of the nonfarm nonmanufacturing sector can be expected to have strong labor force effects because it is dominated by trade and services. These industries in turn employ large numbers of secondary wage earners, such as teenagers and individuals with employed spouses, who have significant alternatives to labor force participation. The availability of suitable jobs, in terms of hours, experience needed, location, commitment and working conditions, may significantly affect the decisions of individuals to enter the work force. A shift from manufacturing to nonmanufacturing may then result in larger numbers of secondary wage earners entering the labor force.

Bowen and Finegan (1969), in their study of labor force participation rates, provide substantial evidence on the labor force effects of the industrial composition of employment. From the time-series regressions covering the period 1949–1965, the ratio of manufacturing to total employment has significant effects on the labor force participation rates of different groups. The estimated coefficients for the manufacturing employment ratio are negative and significant for males 14–15, 16–17, 18–19, 20–24 and 65 and over, and for females in all age groups (Bowen and Finegan, 1969, p. 863). The estimated coefficients for the manufacturing employment ratio are positive for males 25–34, 35–44, 45–54 and 55–64 (the coefficient is only significant for males 45–54). Bowen and Finegan conclude that the increases in nonmanufacturing in the postwar period have increased the job opportunities for teenagers, older males and adult women, and consequently have raised their labor force participation rates (p. 511).

Bowen and Finegan also construct measures of the expected male and teenage male industry mix (p. 453) and the female industry mix (p. 772). These measure the proportions of male, teenage male or female workers in a Standard Statistical Metropolitan Area that are expected on the basis of the industrial mix in that area, using national employment proportions for each industry. The mixes are therefore measures of the demands for males, teenage males or females. These mixes are found to affect significantly the labor force participation rates of various groups (pp. 80, 196, 453).

The existence of these labor force effects creates a great problem for the study of earnings inequality. Consider an increase in production and employment in trade and services. This shift draws into the labor force many workers who will then be employed at low-earnings levels. The greater numbers of these low-earnings workers will raise the measure of earnings inequality. But clearly these workers are made better off by the increase in their job opportunities. The normative conclusion to be drawn from the shift from manufacturing to nonmanufacturing is then directly opposite to what one would infer from the change in the measure of earnings inequality. Earnings inequality goes up, but because the demands for workers with earnings in the lower tail has increased, they are made better off. This problem is clearly a fault in the current measures of earnings inequality. They validly measure changes in earnings inequality only for a fixed labor force. Because they do not control for changes in labor force participation rates, they cannot now be validly used to draw normative conclusions.

A second qualification to the interpretation of the distribution of earnings given here is that in some instances similar workers can receive different wages in different industries. Unionization can clearly have this consequence. One effect of unions may be to impose a minimum wage on an industry. Firms in the industry may respond by choosing more productive workers than they would otherwise, as suggested by Pettengill (1979). The less-productive workers not employed in the unionized sector would seek employment in the nonunionized sector, thereby depressing wages in that sector. One would then expect a larger lower tail in the nonunionized industries than in unionized industries. Similar remarks hold with reference to federally imposed minimum wages (see in particular Mincer's analysis of minimum wages (1976)). These observations are consistent with the differences in the distribution of earnings between the manufacturing and nonmanufacturing industries. By and large the manufacturing sector is more heavily unionized than the service industries, and the coverage of the minimum wage laws is more complete in manufacturing. As one would expect from these observations, a a smaller proportion of workers in manufacturing are in the lower tail compared to nonmanufacturing. Along with training, the effects of unions on the distribution of earnings deserve much more detailed examination, and are reserved for later study.

Another reason why the same worker may have different potential earnings in different industries is the presence of compensating wage differences. In an industry where the working conditions are worse, the equilibrium wage rate is higher. The operation of compensating wage differences is well known to most economists, although the aggregate effects on the distribution of earnings have only recently been examined (Sattinger, 1977a). A closely related but distinct argument is that the earnings paid to a worker affect the value of the worker's labor. This possibility has been discussed at length by Marshall (1964), primarily in the context of less-developed countries. Similarly, after discussing several case studies, Tausky (1970) concludes that in more automated work environments, the work required is substantially different in nature. The worker is required to provide mental alertness and rapid judgment in monitoring machinery, instead of muscular effort. In other words, the worker is paid to remain alert and prepared to act, rather than for a particular amount of output. This is an instance where the value of the labor received by the firm depends crucially on the motivation of the employee and not just a physical amount of activity. The consequences of such phenomena for the distribution of earnings within firms have been discussed by Simon (1957) and Leibenstein (1976) and in the organization theory literature (see, for example, March and Simon, 1958).

Some of the evidence presented in this monograph supports the argument that increases in capital intensity in manufacturing industries result in greater earnings being paid to essentially the same workers. The results in table 11.5 indicate that those manufacturing industries with greater increases in capital intensity have had on the average greater reductions in the proportion of workers in the extreme lower tail. Suppose we interpret this result as meaning that the wages paid to the very least skilled workers are increased (as opposed to meaning that as a result of a greater capital to labor ratio, the industry demands fewer of the very least skilled workers). Then one would expect earnings inequality and wage differentials to decline as the manufacturing capital to labor ratio increases. This is exactly the result that has been obtained in the cross-section analysis and in the wage differential estimates.

A final qualification is that the analysis undertaken in this book has been by and large based on the use of a single-dimensional description of productive ability. If there are multidimensional attributes (as there surely are), the analysis becomes substantially more complex.

7. Conclusions

This chapter has examined changes in the distribution of earnings within industries over time. The procedure has been to relate the proportions of workers in the upper or lower earnings tails in 1969 in an industry to the corresponding proportions in 1949. Occasionally, the proportions in 1969 are significantly affected by changes in the capital to labor ratio, the ratio of production workers to total employment, output and productivity. The results indicate that, relative to the differences among industries in their distributions of earnings at one point in time, changes over time are less variable. That is, the primary determinant of the proportion of workers with earnings in a given range in 1969 is the corresponding proportion in 1949. It follows that shifts in production and employment among industries should have greater effects on the distribution of earnings than changes in the distributions of earnings within industries.

However, the particular inferences to be drawn from interindustry shifts in employment depend on the interpretation of the distribution of earnings within an industry. If the distribution of earnings is rigidly determined within industries (so that equivalent workers would be paid different earnings in different industries), then the expansion of a low earnings industry would result in greater earnings inequality. If, instead, the distribution of earnings within an industry represents the distribution of demands for workers of different qualifications, then the expansion of a low earnings industry could result in an increased demand for less-skilled workers, raising their job opportunities and earnings.

If the distribution of earnings is interpreted as reflecting demands, a second complication arises from the potential labor force effects of different industries. Suppose there is an increase in trade and services and that in response the labor force participation rates of young and old males and females are increased. These groups may be employed at low earnings so that the observed effect of the increase in trade and services is to raise the number of low-earnings individuals and raise the level of earnings inequality. The normative conclusion one would want to draw is just the opposite, however; i.e. the increase in job opportunities makes these low-earnings groups better off. This conflict between inequality measures and the appropriate normative conclusions can only be resolved by developing measures of earnings inequality that control for changes in labor force participation rates.

Because of the complexity of the issues, it is best not to draw any final conclusions at this point regarding the effects of sectoral shifts. Labor force effects, the determination of wages for low-income workers and the weighting of nonlabor market activities in a normative inequality measure deserve much more study.

Appendix: Data sources

Tables 11.1–11.3. The 1949 proportions in table 11.2 are calculated from the *1950 US Census of Population, Special Reports, Industrial Characteristics*, US Department of Commerce, Bureau of the Census, table 17, p. 75. The 1969 proportions in table 11.3 are calculated from the *1970 US Census of Population, Subject Reports, Industrial Characteristics*, US Department of Commerce, Bureau of the Census, table 12, p. 77. In table 11.1 the mean earnings for each year are calculated from the same sources. For 1969, the average earnings for each bracket are the same as those used in Chapter 9. For 1949, the bracket means were used as the average earnings for the bracket. For the highest bracket, a Pareto tail was fitted to obtain an estimate of the average earnings. The estimate obtained in this manner is $16,623. The capital to labor ratios were the same as those used in Chapter 7. Tables 11.4 and 11.5 use the same data as tables 11.1–11.3.

Tables 11.6–11.8. The productivity and output variables P_{66}/P_{49} and Q_{66}/Q_{49}, are obtained from data published by John W. Kendrick, *Postwar Pro-*

ductivity Trends in the United States, 1948—69, National Bureau of Economic Research, distributed by Columbia University Press, New York, 1973. The data are given in part III. For services and for finance, insurance and real estate, productivity series are not given in that source. However, using capital stock data later published by Kendrick (1976), the productivity values were calculated using the procedures described by Kendrick. In finance, insurance and real estate, the level of gross factor productivity is estimated to be 76.1 in 1949 and 115.9 in 1966. In services, the corresponding levels are 92.7 and 104.3. The data on ratio of production workers to total employees, N_{69}/N_{49}, are taken from *Employment and Earnings, United States, 1909—75*, US Department of Labor, Bureau of Labor Statistics, Bulletin 1312—10, 1976.

Chapter 12

THE DISTRIBUTION OF EARNINGS BY INDUSTRY

1. Introduction

The previous chapter examined changes in the distribution of earnings within industries over time in order to investigate the effect of changes in capital intensity on the distribution of earnings. While changes in the capital to labor ratio and changes in the ratio of production workers to total employees systematically affected industry demands for workers, those demands differed substantially from industry to industry and remained fairly stable over time. Compared to changes in the capital to labor ratio and the ratio of production workers to total employees, shifts in production and employment among industries can therefore be expected to have much stronger effects on the demands for workers of different productive abilities and hence on the distribution of earnings.

This chapter seeks to explain the differences in the distribution of earnings among industries. As in the last chapter, the point of view taken here is that wage rates are equalized across industries and that differences in the distribution of earnings among industries represent differences in the demands for labor of different qualities or abilities. This underlying assumption is subject to the potential qualification that low-income workers with the same employment characteristics may receive different earnings in different industries, as discussed in the previous chapter. It should be emphasized that the question of whether industries with fewer low-earnings workers are paying less-skilled workers higher wages or are hiring fewer less-skilled workers appears to be unanswered. The formulation of a convincing empirical test of this question is a research project of major importance for the distribution of earnings.

The next section develops a purely neoclassical theory of the demand by a firm for a distribution of workers according to some characteristic. Essentially, the section does for the size distribution of earnings what traditional production function theory has done for factor shares: relate the distribution of earnings to features of the production function.

It is possible to examine the distribution of earnings within an industry in two ways. First, it is possible to study the demand for workers according to some important employee characteristic, such as years of schooling. This analysis is undertaken in section 3. Alternatively, it is possible to study the demand for workers directly in terms of the earnings received by those workers. If earnings are an increasing function of productive ability, then the distribution of earnings within an industry represents the distribution of demands for workers with respect to a transform of productive ability (assuming that employees only differ according to one characteristic, referred to here as productive ability). This analysis is undertaken in section 4.

The distribution of earnings within an industry can be seen from another point of view. Chapter 7 presented some preliminary results on the demands for workers by industry. More capital-intensive industries employed the more-productive workers, as measured by earnings or schooling, although capital intensity alone did not explain much of the variation. The interpretation placed on these results, following the analysis of Chapter 5, is that the more-productive workers are assigned to more capital-intensive jobs in equilibrium. It follows that by studying the distribution of jobs according to capital intensity, one can draw inferences about the distribution of demands for workers of different productive abilities. The analyses of sections 3 and 4 of this chapter will reveal other determinants of the demands for workers according to productive ability, in particular the ratio of production workers to total employment and the level of technological complexity. It should then be possible to study changes in the distribution of employment according to these industrial characteristics and draw inferences for the distribution of demands for workers and the distribution of earnings.

2. A neoclassical theory of the demand for a distribution of workers

The Cobb-Douglas production function was originally put forward as a means of explaining the distribution of income between capital and labor (Cobb and Douglas, 1928). Since then, the neoclassical theory of production has been successively elaborated to account for more than two factors of production (Allen, 1938; Sato and Koizumi, 1973a, 1973b), nonconstant factor shares (Arrow, Chenery, Minhas and M. Solow, 1961) and the effects of scale (Sato, 1977). From the neoclassical point of view, factor shares are explained by various features of the production function and factor supplies.

The difficulty with this theory as it has been developed is that it deals only with homogeneous factors of production. While factor shares have been explained with production functions, the theory of the size distribution of earnings has been developed by appealing to other phenomena. No production function that has been presented would imply that a firm would hire a continuous distribution of workers according to some employment characteristic. The intention of this section is to develop production theory to account for the employment of distributions of workers.

This development can be approached through an extension of the Cobb-Douglas production function. A simple Cobb-Douglas production function (without necessarily constant returns to scale) is given by $Q = Ax_1^{\alpha_1} x_2^{\alpha_2}$, where x_1 and x_2 are the quantities of two factors of production, α_1 and α_2 are the exponents, Q is the amount of production and A is a constant. Extending the production function to n factors of production,

$$Q = Ax_1^{\alpha_1} x_2^{\alpha_2} \ldots x_n^{\alpha_n} = A \exp \sum_{i=i}^{n} \alpha_i \ln x_i.$$

where Π is the symbol for multiplication of the following elements. The expression above may be rewritten as

$$Q = A \prod_{i}^{n} x_i^{\alpha_i} = A \exp \sum_{i=1}^{n} \alpha_i \ln x_i.$$

Instead of having n discrete factors of production, suppose there is a continuous distribution of factors according to some quality variable. Suppose the quality variable is given by g, for productive ability, and suppose g varies from g_0 to g_1. The exponent α can then be expressed as a function of the quality variable, $\alpha(g)$. Assume that $\alpha(g)$ is continuous. The quantity of the factor of quality g used by the firm is then $x(g)$. The extension of the production to the continuous distribution case is then given by

$$Q = A \exp \int_{g_2}^{g_1} \alpha(g) \ln x(g) dg$$

The problem for the firm is to select a density function $x(g)$ so as to maximize production subject to a cost constraint.

Suppose that the cost of a unit of factor of quality g is given by $w(g)$, where $w(g)$ is a continuous function. The cost of a given distribution $x(g)$ is then

$$\int_{g_0}^{g_1} w(g) x(g) dg.$$

To derive the result as a simple problem in the calculus of variations, form the cumulative cost function

$$C(g) = \int_{g_0}^{g} w(t)x(t)\,dt,$$

the cost of all labor of grade g or less. Then

$$C'(g) = w(g)x(g).$$

Form the functional

$$J[C] = \int_{g_0}^{g_1} \alpha(t)\ln x(t)\,dt = \int_{g_0}^{g_1} \alpha(t)\ln(C'(t)/w(t))\,dt.$$

The problem of finding the employment density function $x(g)$ subject to a cost constraint is equivalent to the problem of finding the cost function $C(g)$ that maximizes the functional $J[C]$ subject to the boundary conditions $C(g_0) = 0$ and $C(g_1) = C_0$, where C_0 is the total labor cost. Because the integrand in $J[C]$ does not depend on $C(g)$, the solution to the problem is obtained by setting $\alpha(g)/C'(g) = \lambda$, where λ is a constant of integration chosen to satisfy the boundary conditions (Gelfand and Fomin, 1963, p. 18; Takayama, 1974, p. 414). Then $x(g) = \alpha(g)/\lambda w(g)$. It follows that the optimal density function of workers is given by the exponent function $\alpha(g)$ as modified or distorted by the wage function $w(g)$. Furthermore, the amount of factor income going to workers of quality g, given by $x(g)w(g)$, is a constant amount $\alpha(g)/\lambda$ which is independent of the wage function $w(g)$. These results are directly analogous to the conclusions for factor shares derived from the Cobb-Douglas production function.

Suppose, for example, that the values of $\alpha(g)$ are described by the lognormal probability density function, such that the mean and variance of the logarithms of g are μ and σ^2. Suppose that the wage function $w(g)$ is given by the exponential form ag^b, where a and b are positive constants. Then the distribution of wages in the firm is also lognormal, and the mean and variance of the logarithms of wages are then $\ln a + b\mu$ and $b^2\sigma^2$ (Aitchison and Brown, 1957, theorem 2.1, p. 11).

Furthermore, a theory of individual firm demand for a distribution of workers according to the employment characteristic g can easily be extended to an aggregate demand for labor, via the reproductive properties of the lognormal distribution. Suppose that each firm in an economy has a lognormal distribution of wages among its employees, and suppose that the variance of logarithms of earnings is the same for each firm, σ^2. Suppose there are a large number of firms, and suppose that the distribution of firms' mean earnings is itself lognormally distributed. Let μ_0 and σ_0^2 be the mean and variance of the logarithms of firms' mean earnings. Then for the economy as a whole, the distribution of earnings will also be lognormal. The mean and variance of the logarithms of earnings will be $\mu_0 - \sigma^2/2$ and $\sigma_0^2 + \sigma^2$, respectively (Aitchison and Brown, 1957, pp. 11 and 110). In a similar manner, Lydall (1968, p. 105) applied the Aitchison and Brown result to the distribution of earnings within occupations.

In the production function that has been developed it is not necessary for capital to enter explicitly or separately. Instead, it is possible that the parameters of the distribution $\alpha(g)$ depend on the amount of capital. If this were so, it would be possible to estimate the parameters of the distribution of earnings as functions of the amount of capital.

3. Demands for workers by schooling levels

This section analyzes differences among industries in their employment of workers with different schooling levels. Essentially, by studying the determinants of these demands it should be possible to discover the principles underlying the assignment of college educated and high school educated workers to jobs.

The equations estimated in this section should be regarded as reduced form quantity equations. Ordinarily, a reduced form quantity equation will depend on both demand and supply variables. However, in a cross-section analysis the supply conditions and variables are substantially the same across industries, so that they drop out. The resulting equation therefore describes how differences in the demand variables affect the quantity demanded. The major attention of this book has been directed towards the capital to labor ratio as the determinant of demand. Of course, the capital to labor ratio for a firm or industry is determined endogenously in response to all the factor prices. However, with factor prices substantially the same across industries, differences in the capital to labor ratios among industries can be regarded as being determined exogenously by the technologies of the different industries. In addition to the capital to labor ratio, Chapter 11 revealed that changes in the ratio of production to workers to total employees caused significant changes in the distribution of earnings within an industry. This ratio will be also included as a demand variable here. It is treated as exogenously determined, following the same argument as for the capital to labor ratio.

Table 12.1 presents some preliminary results using the industries studied in Chapters 7 and 11. The first three columns present the results using twenty-five manufacturing and nonmanufacturing industries (the excluded industries are

Table 12.1
Schooling levels by industry, 1969.

	25 industries			20 manufacturing industries		
	Four years high school or more (1)	Four years college or more (2)	Mean schooling (3)	Four years high school or more (4)	Four years college or more (5)	Mean schooling (6)
$\ln(K/L)$, logarithm of capital to labor ratio in industry	0.041* (2.31)	0.017* (3.36)	0.020 (1.81)	0.019 (1.08)	0.017* (2.65)	0.010 (0.838)
$\ln(N)$, logarithm of ratio of production workers to total employment	−0.764* (5.99)	−0.286* (7.67)	−0.516* (6.40)	−0.851* (8.91)	−0.283* (8.15)	−0.562* (8.38)
D_1, dummy variable for nonmanufacturing industry	0.131* (2.85)	0.025 (1.84)	0.080* (2.75)			
D_2, dummy variable for durable goods manufacturing industry	0.027 (0.845)	−0.002 (0.235)	0.009 (0.474)	0.024 (1.07)	−0.002 (0.274)	0.008 (0.572)
Constant	0.177	−0.055	2.16	0.211	−0.054	2.17
Adjusted R^2	0.714	0.807	0.714	0.852	0.858	0.832

Dependent variables: logarithm of proportion of male and female workers with four years college or more (columns 1 and 4), four years college or more (columns 2 and 5), and mean schooling (columns 3 and 6).
Positive values of t-statistics are given in parentheses under estimated coefficients.
Asterisk denotes significance at 0.05 level.

agriculture, rail transport, nonrail transport, communications and services). The last three columns present the results using only the twenty manufacturing industries. The results indicate that schooling levels on average are higher in industries with higher capital to labor ratios. However, the coefficient is significant in only three out of six cases. Nonmanufacturing industries appear to have employees with significantly more schooling, as measured by the proportion of workers with four years high school or more and mean schooling. The coefficient for D_2, the dummy variable for durable goods manufacturing industries, is not significant in any case. The major result from table 12.1 concerns the effects of the ratio of production workers to total employment. The coefficient for the term is significant in all cases and the t-statistics are extremely large. The greater the ratio of production workers to total employment (and the smaller the proportion of nonproduction workers), the lower the schooling levels of the workers employed. In terms of the schooling levels of employees hired, the ratio appears to be much more important than the capital to labor ratio. Furthermore, the explanatory power of these simple demand equations is raised substantially by the addition of the term for the ratio of production workers to total employment.

Let us now examine the determinants of the schooling levels in industries using a more detailed data base, consisting of sixty-five US manufacturing industries. Data on the proportions of employees with four years of college or more and four years of high school or more are taken from the 1970 US census. Corresponding data on capital per worker are taken from the Annual Survey of Manufacturers. The industries were chosen on the basis of being able to match census industry classifications with Standard Industrial Classification codes.

In addition to the capital to labor ratio, previous investigation has revealed that the ratio of production workers to total employment significantly influences the distribution of earnings within an industry. The same variable is therefore included in this analysis.

Work on comparative advantage has suggested that the difficulty of work in an industry will be related to the quality of the labor force assigned to it in equilibrium. The more-productive workers will have a comparative advantage at more difficult jobs and will therefore be found working at those jobs in equilibrium. It seems reasonable to suppose that the difficulty of work in an industry is related to the level of technological complexity, which can be measured by the ratio of research and development expenditures to value added. National Science Foundation figures on the ratio of research and development expenditures to value added have therefore also been included. These figures are not given for each of the sixty-five industries but for broader industry groupings. In addition to its effect on the difficulty of work, technological complexity can also affect the educational level of the work force through the occupational mix required.

Because supply conditions can be expected to vary from region to region, variables for the proportions of employment located in the northeast, south and west have been included. (The excluded region is the north central.)

The model as it has been estimated is:

$$\ln(E_{C,F}) = a_0 + a_i \ln(K/L) + a_2 \ln(N) + a_3 \ln(RD) + a_4\, NE + a_5 S + a_6\, W + e,$$

where

K/L = the capital to labor ratio in the industry, as measured by the total assets per worker;

N = the ratio of production workers to total employment;

RD = the ratio of research and development expenditures to value added;

NE = the proportion of industry employment in the northeast;

S = the proportion of employment in the south;

W = the proportion of employment in the west;

$E_{C,F}$ = proportion of female workers with four years college or more; and

e = an independent, identically distributed normal random error term.

Similarly, $E_{C,M}$ and $E_{C,T}$ are the proportions of male workers and of male and female workers combined with four years college or more. The terms $E_{H,F}$, $E_{H,M}$ and $E_{H,T}$ represent the proportions of female workers, male workers and male and female workers combined with four years high school or more.

The results of ordinary least squares regressions are given in table 12.2. The coefficient for the capital to labor ratio is positive in all cases, as expected, and is significant except in the cases of males taken alone. This reconfirms previous results regarding the assignment of the more-productive (or in this case more highly educated) workers to more capital-intensive jobs. The coefficient for the ratio of production workers to total employment is negative and significant in all cases. Given that nonproduction or supervisory workers tend to be more highly educated, this is precisely the result one would expect. Finally, the coefficient for the measure of technological complexity is positive and significant in all cases. This result is consistent with the effects it was assumed to have on the difficulty of the jobs and the quality of the work force employed. The results appear to be somewhat better for the proportion with four years of high school or more than for the proportion with four years college or more. There does not appear to be any clear-cut pattern in the coefficients for the proportions of employment in each region.

The determination of educational levels in industries can be seen in more detail by breaking it down into two steps. We may first suppose that firms in an industry, on the basis of the capital to labor ratio, ratio of production workers

Table 12.2
Schooling levels, sixty-five manufacturing industries, 1969.

	Four years college or more			Four years high school or more		
	$\ln(E_{C,F})$ females (1)	$\ln(E_{C,M})$ males (2)	$\ln(E_{C,T})$ all workers (3)	$\ln(E_{H,F})$ females (4)	$\ln(E_{H,M})$ males (5)	$\ln(E_{H,T})$ all workers (6)
$\ln(K/L)$	0.211* (2.59)	0.112 (1.84)	0.169* (2.96)	0.065* (2.65)	0.034 (1.72)	0.041* (2.43)
$\ln(N)$	−2.13* (4.12)	−1.31* (3.38)	−1.48* (4.07)	−0.534* (3.45)	−0.490* (3.98)	−0.532* (4.95)
$\ln(RD)$, logarithm of ratio of research and development expenditures to value added	0.130* (2.27)	0.202* (4.71)	0.211* (5.25)	0.078* (4.51)	0.101* (7.36)	0.095* (7.99)
NE, proportion of employment in northeast	−0.632 (0.991)	1.44* (3.01)	0.597 (1.33)	−0.530* (2.78)	0.181 (1.19)	−0.002 (0.018)
S_1, proportion of employment in south	0.226 (0.486)	0.552 (1.58)	0.225 (0.686)	−0.331* (2.36)	−0.177 (1.60)	−0.218* (2.25)
W, proportion of employment in west	1.56 (1.70)	0.062 (0.089)	0.455 (0.707)	0.125 (0.455)	−0.292 (1.34)	−0.253 (1.32)
Constant	0.271	1.23	1.35	4.20	3.86	3.93
Adjusted R^2	0.434	0.515	0.588	0.584	0.706	0.757

Dependent variables: logarithms of proportions of workers (females in columns 1 and 4, males in columns 2 and 5, males and females combined in columns 3 and 6) with four years college or more (columns 1, 2 and 3) and with four years high school or more (columns 4, 5 and 6).

to total employment, technological complexity and other variables, choose the mix of occupations that will be used. From this mix can be calculated the expected proportions of workers in an industry at different educational levels under the assumption that the workers employed in an occupation in an industry are distributed among educational levels as all workers in the occupation. The second step in the determination of educational levels arises because firms can choose to hire workers in an occupation that have higher or lower educational levels than the national average.

Let $X_{C,T}$ be the expected proportions of all workers with four years of college or more. Similarly, let $X_{C,M}$ and $X_{C,F}$ be the expected college proportions for males and females, respectively, and let $X_{H,T}, X_{H,M}$ and $X_{H,F}$ be the expected high school proportions for all workers, males and females, respectively. The expected proportion $X_{C,M}$ is calculated as follows. Let O_i be the nine by one vector of male workers by occupation for industry i. Let $M = (m_{jk})$ be the eleven by nine matrix of educational levels by occupation for males. Element m_{jk} is the proportion of workers of occupational category k with educational level j. The data on the vectors O_i and the matrix M are taken from the 1970 US census.

Then MO_i is the vector of the expected numbers of workers at each educational level. The proportion $X_{C,M}$ for industry i can be calculated directly. The proportions $X_{C,T}$ and $X_{H,T}$ are obtained from the sum of the vectors of the expected numbers of workers at each level for males and females.

The results of ordinary least squares regressions of the expected educational proportions are presented in table 12.3. The coefficients for the production worker and research and development terms have the same sign and continue to be significant. The capital to labor ratio no longer significantly affects the proportion of all workers with four years high school or more, and the coefficient for the proportion of males with four years high school or more is negative but not significant. In the case of the proportion of workers with four years college or more, the explanatory power is better using the expected proportions than the actual proportions.

The dependent variable in the second step is merely the logarithm of the ratio of the actual proportion divided by the expected proportion, e.g. $\ln (E_{C,T}/X_{C,T})$. This measures the educational level chosen for a given occupational mix. Ordinary least squares regressions of these deviations on the variables are presented in table 12.4. The deviations of the actual proportions with four years college or more from the proportions expected on the basis of the occupational mix are more or less unexplained by the variables. For four years high school or more, the variable coefficients of the variable for the variables $K/L, N$ and RD not only have the same signs as before but are generally significant.

Table 12.3

Expected schooling levels, sixty-five or more manufacturing industries.

	Four years college or more			Four years high school or more		
	$\ln(X_{C,F})$ females (1)	$\ln(X_{C,M})$ males (2)	$\ln(X_{C,T})$ all workers (3)	$\ln(X_{H,F})$ females (4)	$\ln(X_{H,M})$ males (5)	$\ln(X_{H,T})$ all workers (6)
$\ln(K/L)$	0.186* (3.76)	0.048 (1.27)	0.099* (2.74)	0.037* (2.04)	−0.0003 (0.038)	0.012 (1.48)
$\ln(N)$	−1.23* (3.95)	−0.935* (3.87)	−1.08* (4.71)	−0.421* (3.62)	−0.225* (4.03)	−0.301* (5.70)
$\ln(RD)$	0.129* (3.72)	0.184* (6.87)	0.186* (7.33)	0.028* (2.20)	0.035* (5.61)	0.033* (5.66)
NE	−0.349 (0.903)	0.813* (2.73)	0.179 (0.636)	−0.370* (2.58)	0.243* (3.51)	0.060 (0.917)
S	0.213 (0.756)	0.294 (1.35)	0.085 (0.412)	−0.133 (1.27)	0.062 (1.23)	−0.008 (0.161)
w	0.932 (1.68)	0.160 (0.374)	0.460 (1.14)	0.252 (1.22)	−0.0006 (0.006)	0.060 (0.643)
Constant	−3.25	−3.01	−2.90	−0.526	−0.794	−0.730
Adjusted R^2	0.535	0.631	0.694	0.434	0.590	0.663

Dependent variables: Logarithms of proportions of workers with described schooling levels expected on basis of occupational mix.

Table 12.4
Deviations of actual from expected schooling levels, sixty-five manufacturing industries, 1969.

	Four years college or more			Four years high school or more		
	$\ln\left(\dfrac{E_{C,F}}{X_{C,F}}\right)$ females (1)	$\ln\left(\dfrac{E_{C,M}}{X_{C,M}}\right)$ males (2)	$\ln\left(\dfrac{E_{C,T}}{X_{C,T}}\right)$ all workers (3)	$\ln\left(\dfrac{E_{H,F}}{X_{H,F}}\right)$ females (4)	$\ln\left(\dfrac{E_{H,M}}{X_{H,M}}\right)$ males (5)	$\ln\left(\dfrac{E_{H,T}}{X_{H,T}}\right)$ all workers (6)
$\ln(K/L)$	0.025 (0.399)	0.064 (1.79)	0.071* (2.13)	0.027* (2.03)	0.034* (2.44)	0.029* (2.39)
$\ln(N)$	-0.893* (2.22)	-0.373 (1.65)	-0.403 (1.92)	-0.113 (1.32)	-0.264* (3.01)	-0.231* (3.02)
$\ln(RD)$	0.001 (0.024)	0.018 (0.729)	0.026 (1.10)	0.049* (5.18)	0.066* (6.75)	0.062* (7.31)
NE	-0.283 (0.569)	0.627* (2.24)	0.418 (1.61)	-0.159 (1.51)	-0.061 (0.567)	-0.062 (0.657)
S	0.013 (0.035)	0.258 (1.26)	0.140 (0.738)	-0.198* (2.56)	-0.239* (3.02)	-0.211* (3.04)
W	0.624 (0.874)	-0.098 (0.245)	-0.005 (0.014)	-0.127 (0.837)	-0.292 (1.88)	-0.313* (2.30)
Constant	3.52	4.24	4.25	4.73	4.66	4.66
Adjusted R^2	0.038	0.140	0.165	0.510	0.682	0.704

Dependent variable: logarithms of ratios of actual proportions of workers with described schooling level to proportions expected on basis of occupational mix.

The major conclusions to be drawn from tables 12.2, 12.3 and 12.4 are that the differences in the demands for workers by educational level can be substantially explained by the capital to labor ratio, the ratio of production workers to total employment, and the ratio of research and development to value added. In the case of the proportions of workers with four years high school or more, the variables operate both through the choice of occupational mix within an industry and the choice of the educational level for a given occupational mix. In the case of the proportion of workers with four years college or more, the variables operate mainly through the choice of occupational mix. The results of this section reconfirm the previously postulated and observed relationship between capital intensity and the productive ability of workers, measured here by educational level. However, the results also indicate that other characteristics of an industry, the technological complexity and the division of employment between production and nonproduction work, are potentially more important in determining the assignment of workers to jobs. Furthermore, the characteristics of industries that have been examined here are substantially uncorrelated, as indicated by the correlation coefficients in table 12.5. Technological complexity and the division of employment between production and nonproduction work therefore represent important areas for future research.

4. The demands for workers by earnings levels

This section investigates the demands for workers in an industry directly in terms of earnings levels. The proportion of workers with earnings below (or above) a certain level is regarded as measuring the proportion of workers with productive ability below (or above) a particular unobserved level.

Table 12.5
Correlation coefficients for variables in tables 12.2–12.4.

	$\ln(K/L)$ (1)	$\ln(N)$ (2)	$\ln(RD)$ (3)	NE (4)	S (5)	W (6)
$\ln(K/L)$	1.00					
$\ln(N)$	−0.170	1.00				
$\ln(RD)$	0.121	−0.178	1.00			
NE	−0.093	−0.096	0.034	1.00		
S	0.083	0,039	−0.308	−0.445	1.00	
W	−0.045	0.058	−0.025	−0.249	−0.106	1.00

Table 12.6
Mean earnings by industry, 1949 and 1969.

	25 industries		20 manufacturing industries	
	1949 (1)	1969 (2)	1949 (3)	1969 (4)
ln(K/L)	0.074* (2.85)	0.083* (3.19)	0.116* (3.08)	0.137* (4.35)
ln(N)	−1.44* (5.30)	−1.04* (5.46)	−1.47* (5.40)	−0.901* (5.26)
D_1	0.120 (1.70)	0.179* (2.62)		
D_2	0.063 (1.24)	0.135* (2.86)	0.073 (1.46)	0.143* (3.57)
Constant	0.499	1.35	0.386	1.25
Adjusted R^2	0.617	0.730	0.698	0.825

Dependent variable: logarithm of mean earnings, males and females combined.

The results using mean earnings are presented in table 12.6. The industries used for the observations are the same as those in table 12.1. As in Chapter 7, the results show that mean earnings (and mean productive ability, if the relation between the two is linear) depend positively and significantly on the capital to labor ratio. Furthermore, industries with higher ratios of production workers to total employment have significantly lower mean earnings. These results are consistent with the results for schooling in the previous section. It also appears from the 1969 results that there are significant differences between manufacturing and the five nonmanufacturing industries and between durable goods manufacturing industries and other industries in the mean earnings of employees.

Separate investigation of the upper and lower tails provides a clearer picture of the effects of the above variables on the demand for employees by earnings levels. Tables 12.7 and 12.8 give the results for the upper and lower tails for 1949 and 1969 using twenty-five manufacturing and nonmanufacturing industries. Tables 12.9 and 12.10 provide corresponding results for twenty manufacturing industries. The upper and lower ranges for the upper and lower tails are the same as those used in the analysis of changes in the distribution of earnings over time in Chapter 11.

As expected, industries with higher capital to labor ratios have fewer workers in the lower tail and more workers in the upper tail. The estimated coefficients are significant in almost all cases, the exceptions being the two upper tails for

Table 12.7
Proportions of workers in upper and lower tails, twenty-five industries, 1949.

	Less than $500 (1)	Less than $1,500 (2)	Less than $2,500 (3)	More than $3,500 (4)	More than $4,000 (5)	More than $4,500 (6)
$\ln(K/L)$	−0.318* (2.47)	−0.280* (2.81)	−0.160* (2.44)	0.149* (2.16)	0.141* (2.16)	0.131* (2.25)
$\ln(N)$	1.11 (0.819)	2.41* (2.29)	2.01* (2.90)	−4.32* (5.93)	−4.77* (6.89)	−4.94* (8.06)
D_1	0.202 (0.572)	0.007 (0.025)	−0.057 (0.321)	0.552* (2.92)	0.618* (3.45)	0.647* (4.08)
D_2	−0.292 (1.15)	−0.246 (1.25)	−0.130 (1.01)	0.212 (1.56)	0.157 (1.22)	0.100 (0.877)
Constant	−2.02	−0.424	0.089	−2.95	−3.43	−3.86
Adjusted R^2	0.165	0.343	0.361	0.645	0.704	0.764

Dependent variables: logarithms of proportions of all workers with earnings in described range.

Table 12.8.
Proportions of workers in upper and lower tails, twenty-five industries, 1969.

	Less than $1,000 (1)	Less than $4,000 (2)	Less than $7,000 (3)	More than 10,000 (4)	More than $12,000 (5)	More than $15,000 (6)
$\ln(K/L)$	−0.323* (2.80)	−0.294* (3.47)	−0.151* (2.98)	0.162* (2.53)	0.100 (1.81)	0.020 (0.428)
$\ln(N)$	1.03 (1.23)	1.71* (2.77)	1.34* (3.64)	−2.97* (6.36)	−3.09* (7.71)	−3.05* (8.96)
D_1	0.196 (0.652)	−0.74 (0.335)	−0.158 (1.19)	0.683* (4.08)	0.746* (5.18)	0.729* (5.97)
D_2	−0.331 (1.59)	−0.331* (2.16)	−0.167 (1.83)	0.386* (3.33)	0.348* (3.50)	0.256* (3.03)
Constant	−1.91	−0.058	0.241	−3.20	−3.62	−4.03
Adjusted R^2	0.331	0.555	0.581	0.766	0.805	0.820

Dependent variables: logarithms of proportions of all workers with earnings in described range.

Table 12.9
Proportions of workers in upper and lower tails, twenty manufacturing industries, 1949.

	Less than $500 (1)	Less than $1,500 (2)	Less than $2,500 (3)	More than $3,500 (4)	More than $4,000 (5)	More than $4,500 (6)
$\ln(K/L)$	−0.445* (2.24)	−0.429* (2.94)	−2.94* (3.28)	0.292* (3.12)	0.283* (3.09)	0.254* (2.99)
$\ln(N)$	1.20 (0.840)	2.56* (2.45)	2.11* (3.26)	−4.42* (6.55)	−4.81* (7.30)	−4.94* (8.07)
D_2	−0.320 (1.23)	−0.280 (1.46)	−0.160 (1.36)	0.244 (1.98)	0.189 (1.57)	0.128 (1.15)
Constant	−1.69	−0.023	0.445	−3.32	−3.79	−4.16
Adjusted R^2	0.185	0.452	0.555	0.762	0.790	0.814

Dependent variables: logarithms of proportions of workers with earnings in described range.

Table 12.10
Proportions of workers in upper and lower tails, twenty manufacturing industries, 1969.

	Less than $1,000 (1)	Less than $4,000 (2)	Less than $7,000 (3)	More than 10,000 (4)	More than $12,000 (5)	More than $15,000 (6)
$\ln(K/L)$	−0.429* (2.92)	−0.460* (4.53)	−0.259* (4.14)	0.280* (3.33)	0.198* (2.76)	0.093 (1.51)
$\ln(N)$	0.611 (0.767)	1.28* (2.34)	1.10* (3.23)	−2.75* (6.02)	−2.91* (7.48)	−2.90* (8.67)
D_2	−0.345 (1.86)	−0.355* (2.76)	−0.184* (2.31)	0.404* (3.79)	0.363* (3.99)	0.267* (3.42)
Constant	−1.75	0.273	0.465	−3.46	−3.83	−4.18
Adjusted R^2	0.408	0.707	0.722	0.824	0.854	0.861

Dependent variables: logarithms of proportions of all workers with earnings in described range.

twenty-five industries in 1969 and the highest upper tail for twenty-five industries for 1969 (tables 12.8 and 12.10, respectively). The influence of the capital to labor ratio on industry demands for workers by earnings levels appears to be stronger for the lower tail than for the upper tail. That is, the capital to labor ratio explains demands for the less-productive workers better than it explains demands for the more-productive workers, as measured by their earnings levels.

The ratio of production workers to total employees negatively and significantly affects the proportions of employees in the lower tail, but the estimated coefficients are not significant for the very lowest tail. In general, the effect of the ratio of production workers to total employees is much stronger in the upper tail than in the lower tail. This result certainly conforms to expectations: the highest salaries in an industry usually go to the nonproduction employees in management.

The estimated coefficients for D_1 indicate that the five nonmanufacturing industries have significantly more employees in the upper tail. There does not appear to be any difference with respect to the lower tail.

Compared to other industries, durable goods manufacturing industries on the average have more workers in the upper tail and fewer workers in the lower tail. These results are consistent in all four tables, although the estimated coefficients are not always significant.

The results obtained using the sixty-five manufacturing industries of section 3 are presented in table 12.11. These results confirm the effects of the capital to labor ratio and the ratio of production workers to total employment on the proportions of workers in the upper and lower tails. Furthermore, the ratio of

Table 12.11
Proportions of workers in upper and lower tails, sixty-five manufacturing industries, 1969.

	Less than $1,000 (1)	Less than $4,000 (2)	Less than $7,000 (3)	More than $10,000 (4)	More than $12,000 (5)	More than $15,000 (6)
$\ln(K/L)$	−0.126* (2.42)	−0.161* (3.51)	−0.099* (3.43)	0.151* (3.51)	0.130* (2.44)	0.087 (1.71)
$\ln(N)$	−0.003 (0.008)	0.287 (0.989)	0.330 (1.81)	−0.802* (2.95)	−0.764* (2.26)	−0.990* (3.07)
$\ln(RD)$	−0.222* (6.04)	−0.190* (5.89)	−0.102* (5.03)	0.126* (4.18)	0.092* (2.46)	0.074* (2.07)
NE	0.135 (0.330)	0.695 (1.94)	0.505* (2.24)	−0.729* (2.17)	−0.452 (1.08)	0.022 (0.055)
S	0.252 (0.846)	0.638* (2.43)	0.576* (3.50)	−1.12* (4.56)	−1.05* (3.45)	−0.664* (2.28)
W	0.936 (1.60)	0.570 (1.11)	0.179 (0.555)	−0.260 (0.540)	−1.13 (1.89)	−0.685 (1.20)
Constant	−3.82	−2.30	−1.10	−1.04	−1.68	−2.85
Adjusted R^2	0.479	0.575	0.591	0.636	0.456	0.412

Dependent variable: logarithms of proportions of workers with earnings in described range.

research and development to value added, which has been taken as a measure of technological complexity or difficulty, significantly affects the proportions of workers in the tails. The greater the ratio, the lower the number of workers in the lower tails and the greater the proportion of workers in the upper tails. The results are therefore similar to those obtained using educational levels as the measure of productive ability or labor quality.

A potential qualification to the results obtained for the lower tails in sections 3 and 4 of this chapter is that lower earnings for workers may result from incomplete employment for workers rather than lower wage rates. That is, workers who have been partially unemployed in an industry may have low yearly total earnings, although their wage rates may be high. This qualification is particularly relevant to the very lowest tail. A more detailed study of the lower tails would therefore require an investigation of the distribution of unemployment among workers in different industries.

5. Unionization and concentration

This section briefly considers the effects of unionization in labor markets and concentration in product markets on the distribution of earnings within industries. These effects are considered in a separate section because they are not necessarily consistent with the interpretation that the distribution of earnings within an industry reflects the distribution of demands for workers according to productive ability.

Wage rates determined by bargaining between firms and unions represent a potential departure from perfectly competitive labor markets. Unions can be expected to obtain higher wage rates than would otherwise prevail. Firms may partially compensate for the higher wage rates by hiring more skilled or experienced labor. Alternatively, unions may effectively compensate for firm monopsony power in labor markets, so that the results would be substantially the same as in perfectly competitive labor markets.

The effects of concentration in product markets is not immediately obvious, but some economists may argue that economic profits on the part of imperfectly competitive industries may be partially appropriated by employees in the industry.

Tabel 12.12 presents the results for twenty manufacturing industries. The measure of unionization for each industry is a weighted average of percentage of unionization among subindustries, using value of shipments as weights. The data, for 1958, were originally developed by Lewis (1963) and are used elsewhere by Kendrick (1973, p. 136). The concentration ratios, for 1966, have been calcu-

Table 12.12
Effects of concentration and unionization, twenty manufacturing industries.

	Less than $1,000 (1)	Less than $4,000 (2)	Less than $7,000 (3)	More than $10,000 (4)	More than $12,000 (5)	More than $15,000 (6)
$\ln(K/L)$	−0.292 (1.70)	−0.328* (3.02)	−0.187* (2.96)	0.162 (1.94)	0.098 (1.35)	0.051 (0.709)
$\ln(N)$	0.800 (0.967)	1.52* (2.92)	1.34* (4.41)	−3.03* (7.53)	−3.14* (8.99)	−3.05* (8.85)
D_2	−0.303 (1.61)	−0.320* (2.70)	−0.175* (2.54)	0.379* (4.14)	0.341* (4.30)	0.264* (3.36)
Logarithm of unionization, 1958	−0.539 (1.16)	−0.605 (2.05)	−0.484* (2.83)	0.636* (2.80)	0.522* (2.65)	0.305 (1.57)
Logarithm of product market concentration	−0.147 (0.608)	−0.084 (0.548)	0.063 (0.716)	0.005 (0.045)	0.017 (0.167)	−0.052 (0.521)
Constant	0.534	2.61	1.98	−5.69	−5.70	−5.10
Adjusted R^2	0.417	0.760	0.798	0.875	0.843	0.865

Dependent variables: logarithms of proportions of employees with earnings in described range, 1969.

lated by Kendrick (1973, p. 139) and are the average percentages of shipments in each sector accounted for by the largest four firms in a four-digit subindustry.

As expected, unionization reduces the number of workers in the lower tails (significantly in the case of workers earning less than $7,000) and raises the number of workers with earnings in the upper tails (significantly in the case of the ranges greater than $10,000 and greater than $12,000). The coefficients for the product market concentration terms are not significant at conventional levels, so there is no evidence that concentration affects the distribution of earnings within industries.

The estimated coefficient for the capital to labor ratio remains significant at conventional levels for two ranges of the lower tail (less than $4,000 and less than $7,000), but is no longer significant for the upper tail. The coefficients for the other variables, ratio of production workers to total employment and the dummy variable for durable goods manufacturing, generally retain their former values and significance.

For all thirty industries, a different measure of unionization is used. It has been obtained by dividing union membership by total employment in each industry. For the twenty manufacturing industries the estimated coefficient for

Table 12.13
Effects of unionization, thirty industries.

	Less than $1,000 (1)	Less than $4,000 (2)	Less than $7,000 (3)
$\ln(K/L)$	−0.430* (5.05)	−0.400* (5.75)	−0.214* (4.54)
D_1	0.341 (1.62)	0.126 (0.730)	0.013 (0.114)
D_2	−0.359 (1.92)	−0.348* (2.28)	−0.174 (1.68)
Logarithm of unionization	−0.295* (3.56)	−0.214* (3.16)	−0.109* (2.37)
Constant	−2.17	−0.452	−0.077
Adjusted R^2	0.589	0.605	0.468

Dependent variable: logarithm of proportion of workers with earnings in described range.

this measure of unionization is never significant at conventional levels. The results for all thirty industries for the lower tails are presented in table 12.13. The coefficient for the measure of unionization is negative and significant at conventional levels, indicating that the more-unionized industries tend to have fewer workers in the lower tails, everything else the same. The estimated coefficients for the measure of unionization were not significant for the upper tails.

In conclusion, there is no evidence that product market concentration affects the distribution of earnings within industries. Unionization significantly affects the proportions of workers in the upper and lower tails. However, the results with unionization included do not substantially revise previous conclusions.

6. Conclusions

Chapter 11 investigated the effects of changes in variables on the distribution of earnings within an industry. For example, a change in the capital to labor ratio in an industry can, via the capital-skill complementarity mechanism, raise the demand for more-skilled workers and reduce the demand for less-skilled workers. The results of Chapter 11 supported the hypothesis of capital-skill complementarity. The chapter also revealed that changes in output, productivity and the ratio of production workers to total employment affect the distribution of earnings within individual industries.

In contrast, this chapter has investigated the source of variation in the distributions of earnings among industries. More capital-intensive industries use fewer low-earnings or less-educated workers and use more high-earnings or more-educated workers. Similarly, industries with a higher ratio of research and development to value added show the same pattern. Also, industries with higher ratios of production workers to total employment use more low-earnings and less-educated workers and fewer high-earnings or more-educated workers, everything else the same.

Chapters 11 and 12 therefore present two ways in which the structure of the economy can affect the demands for workers of different employment characteristics and hence the distribution of earnings. First, changes in industry characteristics over time can affect the distribution of earnings within industries. Secondly, the distribution of employment among industries with respect to the capital to labor ratio, the ratio of production workers to total employment and the ratio of research and development to value added affects the aggregate distribution of demands for workers of different employment characteristics. That is to say, taking the distribution of demands within industries as given, sectoral shifts in output and employment among industries can also affect the aggregate demands for workers and hence the distribution of earnings.

This monograph has concentrated on the ways in which capital can affect the distribution of earnings among workers. The empirical evidence indicates that sectoral shifts among industries according to capital intensity affect the distribution of earnings much more strongly than changes in the distribution of earnings within industries as a result of capital accumulation. The latter could not be detected with certainty in the aggregate inequality investigations of Chapters 8 and 9. The corresponding investigations of the effects of technological change and the division of employment between production and nonproduction workers will be left to future work, although the latter subject will receive some preliminary consideration in the next chapter.

Appendix: Data sources

Tables 12.1, 12.6–12.10. The schooling data in table 12.1 are taken from the *1970 Census of Population, Industrial Characteristics*, table 3, p. 11. The remaining data are the same as used in Chapter 11.

Tables 12.2–12.5, 12.11. Proportions of workers with four years college or more and four years high school or more are from the *1970 Census of Population, Industrial Characteristics*, cited above. Data on capital per worker are taken from the *Annual Survey of Manufactures, Book Value of Fixed Assets and*

Rental Payments for Building and Equipment, US Department of Commerce, Bureau of the Census, 1971. Data on the ratio of research and development to value added are from *Research and Development in Industry, 1967, Surveys of Science Resources Series*, National Science Foundation. Data on regional proportions are taken from the *1970 Census of Population, United States Summary, Detailed Characteristics*, table 298, p. 1264. The figures on expected educational levels are constructed from the *1970 Census of Population, Occupations by Industry*, pp. 265–280, and *Educational Attainment*, table 11, pp. 213–220. Ratios of production workers to total employment are taken from the *Annual Survey of Manufactures, 1971, Industry Profiles*, US Department of Commerce, Bureau of the Census, M71(AS)–10. Proportions of workers in upper and lower tails are taken from the same source as tables 11.2 and 11.3 in Chapter 11.

Tables 12.12 and 12.13. For the manufacturing industries, data on unionization in 1958 and concentration in 1966 are reported in Kendrick (1973, pp. 136–139). The unionization data were originally developed by Lewis (1963). For table 12.13, the measure of unionization is the ratio of union membership to full-time equivalent employment. The union membership, for 1970, is reported in *Handbook of Labor Statistics 1974*, US Department of Labor, Bureau of Labor Statistics, table 149, p. 362. These data are matched with data on employment by industry in *The National Income and Product Accounts of the United States, 1929–1974*, US Department of Commerce, Bureau of Economic Analysis, table 6.8, p. 209.

Chapter 13

HIERARCHIES

1. Introduction

This chapter investigates briefly the implications of hierarchies for the distribution of earnings, in particular the upper tail. The intention is to explain the upper tail of the distribution and the contribution of different industries to earnings inequality through their employment of individuals at high earnings. Much of the attention given to hierarchies by economists has been directed to explaining the distribution of firm sizes (Calvo and Wellisz, 1978; Lucas, Jr., 1977; and Williamson, 1967). Another subject, closely related to the distribution of earnings, is the incentive structure within organizations or hierarchies (Mirrlees, 1976; Stiglitz, 1975). The information and communication aspects of organizations have been discussed by a number of authors (see, for example, Spence, 1975).

The sociological literature has analyzed hierarchies and organizations more extensively, and has developed a number of potentially fruitful hypotheses concerned with economic variables. For example, the decision to quit or remain with an organization, the distribution of pecuniary and nonpecuniary rewards within an organization, inequality in power or authority, job satisfaction, productivity, the selection of organizational goals, and reaction to changes in the environment have all been subjects of investigation (March and Simon, 1958; Tausky, 1970). Despite the common interest in the theory of organizations and hierarchies, the sociological literature is seldom referenced by economists.

This chapter concentrates on two observable aspects of firm hierarchies: their shape and their size. For the shape of hierarchies, Simon (1957) and Lydall (1959, 1968) have developed the relevant theory. The shape of a hierarchy can be described in terms of the distribution of employees by earnings. This distribution follows Pareto's law, so that the relevant descriptive statistic is the parameter of that distribution, referred to here as Pareto's coefficient. Section 2 concerns the determination of this parameter for different industries.

Considering the importance of nonproduction workers for the amount of earnings inequality, the size of hierarchies for different industries deserves greater study. Section 3 measures the size of a hierarchy in an industry simply by the proportion of nonproduction or supervisory workers. The major question concerns the relationship between the capital to labor ratio and the division of employment between production and nonproduction workers.

2. Pareto coefficient

Pareto's law is one of the earliest empirical descriptions of the distribution of income. It does not apply to the entire distribution, as once thought, but provides a reasonably accurate description of the upper tail. Lydall (1959, 1968, pp. 125–133) has developed a model which explains why Pareto's law holds for the upper tail. (Simon, 1957, had earlier presented a model of a hierarchy using similar assumptions, but had not related it to the Pareto distribution.) Lydall's model arises from the pyramidal structure of hierarchies. A consequence of Lydall's model is that the Pareto coefficient, a parameter appearing in the Pareto distribution and which can be estimated from earnings data, describes the shape of an organizational hierarchy.

Lydall's model is as follows. Suppose there are several distinct levels in the hierarchy. Let x_i be the wage for employees at level i and let y_i be the number of employees at level i. The two major assumptions of the model concern two fixed ratios. First, a fixed ratio holds between the number of employees at one level and the number of employees in the next lower level: $y_i/y_{i+1} = n$, where n is a constant greater than one. This constant describes the average number of employees working under a particular employee, or the span of control. Secondly, there is a fixed ratio between the earnings of an employee at one level and the earnings of an employee in the next lower level. This ratio is such that $x_{i+1}/nx_i = p$, where p is the same for all levels and is less than one.

Let Q_i be the proportion of all employees in grades i and above. Then $\ln Q_i$ approximately equals $\lambda \ln x_1 - \lambda \ln x_i$, where x_1 is the wage at the lowest level and $\lambda = \ln n/(\ln n + \ln p)$. This is a discrete version of the Pareto distribution, which is given by $N = A x^{-\alpha}$, where x is the earnings level, N is the number of workers with earnings above x, and A and α are parameters. The parameter α in the distribution, referred to here as Pareto's coefficient, is a measure of the amount of inequality in the distribution. The smaller the value of α, the greater the earnings inequality. In Lydall's model, λ plays the role of Pareto's coefficient. It follows that earnings will be more equally distributed in the hierarchy the greater the value of n and the lower the value of p.

The above result holds for a single hierarchy or a single firm. Fortunately, Lydall (1968, p. 275) presents an extension which allows the model to be extended to the industry. In this extension, firm sizes can differ within an industry. However, if λ is the same for all firms and the earnings for the bottom level is the same, then the Pareto distribution will also describe the distribution of earnings for the industry, with λ as the Pareto coefficient.

Lydall's model gives no explanation of why λ or n and p should vary among industries, or how these parameters are related to characteristics of industries. This section now considers some possible connections.

The simplest view of a hierarchy is as an instrument of control, a means of reducing the variability of actions at the level of production workers. A consequence of this view is that the major activity of employees in a hierarchy is supervision or control, and the only purpose of wage differentials is to legitimize the authoritarian relationship among employees at different levels in the hierarchy. The problem with this interpretation of hierarchies is that it presumes that all information or instruction passes downward from upper levels. Instead, the problem of organizing production involves coordinating separate activities and planning for future activities. In turn, this coordination and planning requires flows of information not only downward but upward and horizontally.

These ideas can be developed more fully as follows. Suppose first that there are only two activities of the nonproduction employees. These may be termed listening and talking. For example, an employee at one level may collect information from his or her subordinates (listening), process the information (and perhaps reach some intermediate decision), and convey the abstracted information to his or her superior (talking). Alternatively, the employee could receive some general instruction from his or her superior (listening), elaborate on the instructions by filling in details, and convey those instructions to his or her subordinates. This simple picture of an organization could be made formal very easily by specifying and defining the necessary parameters. The implications of such a model arise because the ratios of listeners to talkers are fixed by the nature of the activity. While it is possible to talk to several people at the same time, it is not possible to listen to several people at the same time. If the organization were such that only information and instructions went down through the organization, then an employee would be engaged solely in listening to his or her superiors and conveying that information to his or her subordinates. The span of control could then be very large, with many employees serving under one superior, and the relation between employees at different levels would be very unequal and authoritarian.

In contrast, suppose much of the activity of the firm consisted in conveying information upward. Then an individual employee could not have very many subordinates, because he or she would be required to listen to each individually. The result would be a more vertical hierarchy, with fewer employees under a supervisor. The relations between employees at different levels would be more equal and democratic, since there would be a greater exchange of information between the two. The ratio of listening to talking required for the hierarchy of a firm would then explain the size distribution of employees at each level and the nature of the relations between employees.

It seems likely that the ratio of upward to downward communication is determined by the characteristics of the technology of the industry, although no formal model will be presented here. While there are many reasonable conjectures regarding the relation of the Pareto coefficient to industry characteristics, the intention of this section is merely to reveal the empirical relations for future theoretical work. The results of ordinary least squares estimates of the relation between the Pareto coefficient and industry characteristics are given in table 13.1, using the data for the thirty industries investigated in Chapters 11 and 12. The Pareto coefficients used in table 13.1 are calculated from the two top brackets of the distribution of earnings in an industry for males and females combined.

Table 13.1
Pareto coefficients, 1969.

	30 industries (1)	25 industries (2)	20 manufacturing industries (3)
$\ln(K/L)$, logarithm of capital to labor ratio	0.147* (3.67)	0.073 (1.65)	0.100* (2.25)
$\ln(N)$, logarithm of ratio of production workers to total employment		−0.858* (2.67)	−0.908* (3.74)
D_1, dummy variable for nonmanufacturing industries	0.043 (0.451)	0.192 (1.66)	
D_2, dummy variable for durable goods manufacturing industries	0.243* (2.78)	0.237* (2.97)	0.242* (4.27)
Constant	0.490	0.438	0.347
Adjusted R^2	0.377	0.440	0.705

Dependent variable: logarithm of Pareto coefficient, various groups of industries, 1969.

The results indicate that the Pareto coefficient tends to be larger in more capital-intensive industries, everything else the same. If p is the same among all industries (and it need not be), then more capital-intensive industries have greater spans of control (i.e. an employee has more subordinates to supervise) and have greater earnings equality within the hierarchy. The coefficients for the ratio of production workers to total employment are negative and significant. The smaller the hierarchy, using this ratio as a measure of size, the lower will be the Pareto coefficient and the greater the inequality in the hierarchy. Also, the durable goods manufacturing industries have significantly larger Pareto coefficients, everything else the same. In the absence of a formal model, the interpretation of the results is not certain. Nevertheless, one can conclude that the distribution of earnings within an industry depends on the shape of hierarchies for firms in the industry, and the shape of hierarchies, as measured by the Pareto coefficient, depends on observable features of the industry. The particular details of the determination of the Pareto coefficient for industries require further investigation.

3. Nonproduction workers

This section investigates the size of hierarchies, as measured by the division of total employment between production workers and nonproduction or supervisory workers. Previous chapters have already presented substantial evidence concerning the effects of the ratio of production workers to total employment on the distribution of earnings within industries. Chapter 11 demonstrated that changes in this ratio partially explain changes in the upper tails of the distribution of earnings within industries (see, for example, tables 11.7 and 11.8). Chapter 12 showed that industries with higher proportions of production workers had more workers in the lower tails and fewer in the upper tails (see tables 12.6—12.11). Furthermore, the demand for workers according to educational level depends much more strongly on the division of employment between production and nonproduction workers than on the capital to labor ratio (tables 12.1—12.4).

The general trend in the ratio of production workers to total employment is upward, as indicated in table 13.2. Nonproduction or supervisory workers are generally white-collar workers with higher educational levels and higher earnings. The upward trend in nonproduction and supervisory workers should therefore have very strong effects on the demands for workers and hence the distribution of earnings. Using the data on income inequality (covering 1949—1969) from Chapter 8, the ratio of production workers to total employment for both manu-

Table 13.2
Ratio of production or nonsupervisory workers to total employees.

	Total private nonfarm	Manufacturing	Nonfarm non-manufacturing
1950	0.876	0.822	0.911
1960	0.839	0.749	0.892
1970	0.826	0.725	0.876

facturing and nonmanufacturing industries has a significant coefficient of the expected sign, but only if the other demand variables (the capital to labor ratio and capital concentration) are excluded. Nevertheless, on the basis of the disaggregated analyses, one should expect that the distribution of earnings for the economy depends on the division of employment between production and nonproduction workers.

A complete explanation of this earnings inequality requires also that this division itself be explained. If the proportion of production workers is determined entirely by the capital to labor ratio (so that industries with the same capital to labor ratio would have the same ratio of production workers to total employment), then knowledge of this proportion would add no information on industry demands for workers beyond the information contained in the capital to labor ratio. Let us now examine the determinants of the division of employment between production and nonproduction workers.

The standard neoclassical way of analyzing the number of nonproduction workers is to specify a production function with three factors: capital, production workers and nonproduction workers. From the estimation of the production function or the dual cost function, it is possible to obtain point estimates of the partial elasticities of substitution or the partial elasticities of complementarity among the three factors. From the relative values of these estimates one can infer the relation between capital intensity (or the cost of capital) and the ratio of production worker wages to nonproduction worker wages (or the ratio of production workers to nonproduction workers). This approach has been taken by a number of authors (Berndt and Christensen, 1974a, 1974b; Clark and Freeman, 1977; Denny and Fuss, 1977; Freeman and Medoff, 1978; Hansen, Klotz and Madoo, 1975; Kesselman, Williamson and Berndt, 1977; and Lee, 1976). This work has been summarized by Hamermesh (1976) and Hamermesh and Grant (1978).

Probably the most reliable estimate is provided by Berndt and Christensen (1974a), using time-series data for manufacturing from 1929 to 1968. The estimated partial elasticities of substitution in 1968 are 2.92 between production workers and capital, -1.94 between nonproduction workers and capital, and 5.51 between production and nonproduction workers. These estimates imply that a 10 percent reduction in the cost of capital will lead to 29.2 percent reduction in the number of production workers and a 19.4 percent increase in the number of nonproduction workers, if the wages of production and non-production workers stay the same. It follows that capital accumulation will be accompanied by an increase in the ratio of nonproduction workers to produc-tion workers. Also, an increase in the wages for production workers would lead to a large increase in the numbers of nonproduction workers because of the high degree of substitutability between the two. These two observations could easily explain the large increase in the proportion of nonproduction workers in the postwar period.

While the neoclassical approach explains changes in the ratio of nonproduc-tion workers to production workers over time, it generally suffers from an excess of aggregation. If individual manufacturing industries differ substantially in the ratio of nonproduction workers to production workers for the same factor prices, the increase in the proportion of nonproduction workers over time can come about in two ways. First, there can be a sectoral shift towards industries which use more nonproduction workers, and secondly there can be increases in the proportion of nonproduction workers within industries. It is useful to sepa-rate out the two sources of changes in the ratio of nonproduction workers to production workers. As a first step, this section investigates the differences among industries in the changes in the nonproduction worker proportion over time. The following direct approach is taken. Suppose that for each industry there must be a given number of nonproduction workers for each hundred production workers and a given number of nonproduction workers for each million dollars of capital. To be specific, let L_1 be the number of nonproduction workers, L_2 be the number of production workers and K be the amount of capital. Then L_1 is assumed to be a linear combination of L_2 and K: $L_1 = a_1 L_2 + a_2 K$, where a_1 and a_2 are parameters that can differ from industry to industry. This relation is assumed to hold for all factor prices. Because both labor and capital have increased over time, both sides of the equation can be divided by the number of production workers, L_2, in order to avoid heteroscedasticity. The resulting expression as it will be estimated is

$$L_1/L_2 = a_1 + a_2 K/L_2 + e, \tag{13.1}$$

where

L_1 is the number of nonproduction workers,
L_2 is the number of production workers,

K is the amount of capital,

e is an identically distributed normal random error term.

For each industry, data from 1948 to 1970 are used to estimate the above relation. The results of ordinary least squares regressions for twenty-five manufacturing and nonmanufacturing industries are presented in table 13.3. In general, the simple model explains changes in the ratio of nonproduction to production workers fairly well, the exceptions being apparel, furniture and fixtures, leather, miscellaneous manufacturing and finance. The coefficient for the capital per production worker variable is positive and significant in almost all cases. An increase in capital per production worker therefore results in an increase in the proportion of nonproduction to production workers. By multiplying (13.1) through by $L_2/(L_1+L_2)$, it can be seen that a positive value of a_2 also implies that an increase in the capital to labor ratio (with labor including both production and nonproduction workers) leads to an increase in the ratio of nonproduction workers to total employees.

This result reveals an important mechanism by which increases in capital intensity can raise the productive ability of the workers demanded in an industry. As capital intensity increases, nonproduction workers partially replace production workers, and the nonproduction workers are generally more highly paid and educated. The consequence is equivalent to capital-skill complementarity.

At the same time, the coefficients for the constant term and for capital per production worker vary substantially from industry to industry. That is, eq. (13.1) cannot describe the ratio of nonproduction to production workers in all industries, with the same coefficients for each industry. Pooling all twenty-five industries and estimating (13.1) yields

$$L_1/L_2 = 0.236 + 0.00133\,(K/L_2), \quad \text{with } R^2 = 0.075.$$

$$\quad(28.76)\qquad(6.81)$$

It follows that changes in capital intensity in the economy will not accurately predict changes in the division of employment between nonproduction and production workers: the prediction also requires information on changes in the industry composition of employment.

Table 13.3 indicates that the estimated constant term a_1 in (13.1) is positive for most industries. For those industries with positive values of a_1, production and nonproduction workers are in a sense complements. More production workers require more nonproduction workers (although the two factors are not com-

Table 13.3
Ratio of nonproduction to production workers, 1948–1970.

Industry	Estimated coefficient (times 1000)		Positive values of t-statistics		R^2	Durbin-Watson Statistic
	Constant	Capital per production worker	Constant	Capital per production worker		
	(1)	(2)	(3)	(4)	(5)	(6)
1. Food and kindred	−40.8	21.5	1.96	23.31	0.963	0.673
2. Tobacco	−103.3	5.83	2.86	6.47	0.666	0.583
3. Textiles	−57.9	18.1	5.82	16.34	0.927	0.808
4. Apparel	88.3	9.43	11.3	4.66	0.509	0.434
5. Lumber and wood	8.38	9.71	1.42	19.06	0.945	0.994
6. Furniture and fixtures	262	−9.29	4.72	1.28	0.073	0.381
7. Paper	−111	12.9	8.55	27.1	0.972	0.768
8. Printing and publishing	181	26.2	6.08	12.6	0.882	0.340
9. Chemicals	57.6	11.1	5.07	46.1	0.990	0.848
10. Petroleum	105	3.46	4.40	17.07	0.933	0.240
11. Rubber and plastics	88.2	14.7	4.70	10.15	0.831	1.02
12. Leather	87.6	9.24	3.89	2.00	0.160	0.127
13. Stone, clay and glass	38.1	8.68	6.22	29.1	0.976	0.831
14. Primary metals	36.1	5.69	4.78	24.1	0.965	0.653
15. Fabricated metals	85.8	12.8	5.98	13.3	0.894	0.636
16. Machinery, except electrical	−2.63	21.6	0.150	22.8	0.961	0.647
17. Electrical equipment	165	20.2	5.90	9.31	0.805	0.421
18. Transportation equipment	98.0	16.9	2.68	7.55	0.731	0.224
19. Instruments	13.5	34.1	0.68	24.15	0.965	1.04
20. Miscellaneous manufacturing	75.2	11.4	1.17	2.35	0.209	0.077
21. Mining	−73.8	6.32	4.66	18.9	0.944	0.771
22. Contract construction	94.0	13.2	19.9	14.8	0.912	0.301
23. Utilities	−34.6	8.46	9.87	44.8	0.990	0.455
24. Trade	−95.1	18.2	4.89	10.0	0.827	1.20
25. Finance	388	−1.17	4.22	1.74	0.126	0.057

Table 13.4

Ratio of nonproduction to production workers, Cochrane-Orcutt regressions.

Industry	Estimated coefficients (times 1000)			Positive value of t-statistics			R^2	Durbin-Watson Statistic	Rho used in transformation
	Constant	Capital per production worker	Time	Constant	Capital per production worker	Time			
1. Food and kindred	438	5.15	− 2.50	4.83	1.59	1.07	0.989	1.09	0.907
2. Tobacco	35.9	0.532	5.86	1.55	0.793	8.76	0.960	1.76	0.476
3. Textiles	50.1	2.55	2.57	6.11	2.27	15.7	0.994	1.83	−0.211
4. Apparel	121	− 2.29	− 1.14	12.4	0.805	3.15	0.876	1.53	0.715
5. Lumber and wood	48.9	3.95	2.06	5.00	2.97	3.86	0.975	1.71	0.418
6. Furniture and fixtures	144	3.59	1.97	7.26	1.75	2.94	0.901	2.30	0.678
7. Paper	86.9	4.06	3.79	2.90	3.82	4.74	0.995	1.30	0.862
8. Printing and publishing	294	17.3	1.41	6.51	4.74	1.74	0.967	1.71	0.643
9. Chemicals	160	7.95	3.81	3.31	5.41	1.57	0.994	1.65	0.747
10. Petroleum and coal	210	3.52	− 5.95	3.03	3.94	1.13	0.986	1.89	0.848
11. Rubber and plastics	142	10.0	0.694	7.62	6.01	1.29	0.914	2.36	0.467
12. Leather	78.0	3.82	2.82	9.13	2.51	8.09	0.959	2.25	0.648
13. Stone, clay and glass	66.6	6.51	1.30	5.50	7.35	2.37	0.985	2.04	0.293
14. Primary metals	65.1	4.55	0.800	5.06	10.60	1.37	0.984	1.75	0.710
15. Fabricated metals	70.8	14.7	− 0.855	1.97	4.93	0.683	0.935	1.97	0.666
16. Machinery, except electrical	116	15.8	0.063	3.16	10.4	0.034	0.986	1.95	0.849
17. Electrical equipment	230	25.4	− 8.76	1.74	3.22	1.01	0.921	1.49	0.877
18. Transportation equipment	401	12.8	−10.3	3.34	4.25	1.56	0.957	1.58	0.900
19. Instruments	198	13.2	8.81	3.88	4.41	3.32	0.990	1.66	0.834
20. Miscellaneous manufacturing	87.0	5.50	5.48	6.31	5.41	21.2	0.980	1.79	0.273
21. Mining	50.2	1.51	7.95	1.55	2.32	4.28	0.989	1.51	0.823
22. Contract construction	95.5	11.3	0.683	5.62	2.40	0.477	0.973	1.13	0.842
23. Utilities	− 23.1	8.48	− 0.725	0.705	3.00	0.437	0.996	1.74	0.823
24. Trade	− 63.3	13.8	1.16	1.18	2.35	1.38	0.892	2.39	0.191
25. Finance	141	0.321	3.40	5.06	1.61	9.22	0.990	1.64	0.828

Dependent variable: ratio of nonproduction to production workers, 1948–1970.

plements in the technical sense, since the estimations here use no price information). When a_1 is negative, more production workers reduce the need for nonproduction workers, presumably by taking over their role.

The Durbin-Watson statistics in column 6 of table 13.3 show that there is a definite serial correlation of the residuals. As a means of investigating the validity of the previous results, expression (13.1) is re-estimated with a time trend using the Cochrane-Orcutt procedure to eliminate first-order autocorrelation of the residuals. Columns 7, 8 and 9 of table 13.4 present the R^2, Durbin-Watson statistic and rho used in the transformation.

Columns 1—6 of table 13.4 present the estimated coefficients using the transformed data. The table reconfirms the results from table 13.3. The coefficients for capital per production worker are positive in all but one case, apparel. Furthermore, the estimated constant term is positive in all but two cases, utilities and trade.

The time trend is positive except in seven cases and is significant half of the time. This result is consistent with technological change which favors nonproduction workers. For example, more advanced production techniques may require more planning, market evaluation and coordination, in turn requiring more nonproduction workers.

Alternatively, the positive time trend could indicate that, in response to the reduction in the relative factor price of nonproduction workers over time, firms have substituted them for other factors. Since this possibility was ruled out in the assumptions lying behind (13.1), this interpretation must be investigated using more extensive data.

Given that the division of employment in an industry between production and nonproduction workers depends so strongly on the capital to labor ratio, can the proportion of nonproduction workers be considered a demand variable independent of capital intensity? The answer is that although capital intensity and the proportion of nonproduction workers are strongly related over time in an industry, the two variables are not highly correlated among industries. This section has already presented some evidence on this point: the coefficients in the estimated relations vary substantially from industry to industry. Tables 12.5 in the previous chapter provides additional evidence. The correlation between capital intensity and the ratio of production workers to total employment is low, -0.170 for the sixty-five manufacturing industries. It follows that the capital intensity of the economy does not completely determine the proportion of nonproduction workers: the latter also depends upon the division of employment among industries according to their use of nonproduction workers.

4. Conclusions

This chapter has attempted to develop a means by which the upper tail of the earnings distribution can be studied. Within an industry, the upper tail can be described with reference to two features of hierarchies, their shape and their size. Under certain assumptions an industry will have the same upper tail in its earnings distribution as its member firms, and the Pareto distribution will describe it. Section 2 established that the shape of a hierarchy, as measured by a coefficient of the Pareto distribution, depends systematically on features of the industry. The section did not develop the formal model of the determinants of the Pareto coefficient.

Section 3 measures the size of a hierarchy by the number of nonproduction workers. Over time, the ratio of nonproduction to production workers in an industry is primarily determined by the ratio of capital to production workers. However, the coefficients of this relationship vary substantially from industry to industry. Furthermore, the correlation between the capital to labor ratio in an industry and the ratio of production workers to total employment is low. It follows that the capital to labor ratio for the economy does not alone determine the total demand for nonproduction workers. One must also know the distribution of employment by industry. The division of employment between nonproduction and production workers in an industry therefore provides added information on the demands for workers of different productive abilities.

Appendix: Data sources

Table 13.1. The Pareto coefficients are calculated from the top two upper tails of the distribution of earnings by industry, published in the *1970 Census of Population, Industrial Characteristics*, US Bureau of Commerce, table 12, p. 77. Some of this data is presented in Chapter 11, tables 11.2 and 11.3. The data for the capital to labor ratio and the ratio of production workers to total employment are the same as used in Chapters 11 and 12.

Table 13.2. These ratios are calculated from data in *Employment and Earnings, United States, 1909–1975*, US Department of Labor, Bureau of Labor Statistics, Bulletin 1312–10.

Tables 13.3 and 13.4. The ratios of nonproduction to production workers for manufacturing are provided in the *Handbook of Labor Statistics, 1974*, US Department of Labor, Bureau of Labor Statistics, Bulletin 1825, table 43, pp. 110–111. The ratios for nonmanufacturing industries are calculated from data in *Employment and Earnings*, cited above. The capital and employment data are the same as used in Chapter 7 to calculate the capital concentration variable in table 7.5.

Chapter 14

TO BE CONTINUED

1. Introduction

Readers are undoubtedly familiar with reproductions of three or four hundred year old maps which show an explorer's outline of one continent or another. With our current state of geographical wisdom, these maps amuse us by presenting a view of a continent which we now recognize as distorted and all out of proportion. Bays and inlets actually visited by the explorer are shown in great detail as taking up disproportionately large areas, while vast expanses of land are shown featureless. A smooth coastline connects those parts which are known.

In a similar way, the study of the determination of the demands for workers of different productive abilities may be substantially revised by future work. This monograph has emphasized the importance of capital variables. The formal models of Chapters 4, 5 and 6 lead one to believe that capital is all-important in the determination of earnings inequality. This is in the nature of abstraction, which after all is a process of throwing away information. A formal model directs one's attention to certain phenomena and leads one to ignore others. The disaggregated analysis of Chapters 11, 12 and 13 suggests that other variables are potentially more important than capital in affecting earnings inequality. It is possible that at some future date the relative importance of these or other variables may be found to exceed the importance of the capital variables. Such revisions should be expected.

This chapter attempts to summarize the conclusions that have been established and indicate the areas where work remains to be done. The substantial number of questions that are currently unanswered explains the title of this chapter. Relative to the study of individual supply behavior, the study of the demands for workers with different production characteristics and the general equilibrium determination of the distribution of earnings is just beginning.

2. The effects of capital variables

The most important question that can be posed in this monograph concerns the effects of capital accumulation on earnings inequality. As capital accumulates, does earnings inequality inevitably increase? It is necessary to recognize that capital accumulates in two ways. First, there can be an even increase in the capital to labor ratio in all industries, i.e. each industry's capital to labor ratio increases by the same proportion. Then the capital to labor ratio for the economy would increase, but there would be no change in the distribution of capital among jobs, as measured by capital concentration. Secondly, there can be a shift in production and employment from less capital-intensive to more capital-intensive industries. This would result in an increase in both the aggregate capital to labor ratio and capital concentration.

In the context of an aggregate model, Chapter 4 yields the result that if the capital-skill complementarity hypothesis holds, increases in capital intensity result in greater earnings inequality, everything else the same. The theory developed in Chapter 6 suggests that earnings inequality depends positively on capital concentration. Because of the nature and complexity of the model, however, Chapter 6 gives no clear indication of the effect of capital intensity on earnings inequality.

Both capital concentration and the capital to labor ratio are investigated using aggregate data in Chapters 8 and 9. The results are generally consistent. Earnings and income inequality depend positively and significantly on the concentration of capital among jobs. This result holds when the measure of income or earnings inequality is the variance of logarithms (as in Chapter 8), the coefficient of variation or the Gini coefficient (in Chapter 9). The empirical evidence therefore strongly supports the theories developed in Chapters 5 and 6.

Evidence on the effect of the aggregate capital to labor ratio, holding capital concentration constant, is mixed. The estimated coefficients for the term are generally positive but are not always significant. The aggregate empirical work of Chapters 8 and 9 therefore does not establish the validity of the aggregate theory of Chapter 4 with regard to the influence of capital intensity.

The mechanisms by which capital affects the distribution of earnings are revealed at several points in the empirical work. The results of Chapters 7 and 12 show that more capital-intensive industries employ fewer low-earnings and more high-earnings workers, as measured by the proportions in the lower and upper tails of the distributions of earnings by industry. More capital-intensive industries also employ more highly educated workers, as measured by the proportions with four years high school or with four years college. These results support the arguments of Chapter 5 that more-productive workers will be employed at more capital intensive jobs in equilibrium.

The capital variables do not appear to affect educational differentials, but they do affect the amount of income inequality within schooling levels. The effect is stronger on the earnings inequality for workers with four years high school than for four years college. The interpretation placed on this result is that higher values of the capital to labor ratio and capital concentration raise the wage differentials for unobserved differences in productive ability.

The disaggregated analysis of Chapter 11 provides a means of investigating the effects of changes in the capital to labor ratio separately from the effects of changes in the distribution of employment among industries. The results indicate that industries with larger increases in the capital to labor ratio between 1949 and 1969 employed fewer workers in the lower tail and more in the upper tail of the earnings distribution for the industry, although the relation is generally weak. The effects of changes in the capital to labor ratio on the distribution of earnings in an industry are small compared to the differences in the distributions among industries. It follows from the disaggregated analysis that interindustry shifts in employment and production should have stronger effects on earnings inequality than changes within industries. This would explain the relatively better results for the capital concentration term than the capital to labor ratio in the aggregate investigations.

The evidence that has been obtained here suggests that the process of accumulation raises earnings inequality. This result does not necessarily arise because of capital-skill complementarity, which may or may not hold. Instead, it arises because the process of capital accumulation appears to result in shifts of employment towards the more capital-intensive industries, thus raising the level of capital concentration. Table 7.3, which shows that capital concentration has increased over time, provides evidence for this conclusion. Whether capital concentration increases with capital accumulation during other stages of development for an economy is a subject for further investigation.

3. The effects of schooling variables

Earnings inequality in the United States has failed to decline in the postwar period despite substantial increases in educational levels. This simple observation has led many economists to doubt the effectiveness of raising educational levels in reducing earnings and income inequality. In response, theories of internal labor markets, job queues and screening have become popular. The results of the empirical work in this book reconfirm the earlier belief in the positive effect of rising educational levels on reducing earnings inequality.

When the basic demand variables are included (the capital to labor ratio and capital concentration), the estimated coefficient for the mean schooling level is almost always negative, indicating that increases in the mean level of schooling reduce earnings and income inequality. This holds true for the time-series estimates covering 1949–1969 and the cross-section estimates for 1959. For the 1969 cross-section estimates, the coefficient is occasionally positive, but it is negative when just the mean and standard deviation of schooling and capital to labor ratio and capital concentration terms are included, using the coefficient of variation as the measure of inequality (table 9.6, columns 3 and 8). Furthermore, educational differentials and income inequality by schooling level depend negatively and significantly on the mean schooling level. Finally, the poverty rates depend negatively and significantly on the mean schooling level.

In contrast, the standard deviation of schooling does not have the strong effect on earnings and income inequality that it is supposed to have according to the human capital analysis. The estimated coefficient for the variable often does not have the correct sign and is insignificant in the time series and 1959 cross-section analysis, although the coefficient is generally positive and significant for the 1969 cross-section regressions. Furthermore, there appears to be substantial instability between the 1959 and 1969 regressions. The reasons for the weak effect of the standard deviation of schooling are revealed in the disaggregated analysis of table 9.11. Workers in the upper and lower tails of the schooling distribution have substantially different effects on earnings and income inequality, unlike what one would expect from the human capital analysis. An increase in the number of workers in the lower tail has the expected result of raising both earnings inequality and schooling inequality. However, an increase in the number of workers in the upper tail raises schooling inequality but may not raise earnings inequality, because the greater numbers of more-educated workers reduce the returns to education. The consequence is that the estimated coefficients for the schooling variabless depend on the source of variation in their values, i.e. whether the differences in the values of the schooling variables arise from differences in the number of workers in the upper tail or in the lower tail. A change in the source of this variation between 1959 and 1969 would explain the instability in the estimated coefficients. A more revealing way of investigating the effects of schooling is to use measures of the upper and lower tail of the distribution. When this is done, the coefficients are stable and show the same signs between 1959 and 1969.

4. Revisions in human capital theory

The results in this book lead to a substantial revision of the theory and conclusions of the human capital school of thought concerning earnings inequality.

Chapter 2 reveals that there are in fact two human capital models of earnings inequality. In the Mincer model, educational differentials (wage rate versus schooling level, or the rate of return) are completely determined by the supply behavior of individuals, so that the supply curves for workers at each educational level are perfectly elastic and horizontal. The quantities at each educational level are then completely determined by the location of the demand curves. In the Becker-Chiswick model, the educational differentials are completely determined by the horizontal demand curves, and the locations of the supply curves then determine the quantities at each educational level. The point of Chapter 2 is that although the human capital models can explain either the educational differentials (factor prices) or numbers of workers at each schooling level (factor quantities), it is impossible to explain both within the same consistent model. That is, it is impossible to construct a complete theory of the distribution of earnings by studying only the supply behavior of individuals.

The human capital work on earnings inequality is based on the Becker-Chiswick model. The rates of return to schooling are assumed to be determined exogenously, and the model proceeds by relating the earnings inequality to the exogenously determined distribution of schooling. Chapter 2 indicates that this model requires the efficiency units hypothesis to hold. Chapter 4 presents the conditions under which an aggregate production function will exhibit the efficiency units hypothesis. That analysis reveals that only for very special production functions will the relative earnings of two workers be unaffected by changes in either the capital to labor ratio or the average productive ability of workers.

At several points in the empirical work of this book, failures of the human capital approach have been isolated. The most prominent failure arises in the relation between mean schooling and earnings inequality, a relation which lies at the heart of the human capital approach. Under the assumption that rates of return are determined exogenously, the human capital theory predicts that earnings inequality will be greater when the mean level of schooling is greater, everything else the same. This conclusion is superficially consistent with the course of earnings inequality in the postwar period in the United States. However, this result is not consistently obtained even in the human capital empirical work. The results produced in this book indicate that when the earnings inequality equation is properly specified (with both supply and demand variables included and without a separately estimated rate of return), the estimated coefficient for the mean level of schooling is generally negative, indicating that an increase in the mean level will reduce earnings inequality, everything else the same.

A second point of dispute centers on whether the rate of return to schooling is exogenously determined, as it must be for the Becker-Chiswick approach to be valid. Although Chiswick is aware of a large negative correlation between mean schooling and the rate of return to schooling across states, he dismisses the correlation as arising from mobility. In contrast, the empirical work presented here indicates that the rate of return to schooling is endogenously determined. It depends negatively and significantly on the mean level of schooling, everything else the same. The significance of this result is that as the mean level of schooling changes, not only the numbers of workers at different educational levels but the earnings received at each educational level change. In working out the effects of a change in the mean level of schooling, the Becker-Chiswick analysis holds the rate of return constant, so that only one effect of the change is observed.

A third failure of the human capital approach is in predicting the effects of changes in the upper and lower tails of the distribution of schooling. With the rate of return to schooling fixed, an increase in the number of workers in the upper tail of the distribution of schooling (that is, an increase in the number of highly educated workers) should have the same effect on earnings inequality as an increase in the number of workers in the lower tail. As mentioned in section 3, this result does not hold. Instead, an increase in the number of workers in the upper tail generally has negligible effects on earnings inequality, while an increase in the number of workers in the lower tail strongly raises earnings inequality. The reason for the difference in results lies in the effects on the rate of return to schooling. In the case of the lower tail, the increase raises the number of individuals in that group and reduces the earnings they receive, so that both effects work in the same direction. In the case of the upper tail, the increase raises the number of workers in that higher earnings group but reduces the earnings they receive, so that the two effects work in opposite directions and cancel out. The different effects of the upper and lower tails are precisely what one would expect from a simple supply and demand analysis.

The distribution of earnings cannot be analyzed by only studying the behavior of individuals in their work decisions. To do so produces substantially incorrect conclusions, as outlined above. One must study the interaction between the work behavior of individuals and the economy in which they are employed.

5. Work to be done

When I began on this project, I had no expectations that there would be so much unfinished business at the end. At several points in the analysis it has been necessary to leave developments to further research. The intention of this section is to summarize what work remains to be done and where the discussion that has been presented in this book is incomplete.

There has been little consideration in this monograph of the course of earnings inequality during growth and development of an economy. Despite the common interest, the literature on the relation between development and earnings inequality has evolved separately from the theory of earnings inequality in developed economies. The theory worked out in this monograph perhaps provides a means of integrating the two approaches. In particular, the general conclusion that earnings inequality is strongly affected by sectoral shifts in production and employment is clearly relevant to Kuznets's theories (1955, 1963) (see also the related work by Chenery et al., 1974; Chenery and Syrquin, 1975; and Ritzen, 1977). The major reason why the growth and development literature has been avoided here is that it involves a substantially different body of knowledge with which this author is not adequately familiar. The implications of the theory in Chapter 6 for the course of earnings inequality during development are therefore left to future study.

Another important question which has been neglected is the role of training and job experience. Partly this neglect is the result of the fact that the data which have been used here are not adequate to answer questions concerning their determinants. However, there are clearly several important hypotheses concerning the relation between the amount of capital a worker's labor is combined with and the optimal amount of training. The human capital analysis of the worker decision to receive training has described the supply side of the training decision, i.e. the pecuniary conditions that must be offered for the worker to be willing to be trained. However, the demand conditions have not been described (except for the conditions that must hold at the margin, for example that the extra cost to the firm of training one more worker must equal the expected extra return). For given wage conditions, how much training will a firm seek to give its workers? A complete theory of training would require an explanation of both the supply decisions of workers and the determinants of the amount of training given by firms. A microeconomic theory of the optimal amount of training is too important to be crowded into a discussion of earnings inequality, and therefore is left to a later and more extensive treatment.

A third area concerns fluctuations in employment: the distribution of unemployment is an important part of the distribution of earnings. The theory of quits and layoffs has been extensively developed in the literature as an aspect of labor markets. However, there is an older neoclassical theory relating fluctuations in employment to fluctuations in production. If the production function for a firm is linearly homogeneous, then the capital to labor ratio determines the elasticity of output with respect to a change in employment. Working backwards produces a relation between fluctuations in demand and fluctuations in employment. The implications of this result for differences in employment instability among industries deserves to be worked out.

This monograph has concentrated on the problem of describing the determination of the distribution of earnings. There are clearly many normative conclusions that can be drawn, but these should not be rushed. There appear to be several uncertainties about the descriptive part of the problem. First, what determines the distribution of earnings within an industry? Is this distribution simply the reflection of the demand for workers at different earnings levels, or are similar workers in fact being paid differently? In particular, are the lower proportions in the lower tail for manufacturing the result of union activity or labor market segmentation? These questions must be answered before conclusions can be drawn. Another uncertainty concerns the labor force effects of nonmanufacturing versus manufacturing industries. As discussed in Chapter 11, it is possible that the working conditions and opportunities in nonmanufacturing (in particular, trade and services) produce greater labor force participation for secondary wage earners and part-time workers. If so, the consequence of an increase in such industries would be a greater apparent level of earnings inequality, because of the greater numbers of low-earnings workers. However, these workers are clearly better off as a result of the demand for their labor, so the normative conclusions are ambiguous.

The resolution of these ambiguities lies in an analysis of the labor force effects of industrial composition. That is, how are the labor force participation rates of different groups affected by the industrial structure and the corresponding distribution of jobs? The theoretical foundations for this analysis are partly laid down in Chapter 6, section 4, where the unemployment of labor is endogenously determined. The effects of industrial structure on the distribution of earnings could then be disaggregated into two parts: the effect on the composition and size of the labor force and the effect on the distribution of earnings for a fixed group of employed workers. Another consequence of the existence of labor force effects is that earnings inequality must be measured differently. The differential rents theory of Chapter 6 implies that the distribution of earnings would be truncated at the wage rate for the last employed worker. In contrast, in calculating the inequality measure, it is assumed that the employed labor force constitutes an untruncated sample. Clearly, the parameters of the distribution will be calculated differently if the population under consideration is regarded as truncated instead of as the entire sample. The best procedure for estimating the parameters of the distribution would appear to involve choosing those parameters to provide the best agreement between the cumulative density function of the postulated form (e.g. lognormal) and the observed cumulative density function for earnings.

In addition to the traditional policies concerned with the distribution of schooling, the kinds of policy prescriptions that might arise from the analysis involve the distribution of capital among jobs. To what extent should this distribution be distorted in order to bring about less earnings inequality? The answer may be that the distribution should be undistorted instead of distorted. There are potential biases in the US tax laws which favor capital-intensive industries. Foremost is the investment tax credit. Since more capital-intensive industries have greater investments (per dollar of output), one may expect that the tax law favors them. Employment taxes and the minimum wage also clearly work against labor-intensive industries. Another possibility is that labor-intensive firms are inherently more risky, so that there are fewer labor-intensive jobs. The general policy recommendation would then be to encourage labor-intensive firms, thereby increasing the demand for less-skilled workers and raising their earnings. Whether this recommendation is justified requires further analysis.

Finally, there are several shortcomings in the body of the analysis itself. First among these is the failure to integrate the model of Chapter 4 with the model of Chapter 6. To some extent this failure is inevitable, since the one on Chapter 4 is a general equilibrium neoclassical model and the one in Chapter 6 is to some extent classical in nature, with reserve prices of labor and capital. The resolution of this problem probably requires a true disaggregated general equilibrium model, one in which the distribution of demands for workers is not related to the distribution of capital among jobs but to the distribution of demands for final goods. A consequence of the failure to integrate the two models is that there is no explicit functional form to use in estimating the models.

Although the ratio of manufacturing to total nonfarm employment and the manufacturing capital to labor ratio are consistently observed to affect the distribution of earnings or wage differentials in both cross-section and time-series estimates, the explanation for these results given in the text is inadequate and requires further analysis. Also, the theory of the effects of nonproduction workers and technological complexity on the distribution of earnings needs to be completed.

6. Concluding remarks

It was the original intention of this author, in writing this monograph, to change economists' minds about the nature and determinants of the distribution of earnings, about what the important questions are, and about the approach that should be taken in studying the distribution of earnings. The inevitable risk is that, by making statements that are at variance with the reader's initial beliefs and understandings, the reader will be alienated and reject the approach that has been taken here. However, for scholarly advance to take place, the points of dispute must be glaringly spotlighted rather than politely skirted.

The analysis undertaken in this book has treated wages as factor prices, which as all prices perform the role of allocating resources. In this case, wages assign workers to jobs and assure that the numbers supplied of a particular type equal the numbers demanded. Despite the long history of this approach (Jan Tinbergen's original paper having appeared in 1947), its implications for the distribution of earnings have not been fully appreciated. A major goal of this book has been to indicate forcefully the relevance and necessity of a general supply and demand approach. The tactic used to achieve this goal has been critically to analyze the assumptions underlying human capital models and to isolate failures of the human capital approach.

My hope is that the aggressive presentation of differences will produce useful and scholarly debate on the issues involved in the distribution of earnings. My own ideas on the distribution of earnings have changed considerably in the course of this project. I started out firmly believing in capital-skill complementarity and was initially disappointed that it did not show up in the aggregate empirical work. Only the disaggregated analysis provided weak support for the condition, and I am no longer convinced of its general validity. I also started out thinking that capital was the primary determinant of the demands for workers of different qualities. This is in the nature of a formal model: it directs attention to one set of variables and leads one to ignore others. Instead, although capital is a significant determinant of these demands, it now appears that other variables are also important. Finally, I started out with a presumption that labor markets could be treated as being perfectly competitive (at least for white males) so that wage rates for a given type of labor are equalized across industries. This assumption is not essential to the general supply and demand approach, but it greatly simplifies the analysis. I now have doubts about the validity of the assumption for low-income workers. For reasons discussed in Chapter 11, it seems quite likely that the same worker can have different potential earnings in different industries. I am prepared to change my ideas on the distribution of earnings further as debate evolves.

REFERENCES

Adelman, I., Hopkins, M.J.D., Robinson, S., Rodgers, G.B. and Wery, R. (1979). A Comparison of Two Models for Income Distribution Planning. Journal of Policy Modeling, 1, 37—82.

Ahmad, Al-Sammarie and Miller, Herman, P. (1967). State Differentials in Income Concentration. American Economic Review, 57, 59—71.

Aigner, D.J. and Heins, A.J. (1967). On the Determinants of Income Inequality. American Economic Review, 57, 174—184.

Aitchison, J. and Brown, J.A.C. (1957). The Lognormal Distribution. Cambridge University Press, Cambridge.

Akerlof, George A. (1969). Structural Unemployment in a Neoclassical Framework. Journal of Political Economy, 77, 399—407.

Allen, R.G.D. (1938). Mathematical Analysis for Economists. Macmillan, London.

Arrow, Kenneth J. (1973). Higher Education as a Filter. Journal of Public Economics, 2, 193—216.

Arrow, Kenneth J., Chenery, Hollis B., Minhas, Bagicha, and Solow, Robert M. (1961). Capital—Labor Substitution and Economic Efficiency. Review of Economics and Statistics, 43, 225—250.

Atkinson, A.B. (1970). On the Measurement of Inequality. Journal of Economic Theory, 2, 244—263.

Atkinson, A.B. (1975). The Economics of Inequality. Oxford Economic Press, London.

Becker, Gary S. and Chiswick, Barry R. (1966). Education and the Distribution of Earnings. American Economic Review, 56, 358—369.

Becker, Gary S. (1967). Human Capital and the Personal Distribution of Income. University of Michigan Press, Ann Arbor.

Becker, Gary S. (1975). Human Capital: A Theoretical and Empirical Analysis, with Special Reference to Education, 2nd. edn. Columbia University Press for the National Bureau of Economic Research, New York.

Berndt, Ernst R. and Christensen, Laurits R. (1974a). Testing for the Existence of a Consistent Aggregate Index of Labor Inputs. American Economic Review, 64, 391—404.

Berndt, Ernst R. and Christensen, Laurits R. (1974b). The Specification of Technology in U.S. Manufacturing. Unpublished paper, University of Wisconsin.

Blaug, Mark (1976). The Empirical Status of Human Capital Theory: A Slightly Jaundiced Survey. Journal of Economic Literature, 14, 827—855.

Blinder, Alan S. (1977). Toward an Economic Theory of Income Distribution. MIT Press, Cambridge, Mass.

Bluestone, Barry, Murphy, William M. and Stevenson, Mary (1973). Low Wages and the Working Poor, Policy Papers in Human Resources and Industrial Relations 22. University Publications, Ann Arbor.

Boon, G.K. (1964). Economic Choice of Human and Physical Factors in Production. North-Holland Publishing Company, Amsterdam.

Bowen, William G. and Finegan, T. Aldrich (1969). The Economics of Labor Force Participation. Princeton University Press, Princeton.

Bowles, Samuel and Gintis, Herbert (1976). Schooling in Capitalist America. Basic Books, New York.

Bowles, Samuel and Gintis, Herbert (1977). The Marxian Theory of Value and Heterogeneous Labour: A Critique and Reformulation. Cambridge Journal of Economics, 1, 173–192.

Bronfenbrenner, Martin (1971). Income Distribution Theory. Aldine-Atherton, Chicago.

Brown, Henry Phelps (1977). The Inequality of Pay. Oxford University Press, Oxford.

Buchanan, Daniel H. (1947). The Historical Approach to Rent and Price Theory. In: Readings in the Theory of Income Distribution. Blakiston Company, Philadelphia.

Burns, L.S. and Frech III, H.E. (1970). Human Capital and the Size Distribution of Income in Dutch Cities. De Economist, 118, 598.

Cain, Glen G. (1976). The Challenge of Segmented Labor Market Theories to Orthodox Theory: A Survey. Journal of Economic Literature, 14, 1215–1257.

Calvo, Guillermo A. and Wellisz, Stanislaw (1978). Supervision, Loss of Control, and the Optimum Size of the Firm. Journal of Political Economy, 86, 943–952.

Champernowne, D.G. (1953). A Model of Income Distribution. Economic Journal, 63, 318–351.

Champernowne, D.G. (1973). The Distribution of Income Between Persons. Cambridge University Press, New York.

Chenery, Hollis and Syrquin, Moises (1975). Patterns of Development, 1950–1970. World Bank. Oxford University Press, Oxford.

Chenery, Hollis, Ahluwalia, Montek S., Bell, C.L.G., Duloy, John H. and Jolly, Richard (1974). Redistribution with Growth. Oxford University Press, London.

Chiswick, Barry R. (1968). The Average Level of Schooling and the Intra-Regional Inequality of Income: A Clarification. American Economic Review, 58, 495–500.

Chiswick, Barry R. (1974). Income Inequality; Regional Analyses Within a Human Capital Framework. Columbia University Press for the National Bureau of Economic Research, New York.

Chiswick, Barry R. (1976). Review of Jan Tinbergen (1975a). Journal of Political Economy, 84, 422–425.

Chiswick, Barry R. and Mincer, Jacob (1972). Time Series Changes in Personal Income Inequality in the United States from 1939, with Projections to 1985. Journal of Political Economy, 79, 34–66.

Clark, Colin (1940). The Conditions of Economic Progress. Macmillan, London.

Clark, Kim B. and Freeman, Richard B. (1977). Time-Series Models of the Elasticity of Demand for Labor in Manufacturing. Unpublished paper, Harvard University, Cambridge, Massachusetts.

Cobb, C.W. and Douglas, P.H. (1928). A Theory of Production. American Economic Review, 18, 139–165.

Cochrane, D. and Orcutt, G.H. (1949). Application of Least Squares Regression to Relationships Containing Auto Correlated Error Terms. Journal of the American Statistical Association, 44, 32–61.

Conlisk, John (1967). Some Cross-State Evidence on Income Inequality. Review of Economics and Statistics, 99, 115–118.

Conlisk, John (1977). An Exploratory Model of the Size Distribution of Income. Economic Inquiry, 15, 345–366.

Dantzig, George B. (1963). Linear Programming and Extensions. Princeton University Press, Princeton.

Danziger, Sheldon (1976). Determinants of the Level and Distribution of Family Incomes in Metropolitan Areas, 1969. Land Economics, 52, 467–478.

Denison, Edward F. (1974). Accounting for United States Economic Growth, 1929–1969. The Brookings Institution, Washington.

Denny, Michael and Fuss, Melvyn (1977). The Use of Approximation Analysis to Test for Separability and the Existence of Consistent Aggregates. American Economic Review, 67, 404–418.

Doeringer, Peter B. and Piore, Michael J. (1971). Internal Labor Markets and Manpower Analysis. D.C. Heath and Company, Lexington, Mass.

Donges, J.G., Fels, G., Neu, A.D. et al. (1973). Protektion und Branchenstruktur der Westdeutschen Wirtschaft. Kieler Studien 123. J.C.B. Mohr, Tübingen.

Dorfman, Robert (1979). A Formula for the Gini Coefficient. Review of Economics and Statistics, 61, 146–149.

Fallon, P.R. and Layard, P.R.G. (1975). Capital-Skill Complementarity, Income Distribution and Output Accounting. Journal of Political Economy, 83, 279–301.

Farbman, Michael (1975). The Size Distribution of Family Income in U.S. SMSA's, 1959. Review of Income and Wealth, 21, 217–237.

Ferguson, C.E. (1969). The Neoclassical Theory of Production and Distribution. Cambridge University Press, London.

Formby, John P. and Seaks, Terry G. (1978). The Stability of Interstate Variations in the Size Distribution of Family Income, 1950–1970: Comment. Southern Economic Journal, 42, 615–621.

Freeman, Richard B. (1976). The Overeducated American. Academic Press, New York.

Freeman, Richard B. and Medoff, James B. (1978). Substitution Between Production Labor and Other Inputs in Unionized and Nonunionized Manufacturing. Unpublished Paper, Harvard University.

Gastwirth, Joseph L. (1972). The Estimation of the Lorenz Curve and Gini Index. Review of Economics and Statistics, 54, 306–316.

Gelfand, I.M. and Fomin, S.V. (1963). Calculus of Variations. Prentice-Hall, Englewood Cliffs, New Jersey.

Griliches, Zvi (1969). Capital-Skill Complementarity. Review of Economics and Statistics, 51, 465–468.

Griliches, Zvi (1970). Notes on the Role of Education in Production Functions and Growth Accounting. In: Hansen, W. Lee (ed.), Education, Income and Human Capital; Studies in Income and Wealth 35. Columbia University Press for the National Bureau of Economic Research, New York.

Hamermesh, Daniel S. (1976). Econometric Studies of Labor Demand and Their Application to Policy Analysis. Journal of Human Resources, 11, 507–525.

Hamermesh, Daniel S. and Grant, James (1978). Econometric Studies of Labor-Labor Substitution and Their Implications for Policy. Econometrics Workshop Paper no. 7709, Michigan State University.

Hansen, Reed, Klotz, Ben and Madoo, Rey (1975). The Structure of Demand for Low-Wage Labor in U.S. Manufacturing, 1967. Unpublished Paper, the Urban Institute.

Hartog, Joop (1976a). Ability and Age-Income Profiles. Review of Income and Wealth, 22, 61–74.

Hartog, Joop (1976b). Age-Income Profiles, Income Distribution and Transition Proportions. Journal of Economic Theory, 13, 448–457.

Hartog, Joop (1977). On the Multicapability Theory of Income Distribution. European Economic Review, 10, 157–171.

Hartog, Joop (1978). Personal Income Distribution: A Multicapability Theory with an Application to Tax Incidence. Doctoral Dissertation, Erasmus University, Rotterdam.

Haveman, Robert (1977). Jan Tinbergen's 'Income Distribution: Analysis and Policies'. Journal of Human Resources, 12, 103–114.

Hicks, J.R. (1970). Elasticity of Substitution Again: Substitutes and Complements. Oxford Economic Papers, 22, 289–296.

Hirsch, Barry T. (1978a). Earnings Inequality Across Labor Markets: A Test of the Human Capital Model. Southern Economic Journal, 45, 32–45.

Hirsch, Barry T. (1978b). Predicting Earnings Distributions Across Cities: The Human Capital Model Versus the National Distribution Hypothesis. Journal of Human Resources, 13, 366–384.

Hirsch, Barry T. and Hoftyzer, John (1979). The Distribution of Capital and the Distribution of Earnings. Unpublished Paper, University of North Carolina at Greensboro.

Houthakker, Hendrik S. (1952). Compensated Changes in Quantities and Qualities Consumed. Review of Economic Studies, 19, 155–164.

Houthakker, Hendrik S. (1974). The Size Distribution of Labour Incomes Derived from the Distribution of Aptitudes. In: Sellekearts, W. (ed.), Econometrics and Economic Theory: Essays in Honour of Jan Tinbergen. International Arts and Sciences Press, White Plains, New York.

Jencks, Christopher et al. (1972). Inequality: A Reassessment of the Effect of Family and Schooling in America. Basic Books, New York.

Jensen, Arthur R. (1969). How Much Can We Boost IQ and Scholastic Achievement? Harvard Educational Review, 39, 1–123.

Johnson, Harry G. (1973). The Theory of Income Distribution. Gray-Mills, London.

Jovanovic, Boyan (1978a). Job Matching and the Theory of Turnover. Unpublished Paper, Bell Laboratories.

Jovanovic, Boyan (1978b). Turnover and Specific Capital. Unpublished Paper, Bell Laboratories.

Jovanovic, Boyan (1978c). Positive and Negative Sorting by Quality. Unpublished Paper, Bell Laboratories.

Jovanovic, Boyan (1978d). Some Results on the Testing of Workers for the Purpose of Optimal Assignment. Unpublished Paper, Bell Laboratories.

Kendrick, John W. (1961). Productivity Trends in the United States. Princeton University Press (for the National Bureau of Economic Research), Princeton.

Kendrick, John W. (1973). Postwar Productivity Trends in the United States, 1948–1969. National Bureau of Economic Research, Columbia University Press, New York.

Kendrick, John W., Lee, Kyu Sik, and Lomack, Jean (1976). The National Wealth of the United States by Major Sector and Industry. The Conference Board, New York.

Kesselman, Jonathon, Williamson, Samuel H. and Berndt, Ernst R. (1977). Tax Credits for Employment Rather Than Investment. American Economic Review, 67, 339–349.

Kuipers, S.K. (1976). Review of Jan Tinbergen (1975a). De Economist, 124, 168–171.

Kuznets, Simon (1953). Shares of Upper Income Groups in Income and Savings. National Bureau of Economic Research, New York.

Kuznets, Simon (1955). Economic Growth and Income Inequality. American Economic Review, 45, 1–28.

Kuznets, Simon (1963). Quantitative Aspects of Economic Growth of Nations: III, Distribution of Income by Size. Economic Development and Cultural Change, 11, 1–80.

Lee, Jae W. (1976). A Dynamic Analysis of Relative Share of Production Labour to Capital. Applied Economics, 8, 207–214.

Lewis, H.G. (1963). Unionism and Relative Wages in the United States. University of Chicago Press, Chicago.

Leibenstein, Harvey (1976). Beyond Economic Man. Harvard University Press, Cambridge, Mass.

Lucas, Robert E.B. (1977). Is There a Human Capital Approach to Income Inequality? Journal of Human Resources, 12, 387–395.

Lucas Jr., Robert E. (1978). On the Size Distribution of Business Firms. Bell Journal of Economics, 9, 508–523.

Lydall, Harold (1959). The Distribution of Employment Incomes. Econometrica, 27, 110–115.

Lydall, Harold (1968). The Structure of Earnings. Oxford University Press, New York.

Mandelbrot, Benoit (1962). Paretian Distributions and Income Maximization. Quarterly Journal of Economics, 76, 57–85.

March, James G. and Simon, Herbert (1958). Organizations. John Wiley and Sons, New York.

Marin, Alan and Psacharopoulos, George (1976). Schooling and Income Distribution. Review of Economics and Statistics, 58, 332–338.

Marshall, Alfred (1964). Principles of Economics, 8th edn. Macmillan, London.

Marx, Karl (1967). Capital. International Publishers, New York.

Mayazawa, K. (1964). The Dual Structure of the Japanese Economy and its Growth Pattern. The Developing Economies, 2, 147–170.

Mayazawa, K. (1976). Input-Output Analysis and the Structure of Income Distribution. Springer-Verlag, Berlin.

Mayer, Thomas (1960). The Distribution of Ability and Earnings. Review of Economics and Statistics, 42, 189–195.

Mincer, Jacob (1958). Investments in Human Capital and Personal Income Distribution. Journal of Political Economy, 66, 281–302.

Mincer, Jacob (1970). The Distribution of Labor Incomes: A Survey. Journal of Economic Literature, 8, 1–25.

Mincer, Jacob (1974). Schooling, Experience and Earnings. Columbia University Press for National Bureau of Economic Research, New York.

Mincer, Jacob (1976). Unemployment Effects of Minimum Wages. Journal of Political Economy, 84, S87–S104.

Mirrlees, J.A. (1971). An Exploration in the Theory of Optimum Income Taxation. Review of Economic Studies, 38, 175–208.

Mirrlees, James A. (1976). The Optimal Structure of Incentives and Authority Within an Organization. Bell Journal of Economics, 7, 105–131.

Morishima, Michio (1973). Marx's Economics. Cambridge University Press, Cambridge.

Mortensen, Dale T. (1978). Specific Capital and Labor Turnover. Bell Journal of Economics, 9, 572–586.

Näslund, Bertil (1977). An Analysis of Economic Size Distributions. Springer-Verlag, Berlin.

Osberg, Lars S. (1975). A Structural Approach to the Distribution of Earnings. Doctoral Dissertation, Yale University.

Osberg, Lars S. (1976a). Tinbergen and the 'Blurring' of the Human Capital Paradigm. Review of Income and Wealth, 22, 93–97.

Osberg, Lars S. (1976b). Industrial Structure of Micro-Economies and the Distribution of Earnings. Research Report 7613, Department of Economics, University of Western Ontario.

Pen, Jan (1971). Income Distribution. Praeger, New York.

Petersen, Hans-Georg (1979). Effects of Growing Incomes on Classified Income Distributions, the Derived Lorenz Curves, and Gini Indices. Econometrica, 47, 183–198.

Pettengill, John S. (1979). Labor Unions and the Wage Structure: A General Equilibrium Approach. Review of Economic Studies, forthcoming.

Plotnick, Robert D. and Skidmore, Felicity (1975). Progress Against Poverty: A Review of the 1964–1974 Decade. Academic Press, New York.

Reder, Melvin (1968). The Size Distribution of Earnings. In: Marchal, Jean and Ducros, Bernard (eds.). The Distribution of National Income. St. Martin's Press, New York.

Reder, Melvin (1969). A Partial Survey of the Theory of Income Size Distribution. In: Soltow, Lee (ed.). Six Papers on the Size Distribution of Wealth and Income; Studies in Income and Wealth 33. Columbia University Press for the National Bureau of Economic Research, New York.

Reynolds, Morgan and Smolensky, Eugene (1977). Public Expenditures, Taxes and the Distribution of Income. Academic Press, New York.

Ricardo, David (1953). On the Principles of Political Economy and Taxation. In: Sraffa, Piero (ed.). The Works and Correspondence of David Ricardo, vol. I. Cambridge University Press, Cambridge.

Ritzen, J.M.M. (1977). Education, Economic Growth and Income Distribution. North-Holland, Amsterdam.

Rosen, Sherwin (1974). Hedonic Prices and Implicit Markets: Product Differentiation in Pure Competition. Journal of Political Economy, 82, 34–55.

Rosen, Sherwin (1977a). Labor Quality, the Demand for Skills, and Market Selection. National Bureau of Economic Research Working Paper no. 162.

Rosen, Sherwin (1977b). Human Capital: A Survey of Empirical Research. In: Ehrenberg, Ronald G. (ed.). Research in Labor Economics, Vol. 1. JAI Press, Greenwich, Conn.

Rosen, Sherwin (1978). Substitution and the Division of Labour. Economica, 45, 235–250.

Roy, A.D. (1950). The Distribution of Earnings and of Individual Output. The Economic Journal, 60, 489–505.

Roy, A.D. (1951). Some Thoughts on the Distribution of Earnings. Oxford Economic Papers, 3, 135–146.

Sahota, Gian (1977). Personal Income Distribution Theories of the Mid–1970s. Kyklos, 30, 724–740.

Sahota, Gian (1978). Theories of Personal Income Distribution: A Survey. Journal of Economic Literature, 16, 1–55.

Sale, Tom S. (1974). Interstate Analysis of the Size Distribution of Family Income, 1950–1970. Southern Economic Journal, 41, 434–441.

Samuelson, Paul A. (1971). Understanding the Marxian Notion of Exploitation: A Summary of the So-Called Transformation Problem Between Marxian Values and Competitive Prices. Journal of Economic Literature, 9, 399–431.

Sato, R. (1977). Homothetic and Non-Homothetic CES Production Functions. American Economic Review, 67, 559–569.

Sato, R. and Koizumi, T. (1973a). The Production Function and the Theory of Distributive Shares. American Economic Review, 63, 484–489.

Sato, R. and Koizumi, T. (1973b). On the Elasticities of Substitution and Complementarity. Oxford Economic Papers, 25, 44–56.

Sattinger, Michael (1975). Comparative Advantage and the Distributions of Earnings and Abilities. Econometrica, 43, 455–468.

Sattinger, Michael (1976a). Compensating Wage Differences. Stony Brook Working Paper no. 165, State University of New York at Stony Brook.

Sattinger, Michael (1976b). Capital and the Size Distribution of Earnings. Stony Brook Working Paper no. 167, State University of New York at Stony Brook.

Sattinger, Michael (1977a). The Efficiency Units Assumption and the Distribution of Earnings. Stony Brook Working Paper no. 178, State University of New York at Stony Brook.

Sattinger, Michael (1977b). Compensating Wage Differences. Journal of Economic Theory, 16, 496–503.

Sattinger, Michael (1978). Comparative Advantage in Individuals. Review of Economics and Statistics, 60, 259–267.

Sattinger, Michael (1979). Differential Rents and the Distribution of Earnings. Oxford Economic Papers, 31, 60–71.

Sawyer, Malcolm (1976). Income Distribution in OECD Countries. OECD Economic Outlook, Occasional Studies. Organization for Economic Cooperation and Development, Paris.

Schultz, T.P. (1965). The Distribution of Personal Income: Case Study of the Netherlands. PH.D. Dissertation, Massachusetts Institute of Technology.

Seiver, Daniel (1979). The Measurement of Income Inequality with Interval Data. Review of Income and Wealth, 25, 229–233.

Simon, Herbert A. (1956). The Compensation of Executives. Sociometry, 20, 32–35.

Simon, Herbert A. (1957). Models of Man. John Wiley and Sons, New York.

Singh, S.K. and Sale, Tom S. (1978). The Stability of Interstate Variations in the Size Distribution of Family Income, 1950–1970. Southern Economic Journal, 45, 622–629.

Spence, A.M. (1975). The Economics of Internal Organization. Bell Journal of Economics, 6, 163–172.

Sraffa, Piero (1960). Production of Commodities by Means of Commodities. Cambridge University Press, Cambridge.

Stigler, George J. (1956). Trends in Employment in the Service Industries. National Bureau of Economic Research, no. 59. Princeton University Press, Princeton.

Stiglitz, Joseph E. (1975). Incentives, Risk and Information: Notes Towards a Theory of Hierarchy. Bell Journal of Economics, 6, 552–579.

Takayama, Akira (1974). Mathematical Economics. Dryden Press, Hinsdale, Illinois.

Tannen, Michael B. (1976). The Size Distribution of Family Incomes: A Re-examination. Southern Economic Journal, 42, 666–674.

Taubman, Paul (1976a). The Determinants of Earnings: Genetics, Family and Other Environments; A Study of White Male Twins. American Economic Review, 66, 858–870.

Taubman, Paul (1976b). Sources of Inequality in Earnings. North-Holland Publishing Company, Amsterdam.

Taubman, Paul (1978). Income Distribution and Redistribution. Addison-Wesley; Reading, Mass.

Tausky, Curt (1970). Work Organizations. F.E. Peacock Publishers, Itasca, Illinois.

Thurow, Lester (1975). Generating Inequality: Mechanisms of Distribution in the U.S. Economy. Basic Books, New York.

Tinbergen, Jan (1947). Enkele Opmerkingen over de Verdeling der Arbeidsinkomens. Mededeelingen der Koninklijke Nederlandsche Akademie van Wetenschappen, afd. Letterkunde, New Series, vol. 10, no. 8.

Tinbergen, Jan (1951). Some Remarks on the Distribution of Labour Incomes. International Economic Papers, 1, 195–207.

Tinbergen, Jan (1956). On the Theory of Income Distribution. Weltwirtschaftliches Archiv, 77, 155–173.

Tinbergen, Jan (1970). A Positive and a Normative Theory of Income Distribution. Review of Income and Wealth, 16, 221–233.

Tinbergen, Jan (1972). The Impact of Education on Income Distribution. Review of Income and Wealth, 18, 255–265.

Tinbergen, Jan (1974). Substitution of Graduate by Other Labor. Kyklos, 27, 217–226.

Tinbergen, Jan (1975a). Income Distribution; Analysis and Policies. North-Holland Publishing Company, Amsterdam.

Tinbergen, Jan (1975b). Income Differences: Recent Research. North-Holland Publishing Company, Amsterdam.

Tinbergen, Jan (1975c). Substitution of Academically Trained by Other Manpower. Weltwirtschaftliches Archiv, 86, 466–476.

Tinbergen, Jan (1977). Income Distribution: Second Thoughts. De Economist, 125, 315–339.

Tuck, R.H. (1954). An Essay on the Economic Theory of Rank. Basil Blackwell, Oxford.

Welch, Finis (1969). Linear Synthesis of Skill Distribution. Journal of Human Resources, 4, 311–327.

Westergaard-Nielsen, Niels (1975). Indkomstfordeling og Uddannelse. Unpublished graduate thesis, University of Aarhus, Denmark.

Williamson, Oliver E. (1967). Hierarchical Control and Optimum Firm Size. Journal of Political Economy, 75, 123–138.

Winegarden, C.R. (1979). Schooling and Income Distribution: Evidence from International Data. Economica, 46, 83–87.

Wood, A. (1975). Review of Jan Tinbergen (1975a). Economic Journal, 85, 93.

Wood, A. (1978). A Theory of Pay. Cambridge University Press, Cambridge.

Yndgaard, Ebbe (1975). The Outline of a General Disequilibrium Dynamic Model with Personal Income and Wealth Distributions. Warsaw Fall Seminars in Mathematical Economics 1975. Springer-Verlag, 133, 148–159.

Yndgaard, Ebbe (1976a). GDM, a General Disequilibrium Model; Theories on the Distribution of Personal Incomes. Memo 1976–2, Institute of Economics, University of Aarhus.

Yndgaard, Ebbe (1976b). GDM, a General Disequilibrium Model; Assumptions and Principles. Memo 1976–3, Institute of Economics, University of Aarhus.

Yndgaard, Ebbe (1978). GDM, Computerization of Micro-Founded Macro Econometric Models. Institute of Economics, University of Aarhus.

AUTHOR INDEX

Adelman, I. 37
Ahluwalia, M.S. 265
Ahmad, A. 155
Aigner, D.J. 155, 166
Aitchison, J. 132, 228, 229
Akerlof, G. 36
Allen, R.G.D. 35, 36, 52, 226
Arrow, K.J. 70, 226
Atkinson, A.B. 23, 132-134

Becker, G.S. 14, 15, 18, 19, 183, 189
Bell, C.L.G. 265
Berndt, E.R. 252
Blaug, M. 13
Blinder, A.S. 23, 37
Bluestone, B. 217
Boon, C.K. 127
Bowen, W.G. 220
Bowles, S. 17, 139, 217
Bronfenbrenner, M. 23
Brown, H.P. 23
Brown, J.A.C. 132, 228, 229
Buchanan, D.H. 69
Burns, L.S. 155

Cain, G. 217
Calvo, G. 247
Champernowne, D.G. 5, 64
Chenery, H. 226, 265
Chiswick, B. 10, 14, 18, 23, 140-146, 155, 181-185, 189, 192, 264
Christensen, L.R. 252
Clark, C. 135
Clark, K.B. 252
Cobb, C.W. 226
Cochrane, D. 150, 196
Conlisk, J. 67, 155

Dantzig, G.B. 71
Danziger, S. 155
Denison, E.F. 66
Denny, M. 252
Doeringer, P.B. 217, 218
Donges, J.G. 128
Dorfman, R. 132
Douglas, P. 226
Duloy, J.H. 265

Farbman, M. 155
Fallon, P.R. 36, 52
Fels, G. 128
Ferguson, C.E. 45, 54, 55, 62, 88
Finegan, T.A. 220
Fomin, S.V. 228
Formby, J.P. 155, 176
Frech III, H.E. 155
Freeman, R.B. 136, 252
Fuss, M. 252

Gaswirth, J.L. 132
Gelfand, I.M. 228
Gintis, H. 17, 139, 217
Grant, J. 127, 252
Griliches, Z. 36, 52, 90, 126, 127

Hamermesh, D.S. 127, 252
Hansen, R. 252
Hartog, J. 29, 57
Haveman, R.H. 23
Heins, A.J. 155, 166
Hicks, J.R. 36, 51, 55
Hirsch, B.T. 155, 174
Hoftyzer, J. 174
Hopkins, M.J.D. 37
Houthakker, H.S. 28, 29, 32

Jencks, C. 64, 136, 182
Jensen, A.R. 139
Johnson, H.G. 23
Jolly, R. 265
Jovanovic, B. 70

Kendrick, J. 136, 141, 210, 214, 223, 224, 242, 243
Kesselman, J. 252
Klotz, B. 252
Kuipers, S.K. 23
Koizumi, T. 36, 51, 52, 226
Kuznets, S. 10, 140, 147, 152, 153, 179, 265
Layard, P.R.G. 36, 52

Lee, J.W. 252
Lee, K.S. 136
Lewis, H.G. 242
Liebenstein, H. 222
Lomack, J. 136
Lucas, R.E.B. 13, 17
Lucas, Jr., R. 247
Lydall, H. 23, 33, 229, 247, 248-251

Madoo, R. 252
Mandelbrot, B. 29
March, J.G. 222
Marin, A. 184
Marshall, A. 20, 21, 221
Marx, K. 16, 17, 69
Mayazawa, K. 33, 34
Mayer, T. 24, 34, 35
Medoff, J.B. 252
Miller, H.P. 155
Mincer, J. 5, 10, 13-15, 18, 20, 23, 140-146, 183, 216, 217, 221
Minhas, B. 226
Mirrlees, J.A. 67, 247
Morishima, M. 17
Mortensen, D.T. 70
Murphy, W.M. 217

Näslund, B. 33
Neu, A.D. 128

Orcutt, G. 150, 196
Osberg, L.S. 23, 33, 218

Pen, J. 23
Petersen, H. 132
Pettengill, J.S. 221
Piore, M.J. 217, 218

Plotnick, R.D. 4, 139
Psacharapoulos, G. 184

Reder, M. 23, 24, 35
Reynolds, M. 139
Ricardo, D. 9, 16, 27, 69
Ritzen, J.M.M. 7, 37, 265
Robinson, S. 37
Rodgers, G.B. 37
Rosen, S. 13, 20, 28, 32
Roy, A.D. 5, 6, 23, 24, 29-32, 45

Sahota, S. 23
Sale, T.S. 155
Samuelson, P.A. 17
Sato, R. 36, 44, 47, 51, 52, 226
Sattinger, M. 31, 73, 95, 107, 221
Sawyer, M. 132
Schultz, T.P. 155
Seaks, T.G. 155, 176
Seiver, D. 132, 156, 191
Simon, H. 33, 222, 247, 248
Singh, S.K. 155
Skidmore, F. 4, 139
Smolensky, E. 139
Solow, R. 226
Spence, A.M. 247
Sraffa, P. 17
Stevenson, M. 217
Stigler, G. 135
Stiglitz, J. 247
Syrquin, M. 265

Takayama, A. 228
Tannen, M.B. 155
Taubman, P. 14, 20, 64
Tausky, C. 221
Thurow, L. 28, 139, 218
Tinbergen, J. 3, 5-8, 13, 23-29, 72, 73, 139, 142, 184, 268
Tuck, R.H. 24, 32-34

Welch, F. 29
Wellisz, S. 247
Wery, R. 37
Westergaard-Nielsen, N. 32
Williamson, O.E. 247
Williamson, S.H. 252
Winegarden, C.R. 184
Wood, A.J.B. 23

Yndgaard, E. 36

SUBJECT INDEX

Almost-homogeneous production function 44
Almost-homothetic production function 47, 48
Alternative capital variables 175, 176
Alternative schooling variables 177-181
Assignment problem
  absence with efficiency units assumption 20
  and comparative advantage 8, 9, 31, 77-79, 85-88
  and preferences 8, 72-76
  and scale of resources effect 9, 79-90
  arising from Ricardian model 69
  in operations research 71
  in Tinbergen's model 27
  relation to capital-skill complementarity 90, 91, 126-128
Atkinson's inequality measure 132-134

Capital concentration
  and manufacturing ratio 135, 148
  effects on earnings inequality across states 174, 189, 260, 261
  effects on income inequality over time 143, 144, 260, 261
  estimates by state 165, 166
  over time 124-126
Capital-skill complementarity 36, 135, 148
  evidence from industry studies 205, 209
  implications for inequality multiplier 52
  relation to assignment problem 90, 91, 126-128
Capital to labor ratio
  and nonproduction workers 251-258
  and Pareto coefficients 250, 251
  and poverty 187

changes over time 134, 135
  effects on inequality 142-144, 150, 151, 174, 260, 261
  effects on industry earnings distributions 205-210
  effect on inequality multiplier 45-48
  estimated ratios by state 165
  statistics by industry 121-124
  versus earnings by industry 128-132, 237-245
  versus schooling by industry 128, 129, 229-237
Classical income distribution theory 10, 267
Cochrane-Orcutt iterative technique 150, 196
Coefficient of variation 42, 43, 113, 115, 132-134, 156, 172
Comparative advantage 5, 29-32, 77-79
  and difficulty 31
  and efficiency units assumption 20, 21
  as a theory of jobs 6
  in Arrow's screening model 70
  in Roy's model 29-31
Compensating wage differences 73-76, 221
Concentration (product market) 242-244
Constant of integration 95, 105, 106, 109, 110

Demand for distribution of workers 226-229
Difficulty of job or task 31, 56, 57, 77, 78
Dual labor markets 131

Education (see schooling)
Efficiency units assumption
  and demand for labor 17
  and inequality multiplier 60, 68

and labor theory of value 16, 17
in human capital model 17-20
Marshall's objections 20, 21
with preferences 73, 76
Employment fluctuations 265

Gini coefficient 132-134, 156, 172, 173,
    177, 179
Growth accounting 66-68

Hedonic price function 28
Heredity versus environment 4, 5, 64, 65
Heteroscedasticity 172, 253
Human capital
    Becker-Chiswick model 14-20, 116, 117,
        183, 184
    effect of mean schooling on inequal-
        ity 184, 189, 263, 264
    exogeneity of rate of return to school-
        ing 179, 184, 185, 189, 263, 264
    Mincer model 13-15, 116, 117, 216, 217,
        262, 263
    predictions concerning upper and lower
        tail 177-179, 189, 264

Ideology 6, 7
Individual characteristics approach 1-3, 7
Inequality multiplier 8, 39-68
Internal labor market 131, 217, 218, 261
Investment tax credit 267

Labor force effects 220-223, 266
Labor market segmentation 217, 266
Learning by doing 218
Lognormal distribution 108-112, 228

Manufacturing to total employment ratio
    and capital concentration 148, 194, 195
    and labor force effects 215-217
    changes over time 134, 135
    effect on earnings inequality by state 166,
        174-177
    effect on income inequality over
        time 145, 151, 152
    effect on wage differentials 197-200
Measurement of inequality 132-134
    and labor force effects 220, 221
    measures used in analysis 140, 141, 156,
        157
Microsimulation 36, 37
Misspecification biases 142, 145
Mobility of workers 155, 185, 264
Multicollinearity 146, 147, 151, 155, 174

Neoclassical income distribution theory 10,
    40, 267
Nonproduction workers 251-257

On-the-job training 131, 132, 218, 265

Pareto coefficients 106, 107, 248-251
Pareto distribution 11, 104-108
Partial elasticities of substitution and com-
        plementarity
    and nonproduction workers 252, 253
    description 36, 51-52
    relation to inequality multiplier 51-55
Poverty
    and Akerlof's model 36
    empirical analysis 186-188
    research questions 4
    theory of poverty 60-64
Productivity 145, 210-214

Quits and layoffs 265

Reserve prices 10, 27, 97, 101-104
Ricardian differential rents 69, 95

Scale of resources effect
    derivation of results 79-85
    previous work 32-35
    relevance to assignment problem 35
    with Cobb-Douglas production func-
        tion 88-90
    with comparative advantage 85-88
Schooling
    changes in distribution over time 134-136
    distribution by state 164, 165
    effects on inequality 145, 176, 183-186,
        189, 260, 261
    expectations of economists 139, 140
    inequality within schooling levels 182,
        183
    instability in effects 176, 179-181, 262
    predictions of human capital models 183-
        184
    rate of return to schooling 136, 181, 182
Secondary wage earners 220, 266
Sectoral shifts 215-222
    and capital intensity 135, 136, 203
    and Kuznets models 265
Self-selection 30, 31
Stochastic chance model 5, 64
Supply and demand 5, 165, 219
    in Tinbergen's model 24
    versus human capital predictions 177-181

Technological progress 55-57
Tinbergen's model 24-29

Unemployment
  and measurement of inequality 219
  in Akerlof's model 36
  in differential rents model 101-104

Unionization 221, 242-244, 266
Upper income shares 147-151

Variance of logarithms 110, 111, 115, 132-134, 140

Wage differentials 48-50, 193-201

DATE DUE